HERE COMES WHIRLAWAY!

Whirlaway (left) and Dustwhirl at Calumet Farm.

Here Comes Whirlaway!

by Fred C. Broadhead

Sunflower University Press®
1531 Yuma (Box 1009), Manhattan, Kansas 66502-4228 USA

Printed in the United States of America on acid-free paper.

ISBN 0-89745-181-3

Photos courtesy of Keeneland Library Racing Association, Lexington, Kentucky, unless otherwise noted.

Edited by Sandra J. Rose

Layout by Lori L. Daniel

God's humbler instrument,
though meaner clay,
Should share the glory
of that glorious day.

— *On the headstone of Copenhagen,*
the Duke of Wellington's chestnut
throughout the Battle of Waterloo

Contents

Acknowledgments

FOR generous gifts of time, assistance, and cooperation, I wish to extend special thanks and recognition to:

Cleveland Amory — Writer, Critic
Edgar Allen — Director of Media Relations, Churchill Downs, Louisville, Kentucky
Ed Ashford — **The Thoroughbred Record**
Joseph Burnham — Film Producer, Thoroughbred Racing Associations

J. Fred Colwill — Chief of Stewards, Maryland Jockey Club
Johnny Cothorn — Clocker, *Daily Racing Form*, Pimlico Race Course
Theresa Fitzgerald — Librarian, *The Blood-Horse*
Margaret Glass — Secretary, Calumet Farm
Nancy J. Hatley — Typist and Adviser
Johnny Longden — California Thoroughbred Breeders Association
Laura McCutchan — Research Consultant, Louisville (KY) *Courier-Journal*
Dick Nash — Los Angeles Turf Club, Santa Anita Park
Myer Pruce — Johnny Cothorn's associate, Pimlico Race Course
Alfred Shelhammer — Racing Steward, Hollywood and Santa Anita Parks
David Shultz — Librarian, *Daily Racing Form*, Chicago
Sam Siciliano — Public Relations, Publicity Director, Pimlico
Dick Sweeny — WHAS Radio-TV, Louisville, Kentucky
Bill Tanton — Sports Columnist, Baltimore (MD) *Evening Sun*
Bob Varey — Publicity, Public Relations Director, Suffolk Downs
John Wyatt — Chief Photographer, Lexington (KY) *Herald-Leader*

Foreword

HAVING spent more than 30 years researching and writing about the sport of horse racing in general and the Kentucky Derby in particular, I thought I knew something about Whirlaway. I wasn't even born when he won the 1941 Kentucky Derby, but because of my research, I have sometimes felt that I was actually there for the 67th "run for the roses" watching Mr. Longtail himself charge to that eight-length victory in track-record time.

Through the years, I have talked with Eddie Arcaro, Johnny Longden, Wendell Eads, Arthur Craig, and Shelby Clark, former jockeys who rode Whirlaway. Each had interesting stories to tell about this temperamental colt. I've also talked with H. A. "Jimmy" Jones whose father, Ben, worked long hours with Whirlaway to correct his bad habits.

I mention my past experiences only to let you know that I *thought* I new something about Whirlaway until I read Fred C. Broadhead's manuscript. An artist with the written word, Broadhead takes us through Whirlaway's career, from his days as a colt at Calumet Farm to his last years in France. In between, we see him develop into a champion.

Broadhead quotes many of the famous sportswriters of the time, including Red Smith, Grantland Rice, Bryan Field, and Arthur Daley. The chapter on Whirlaway's Derby makes me feel like I was sitting in historic Churchill Downs on that first Saturday in May. As we continue through his career, we learn that he helped raise money for the war-relief effort. For all the records that Whirlaway set in his illustrious career, I believe that Broadhead best puts things in perspective by writing that

> Mr. Longtail's gallant campaign on behalf of the War Emergency Relief Fund for Armed Services personnel in 1942 represents the noblest act of patriotism ever performed by a thoroughbred racehorse.

Whirlaway died in France, the cheers of the crowds at Churchill Downs, Pimlico, Belmont Park, and other racetracks a distant memory. This book brings Whirlaway to life, taking you back in time to follow his 60-race career as if you were there, binoculars in hand, watching his every exciting move. Thanks to Fred C. Broadhead, *now* I finally know the Whirlaway story.

Jim Bolus
Secretary, National Turf Writers
Louisville, Kentucky

Preface

THIS documented narrative is the story of a racehorse named Whirlaway, the only thoroughbred racehorse to merit recognition as a war hero. Whirlaway's noteworthy contribution to the War Emergency Relief Fund during World War II has never been described in print, since it unfolded over 50 years ago. The story was never classified as "secret," but, somehow in the rush of postwar events, it has escaped the columns of leading sportswrit-

ers and historians. No doubt World War II produced an endless number of unsung heroes, but it does stretch the scope of imagination to picture a thoroughbred racehorse as being among that number — maybe a quarter horse or some stronger breed, but not a high-strung, fragile thoroughbred.

I did not gain access to this unusual story from a preset plan of research, but rather from a series of starts, lapses, and new beginnings. The initial motivation for writing the story presented itself in an unsuspecting manner. I happened to be watching television Saturday afternoon, May 6, 1978, as the 104th running of the Kentucky Derby was about to unfold on TV screens across the nation. Preceding the event, much was said about the co-favorites in the race — Affirmed and Alydar. The latter was the first strong entry from Calumet Farm in several years. In the commentary, Lucille (Mrs. Gene) Markey, formerly Mrs. Warren Wright, owner of Alydar, was quoted as saying that of all of the outstanding racehorses from Calumet Farm, Alyder ranked second in her favor, with Whirlaway her number one choice.

With my curiosity piqued, I decided to seek more information about this racehorse, and thus began a research trail that lasted ten years.

Because Whirlaway's racing career took place in the first half of the 20th century, very little has been written about him. Most of my research data was compiled from primary sources — microfilm accounts from newspapers and periodicals, newsreel films, interviews with those who were eyewitnesses to Whirlaway's races or who were a part of the thoroughbred racing scene of that day.

The further I pursued my research on Whirlaway, the more intrigued I became. The details soon began to read like a fairy tale. I not only learned that Whirlaway was Calumet Farm's first Kentucky Derby and Triple Crown winner, but also that he was the leading money-winner of the day, and probably the most popular contemporary racehorse in thoroughbred racing history. These credentials alone established the colt's greatness; but when the trail led to the discovery that Whirlaway had participated in 22 races at 12 different tracks on behalf of the War Emergency Relief Fund in 1942, I decided that such an inspiring story should be told.

Being a member of the World War II generation with history as my major study, I had hoped some day to find the time and occasion for writing a biography of some lesser-known figure from that crisis-filled era. What I least expected was to produce a biography of a racehorse. But with my love of animals, especially horses, I feel fully rewarded for the decade spent putting together the many loose ends of the Whirlaway story.

My hope is to be able to offer a tribute to this majestic creature for those who missed his impact the first time around and for those present and future generations, who have never heard his name.

Throughout history, civilizations have shown much indifference and little respect for the countless number of true heroes in their midst. We have tried to honor war heroes by paying tribute occasionally at the Tomb of the Unknown Soldier. There are rare moments when we recognize heroes while they are still alive, but too often their memorable deeds go with them to the grave. Once in a while we pause and reconsider those who have made significant contributions to human progress and belatedly proclaim them heroes.

But in the long view of history, another less-visible species containing a disproportionate number of unsung heroes should undeniably be the horse. Much of history has been written on the back of a horse. Since domestication around 2000 B.C., this noble four-legged creature has contributed heavily to the march of civilization. Until the early years of the 20th century, the horse was essential for all kinds of transport, for tilling the soil, for powering infant industries, and for entertainment in sporting activities. Even in this seemingly sophisticated space age, half of the world still depends on the horse and other draft animals for transportation and work. Horses may be slower than automobiles, trucks, or tractors, but they are less expensive; they live off the land and propagate their own species; thus, they are a renewable source of energy, a crucial factor in a fuel-hungry society.

In countless wars throughout the centuries, the horse has played a major role. Alfred Tennyson's lines in the "Charge of the Light Brigade" were written for warriors on horseback but should apply equally to the horses they rode into battle:

> Theirs not to make reply,
> Theirs not to reason why,
> Theirs but to do or die.

In the Russian campaign of 1812, Napoleon crossed the Nieman River with 187,000 horses; six months later he recrossed the Nieman with only 1,600. During the first eight months of the Civil War in 1864, the federal Army used up to 40,000 horses. Even in World War II, because they enjoyed greater flexibility in operations over difficult terrain and particularly in severe weather, the Russian Red Army cavalry units employed 200,000 horses effectively against German mechanized vehicles.

For the most part, the equine heroes of war are nameless, but a few did acquire some measure of immortality along with their famous military riders. Alexander the Great rode a horse named Bicephalus; Napoleon, Marengo; General Robert E. Lee, Traveler; General Sheridan, Winchester; and the Duke of Wellington, the powerful chestnut Copenhagen. Comanche, Captain Keogh's tough little mount in Custer's last stand at the Little Big Horn, was the sole survivor of that massacre.

There are horses known only as creations of art and literature, such as Pegasus, the Flying Horse of Greek mythology, and the Bronze Horse in sculptured form at the Metropolitan Museum of Art. But in real life, there has been only one racehorse that has fully merited recognition as a war hero. That special horse was Whirlaway.

So let it be known and the news widely dispersed that once upon a time, a Prince Charming came charging out of the animal kingdom and, endowed by his Creator with rare speed and indomitable courage, made complete his conquest of a thoroughbred-loving nation.

Chapter 1

The World of Whirlaway

THE year 1938 began for Warren and Lucille Wright in the same manner as had the past seven years. The goal of developing winning thoroughbred racehorses was uppermost in their thinking and business operations.

Warren Wright had inherited Calumet Farm as a part of the Calumet Baking Powder fortune left him by his father, Warren Monroe Wright. The elder Wright had

Blenheim II, Whirlaway's sire.

enjoyed success in the trotting horse field, having developed and raised winners in Triple Crown races such as the Hambletonian held in DuQuoin, Illinois, and the Kentucky Futurity, held in Lexington, as well as other races. But when the Warren Wrights left Chicago and made Kentucky's Calumet Farm their home in 1931, they had other ideas about horse racing. Warren Wright had a strong preference for the faster-gaited thoroughbreds over sedate trotters and harness racers.

The new master of Calumet plunged into thoroughbred racing on a lavish scale, committing large outlays of money for the purchase of racing and breeding stock. Every building at Calumet Farm was remodeled or rebuilt, and the grounds were increased to 1,038 acres. The farm soon became a showplace for the care and training of thoroughbreds. From the beginning, Warren Wright worked hard toward the day he would witness a Calumet horse winning the Kentucky Derby.

Even in its early years of operation as a thoroughbred racing farm, Calumet showed signs of becoming a leading racing stable. In 1937, the farm ranked ninth on the charts, posting 63 winners and over $100,000 in winnings. Calumet's first trophy was earned by Hadagal in 1934 as winner of Kentucky's Governor Green Handicap. In the same year, Calumet raced Nellie Flag, regarded as a champion two-year-old filly and considered good enough to start as the favorite in the 1934 Kentucky Derby. Three years later, a Calumet colt named Bull Lea won the Widener Handicap, a major race in Florida. But after seven years of racing, Warren Wright still pursued his number one goal — a Kentucky Derby winner.

As early as 1936, Wright decided to take some bold steps in his quest to post a Derby winner. He organized and headed the American investors syndicate that went to England and purchased Blenheim II, a former winner of the English Derby and the most successful sire in Europe, for $250,000. Calumet Farm acquired one-fourth interest in the stallion. That same year, Calumet also obtained a beautiful broodmare named Dustwhirl, who had shown good speed though had never been entered in a race. However, before coming to Calumet Farm she had produced a couple of stakes winners.

Dan Mahaney, business manager at the Farm, had played an important role in these developments. It was he who suggested in 1937 that Dustwhirl be mated to Blenheim II. Mr. Wright gave his consent to the

Dustwhirl, Whirlaway's dam.

Whirlaway and Dustwhirl shortly after the colt's birth.

idea, and yet another attempt at improving the Calumet breed was launched.

April 2, 1938, started as a routine day at Calumet Farm, but before it had ended, the word went out that a new foal had been born. Everyone in the vicinity gathered at the foaling barn to take a look at the first-born from Dustwhirl and Blenhiem II. The new arrival turned out to be a blaze-faced chestnut colt. Other identifying features of the foal, more unique in nature, were not apparent to the curious onlookers at the time.

As had happened so often in the past, the question was again raised at Calumet Farm — would this baby colt turn out to be a winner? Hope and determination were still alive. The countdown continued.

Whirlaway at birth.

As was custom, the new foal was called by his mother's name, Dustwhirl. This was quickly shortened to Whirly, which remained the colt's name until he received an official one approved by the Jockey Club. That turned out to be one suggested by Mrs. Wright — Whirlaway. The nickname "Whirly" would continue to be the favorite from among a long list that would accrue during his racing career.

If Dustwhirl and Blenheim II could have conjectured as human parents do, they would have expressed high hopes for their newborn son; but considering the uncertain conditions existing in the world of 1938, they could not know what might be in store for their first offspring.

The year of Whirlaway's birth gave forth an early signal that business as usual was not in the offing. On January 17, Benny Goodman and his orchestra had invaded the confines of staid Carnegie Hall in New York City with a concert, which Olin Downes of *The New York Times* characterized as a "new kind of music." This new music, called swing, or the beat of any popular music for that matter, had never before been heard in Carnegie Hall. Since its opening concert in 1891, conducted by the famous Russian composer, Peter Ilyich Tchaikovsky, Carnegie Hall had been reserved for the New York Philharmonic Orchestra and classical music of Bach and Beethoven vintage. Largely as a result of this historic concert, Benny Goodman was hailed as the "King of Swing," and Carnegie Hall was never the same. Goodman is also credited with crossing another musical frontier by becoming the first white conductor to include black musicians in his orchestra — Count Basie, Lionel Hampton, and Teddy Wilson.

Elsewhere on the national scene, the country was still feeling the effects from a recession of the previous year. President Franklin D. Roosevelt was having difficulty for the first time in getting his economic recovery program through Congress. In one of his famous "fireside chats," he appealed directly to the people by radio for support:

> I am constantly thinking of all our people — unemployed and employed alike — of their human problems of food and clothing and homes and education and health and old age. You and I agree that security is our greatest need — the chance to work, the opportunity of making a reasonable profit in our business — whether it be a very small business or a larger one

Whirlaway as a colt.

> the possibility of selling our farm products for enough money for our families to live on decently. I know these are the things that decide the well-being of our people.

On the world scene, the deadly theatrics of military dictators were threatening the freedom and security of increasing thousands of innocent people. In 1936, Hitler's German troops had occupied the west bank of the Rhine and announced to the world that the Treaty of Versailles had been shredded. The Japanese were penetrating farther into China. Italy, under Mussolini, had defied League of Nations sanctions and completed

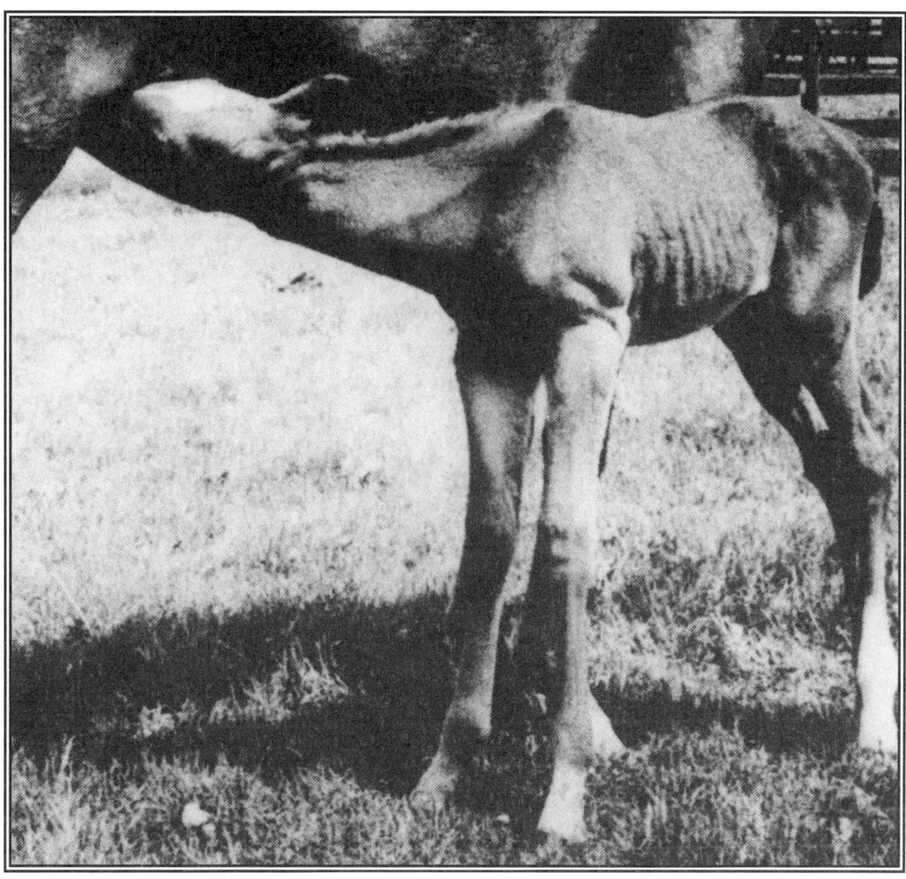

Whirlaway.

the inglorious conquest of Ethiopia. And another military dictatorship was emerging in Spain under Generalissimo Franco and his rebels.

The cares of the nation and the world were far removed from the foaling barn that day at Calumet Farm when Whirlaway made his first appearance. Bert Clark Thayer, eminent horse photographer and writer of the day, who took pictures of Whirlaway throughout his racing career, tells of the time he was photographing Whirlaway's mother, Dustwhirl. The colt kept insisting on getting into the picture, which Thayer said later "foreshadowed his penchant for attracting attention throughout his career."

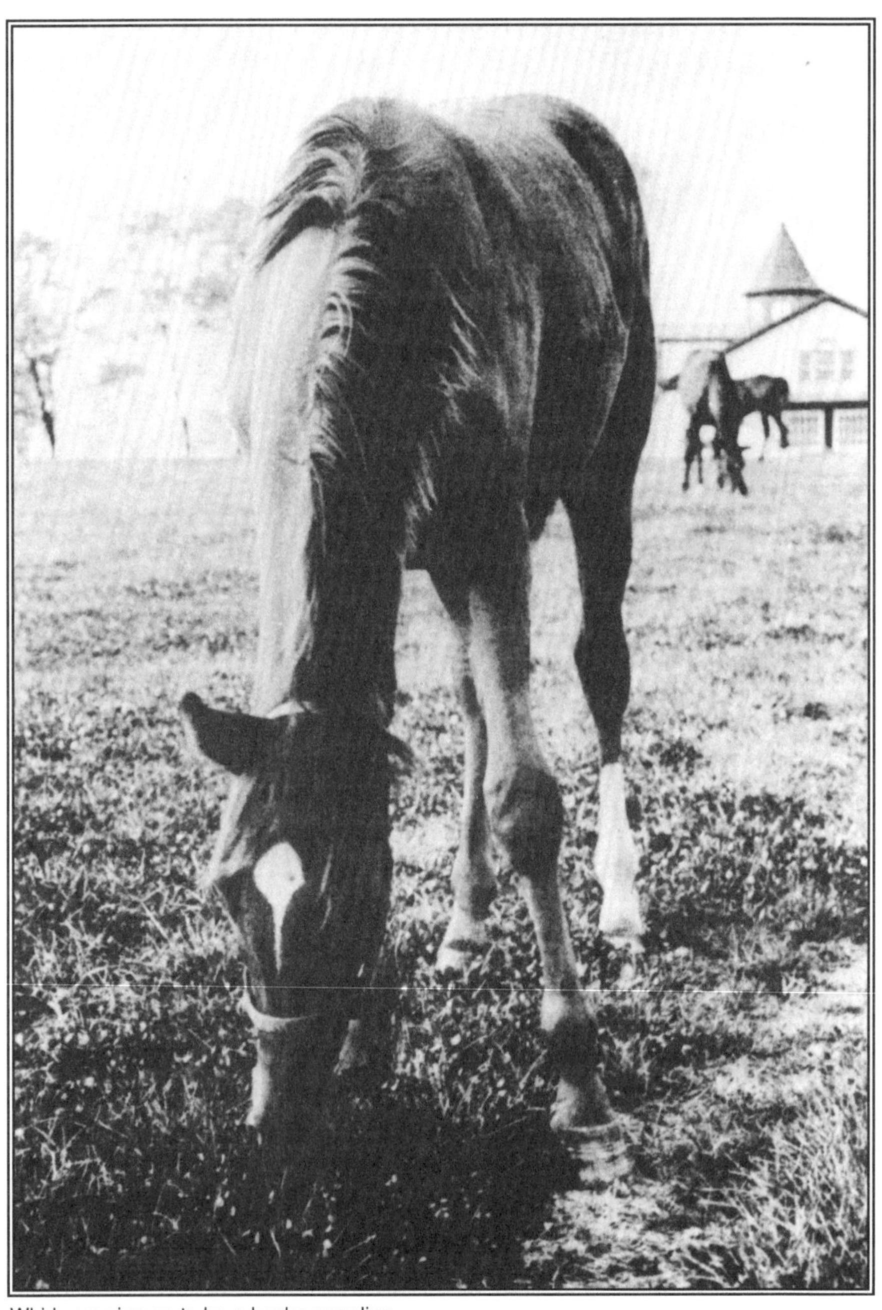

Whirly growing up to be a husky weanling.

A few days after birth, mares and their foals are taken to a special barn where they stay for about six months until the foal is weaned. Zeke Wilson had been in charge of weanlings at Calumet for the previous 19 years. Whirly was Zeke's favorite of the 24 foals that came to his barn in 1938. Zeke said:

> Whirly was gentle in the stall for brushing and cleaning of feet, never mean, but often mischievous and would throw his head. . . . Never had a sick day in his six months' stay at the barn. I thought from the first he might be a fast one. . . .

When Whirlaway grew stronger, he and his mother were put with the other mares and their foals in the big pasture. According to Thayer,

> He had a happy, carefree life, managing to eat a little grass in spite of his long legs, romping and playing the whole summer long, the happiest period of his life.

While Whirly was a resident at Zeke Wilson's foaling barn, Calumet Farm had its hopes dashed again when its entry, Bull Lea, a co-favorite with Fighting Fox, finished eighth in the Kentucky Derby. Lawrin, trained by Ben Jones for Woolford Farms and ridden by Eddie Arcaro, was the surprise winner in the 64th running of the Derby. This combination of Jones and Arcaro would later greatly influence the racing career of the newborn foal playing and grazing in the big pasture at Calumet Farm.

Many would agree that 1938 was a year of momentous events in the United States and throughout the world, a year of unresolved issues and problems that would, in the immediate years ahead, lead to global disillusionment and tragedy, but a year in which the advent of Whirlaway had little significance beyond the rolling acres of Calumet Farm.

Whirlaway grew quickly, as baby colts usually do, and early in 1939 began to take on bodily features and natural traits that would clearly distinguish him as a thoroughbred racehorse. His handlers began to notice his good bone and muscle, his racy look, and how constantly he would outrun all other colts in the paddock races. It was at this point that Bill Reitzman, who was in charge of breeding stock at Calumet, took an

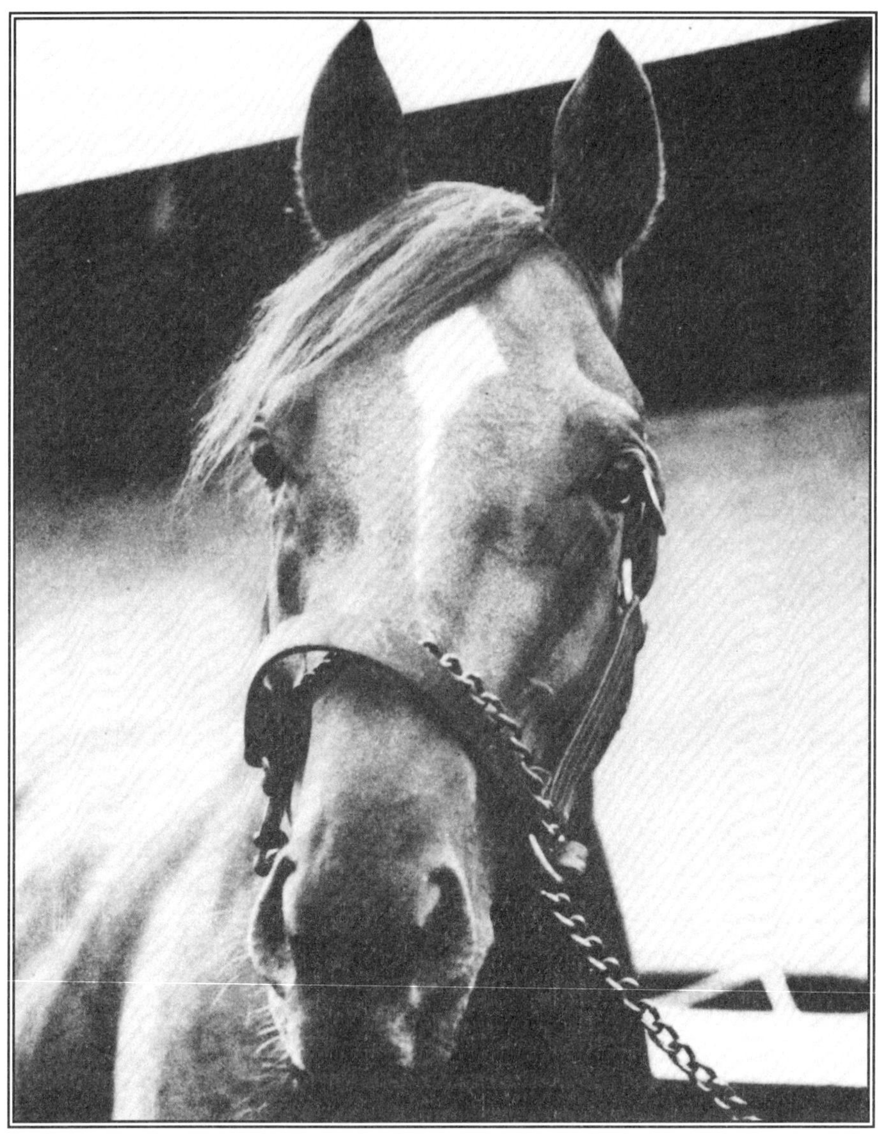

Whirly as a handsome yearling.

interest in this handsome youngster. He was impressed with Whirly's faultless action when in motion and picked this yearling as the one to nurture with his attention and special care.

Then came the beginning of World War II. A poll taken early in 1939 showed a strong preference for isolationism throughout America. Among those surveyed, 80 percent hoped that the Allies would prevail against Nazi aggression, but 90 percent did not want to join them in war.

Calumet Farm was racing some horses during the summer of 1939, but not doing as well as Woolford Stable with Ben Jones as trainer. Warren Wright remembered Jones for his success in training Lawrin, the 1938 Kentucky Derby winner. With that in mind, Wright met with Jones in Chicago and offered him the job of training Calumet horses. An agreement was quickly reached, and during the last week of August, Ben and his son Jimmy (H. A.) took charge of Warren Wright's thoroughbreds.

Almost to the day, as Ben Jones began his new job at Calumet Farm, German troops invaded Poland. With the announcement of this blatant act of aggression against Poland, and in keeping with previous treaty commitments, at 6:00 a.m., September 3, 1939, England and France declared war on Germany, and the most destructive conflict in history was officially under way. Germany crushed Poland within a month, and that tragic country was partitioned by Germany and Russia.

Most Americans were shocked at Germany's ruthless invasion of Poland but still hoped and believed the United States could stay out of the war. As Ben Jones assumed his duties at Calumet Farm in September 1939, he must have had serious thoughts about his future and the prospects for the yearlings he would soon be taking to Florida to begin their training for the upcoming 1940 racing season.

When Ben Jones and Jimmy had arrived at Calumet Farm that August, they were anxious to look over the string of horses at their command and to start planning for the approaching season. After familiarizing themselves with the facilities available, they soon began concentrating on the 20 yearlings called up from their romping and playing in the Farm's big pasture. Out of this class of prospects, one youngster caught Ben's eye as most likely to succeed as a racer. A handsome chestnut, this lone standout turned out to be Zeke Wilson's favorite weanling, Whirly, then called Whirlaway. Jimmy Jones recalled in later years,

> I often think back and wonder what might have been had we not had this one good colt in an otherwise poor collection.

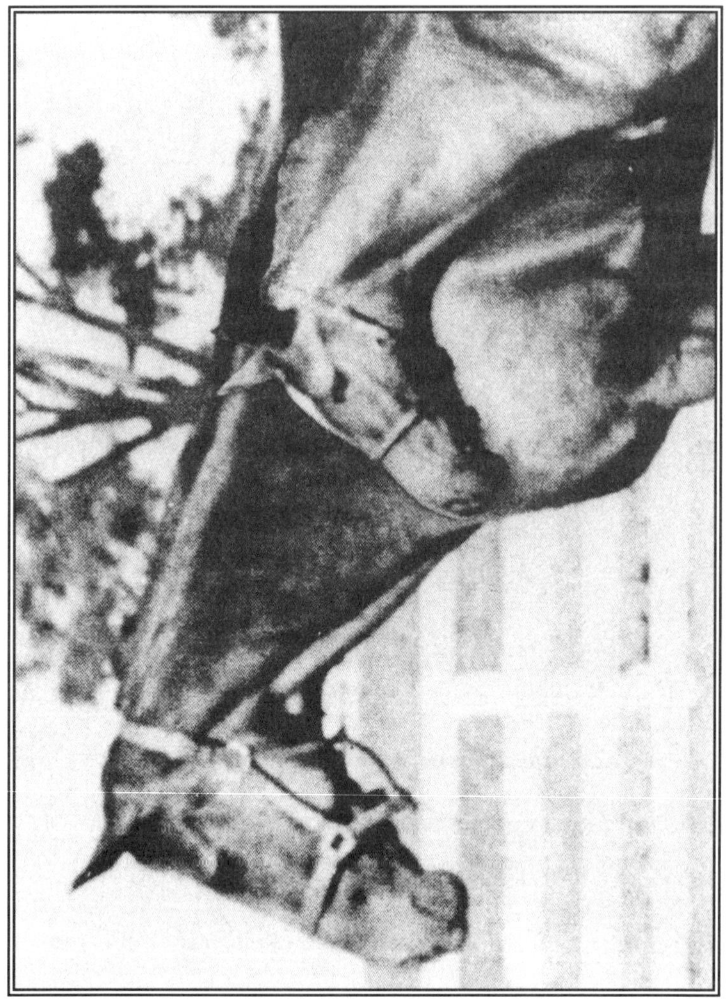

Mother and son.

Whirlaway continued to impress his handlers during the early months of 1940, and speculation grew around the stable that young Whirly might really be the one to reverse the pattern of few winners and large deficits that had befallen Calumet Farm in its first nine years of operation as a thoroughbred racing establishment. Ben Jones soon decided to devote full time to training Whirlaway, while Jimmy took on instructional duties of the other horses.

Called B. A. by some and "Plain Ben" affectionately by others, Ben Jones had been born in Parnell, Missouri, in 1883 and had grown up as a rancher's son. He attended what later became Colorado A & M College, but soon decided that the academic life was not for him. Finally, he turned to training and racing horses in the "bush" tracks of the Southwest and Mexico, known then as the "leaky-roof circuit" because of inferior facilities. The races were mostly small-purse short sprints of a few hundred yards, and Ben had to win many of these to keep his family afloat. Things improved when Jones acquired a well-bred stallion named Seth who sired several good horses. In 1929, this stallion had tied as the leading sire of two-year-olds, which in turn enhanced the reputation of the trainer in his high-risk profession.

The first big break came for Ben in 1932, at the depths of the Great Depression, when Herbert Woolf hired him to train his horses at Woolford Farm near Kansas City. Woolf's horses did well, and by 1938, when the Farm's Lawrin won the Kentucky Derby, Ben had achieved major-league status as a trainer.

Thus it was that Warren Wright at age 64 placed renewed hope for Calumet Farm in this veteran 56-year-old trainer and an untried colt.

By the start of his training period as a two-year-old, Whirlaway had grown into a handsome colt with a glistening coat and an extra-long, full tail. What would be more important to his racing career was that the equine youngster was a model of conformation, without blemish, and was blessed with strong legs and a sound body.

Although Whirlaway appeared to possess the necessary credentials for becoming a winning racehorse, he immediately showed a disdain for his new lifestyle. Some writers have made much of his temperamental behavior as a two-year-old, but Whirlaway was not much different from most thoroughbreds in showing a dislike for the racetrack environment. Sam Riddle, owner of Man O' War, winner of the 1920 Preakness and

Belmont Stakes, almost gave up on him as a two-year-old. The colt fought like a tiger with his handlers and screamed with fervor at being saddled. It took several days of effort to approach him with safety. "Big Red" continued to show discomfort with being saddled throughout his career.

Count Fleet, 1943 Kentucky Derby winner, sired at Mrs. John D. Hertz's Stoner Creek Stud in Kentucky, was so fractious as a yearling, that John D. Hertz tried to sell him. Later Hertz tried to dissuade jockey Johnny Longden from riding the Count, telling Johnny he feared the colt might cause him serious injury.

Perhaps these temperamental thoroughbreds were simply proclaiming their distaste for the strange life into which they were forcibly subjected. R. H. Smythe, eminent horse psychologist, in his book *The Mind of the Horse*, makes this observation concerning the horse's predicament:

> Today, one can only regard the modern horse, wholly dependent on the whims of mankind, removed from its natural environment and living an entirely artificial life, as one of the most extraordinary of all domesticated animals.

After playing and romping over the rolling Calumet hills as a yearling, Whirlaway was quick to register disapproval for the radically different environment set within the highly restricted boundaries of a racing oval. He was a rugged little fellow with a lot of spirit. Sometimes it took several handlers to saddle him. If brought to the track through a particular gate in the morning, he rebelled if he was not taken through the same gate in the afternoon. Perhaps it was his way of insisting on consistent treatment in an unfamiliar setting.

Eddie Arcaro, whose career as a jockey would receive its greatest boost from riding Whirlaway, made a perceptive statement in 1958 concerning the early training of thoroughbreds. When asked by writer Stanley Frank of the *Saturday Evening Post* if he thought racehorses lacked in brain power, he replied:

> No, I don't. I think a thoroughbred is very smart. It's a wonder he doesn't turn into a complete idiot when you analyze what's done to him. . . .

Whirlaway.

He pointed out that a thoroughbred's intensive breed makes him high-strung to begin with. Then at about 16 months old, someone he's always trusted takes him to a starting gate and closes him in a narrow stall that must seem like a prison. With people hollering at him, smacking him on the fanny, and ringing bells to get him accustomed to racing conditions, he's scared to death. But the next day he's expected to go calmly into the gate again. Arcaro concluded,

> . . . He must be intelligent to figure out what the trainer is trying to do, and bear up under the pressure put on him.

In the early months of 1940, Whirlaway and Ben Jones began what would later be recognized as one of the closest and most notable relationships in sports history. This rapport between horse and trainer would represent the highest level of learning environment — that envisioned by an educational philosopher, with the teacher on one end of a log and the student on the other — one-on-one learning. No thoroughbred would ever have a more capable and patient teacher.

It was not long until Ben discovered that this young colt had great potential as a racer. Whirlaway was a rugged, full-spirited juvenile, possessing an unlimited supply of energy. He displayed the ability of being able to run briskly in the morning workout and repeat the same effort in the afternoon, racing for long periods of time without showing signs of tiring.

Teacher and student spent long hours each day preparing for the upcoming racing season. The course of study included standing by the starting gate, walking around the racetrack, being saddled and unsaddled, and watching beside the track while groups of horses galloped by. Slowly but steadily, the young apprentice responded positively to the training program set before him.

Whirlaway reached his second birthday in April 1940, and the day was fast approaching when he would launch his racing career. At that time, the colt's prospects for becoming a successful thoroughbred racehorse were uncertain. However, after the passage of a little over three years and 60 consecutive races, a more definitive assessment of Whirlaway's life on the racing oval could be given.

Chapter 2

The Excitement Begins

WHILE Whirlaway and Ben Jones were engaged in serious training for the beginning of the racing season early in 1940, the war in Europe was spreading rapidly. With the German invasion of the Low Countries and France, sympathy in the United States swung swiftly to the side of the Allies. Volunteer aid and relief societies sprang up in their behalf. People in this country were thinking and discussing the upcoming presidential elec-

tion and the possibility of FDR running for an unprecedented third term. Employment in the nation was improving with the spread of defense industries, but purchasing power was restricted for most people. Jack Dempsey's restaurant in New York City was offering a lunch for 65 cents and a complete dinner for $1.50. In thoroughbred racing news, Seabiscuit won the Santa Anita Handicap in March and became the world's leading money-winner with a total of $437,730. He won over Kayak, who had beaten him the previous year in the same race.

In June 1940, Ben Jones decided it was time for Whirlaway to launch his racing career. The scene was the old Lincoln Fields track near Chicago. The date was June 3, and the race was a five-furlong sprint for maiden two-year-olds. Having just turned two in April, and probably based on his stunning appearance alone, Whirlaway went to the post as race favorite. Jack Richard was chosen to ride the Calumet hopeful in this initial race.

This first race established a pattern that would afford endless discussions about Whirlaway's racing style. Soon after the start of the race, Whirlaway broke to the outside, followed the fence most of the distance, and with a sudden rush of speed in the stretch, came home first.

After the race, trainer Jones said: "I knew he was a winner." But Plain Ben also knew that there was still much work ahead before Whirlaway was ready for serious competition. Jones added that the young colt's tendency to bear out might have been caused by the location of the Calumet barn at Lincoln Fields. The gateway to the barn was located at the turn into the stretch, and Ben believed that once the youngster spotted that familiar gateway, he was inspired to go home.

That maneuver was corrected with the transfer of the Calumet stable to Arlington Park in Chicago after that first race. Whirlaway ran straight in his next two races. Ben Lindheimer, operator of Arlington Park in those days, recalled later how he would sit in the stands in the mornings and watch Whirlaway and Jones work together day after day in the hot sun. This patient one-on-one instruction between teacher and pupil enabled the colt to become thoroughly familiar with all aspects of the racetrack — its contours, the starting gate, the grandstand, and the crowd.

Whirlaway spent the rest of June and most of July at Arlington Park. He won only one of his five races there, but gained much needed experience for the important two-year-old races later in the year. In his last race at Arlington that summer, Whirlaway was ridden by Johnny Longden. This promising young jockey would in later years be recognized as one of the greatest, amassing a grand total of 6,027 winners in a career spanning 40 years. Longden went on to ride Whirlaway in ten of his races in the late summer and fall of 1940. Although the colt was still a somewhat willful and temperamental juvenile, Johnny played a definite role in those races in developing the youngster's exciting racing style, which would soon start attracting large crowds.

After the Arlington Futurity in Chicago, Whirlaway and Calumet stable moved on to Saratoga Springs in upper New York state, location of the oldest thoroughbred racetrack in the United States. This famous spa was, and still is, the scene of what is the most important race in late summer for two-year-olds, the Hopeful Stakes.

Whirlaway's first race at Saratoga was August 3, only one week after racing in Chicago. In the Hotel Stakes over a distance of six furlongs, the Calumet colt finished second to Attention by one-half length. It was in this race that the real potential and style of Whirlaway as a racer began to surface. He stole the show by starting last, was next to last at the quarter pole, but was running over the winner in the closing strides.

A week later, Whirlaway was entered in his second six-furlong sprint at the Saratoga meet, the Saratoga Special. In this particular race, the winner takes all. Bryan Field, turf writer for *The New York Times*, gave this description of the race:

> Sweeping on from last place and around the entire field at the head of the stretch, the Calumet Farm's Whirlaway today overwhelmed his opposition in the Saratoga Special in such smashing style that already he is being hailed as the potential juvenile champion.

As the race began, many had given up hope that Whirlaway would even get in the money. Alfred G. Vanderbilt's entry, New World, was burning up the track and was a couple of lengths ahead of the rest. They were that way at the far turn, and still almost that way at the turn into the stretch. Then, as Field saw it,

> . . . Whirlaway had begun his rush under Johnny Longden and was much closer, albeit still last. Yet in that straight line the son of Blenheim II dashed past all the others, collared New World and left him standing. . . . Whirlaway had a length margin at the end and was going away.

It was an impressive victory for Whirlaway, and it gained for a justly proud Warren Wright his first important trophy after ten long years of waiting. Whirly's effort overshadowed the 61st running of the historic Alabama Stakes run on the same day. It was also the best attendance for the Saratoga meet up to that point.

Two weeks later, on August 24, Whirlaway was entered in the celebrated Hopeful Stakes, Saratoga's classic $43,350 race for two-year-olds. Track conditions were so soggy that many of the horses were withdrawn from the race, including New World. But Whirlaway had not been scratched from any of the previous eight races in which he was entered, and this one would be no exception. By running in the Hopeful, this young colt was continuing to establish a precedent that would last throughout his racing career.

Bryan Field of *The New York Times* wrote about the 1940 Hopeful Stakes:

> Whirlaway won . . . through the mud and rain . . . under rough and tough conditions. He drove through the stretch to win by a length from as keen a colt as Mrs. Parker Corning's Attention.
>
> . . . The running proved his mettle, too. Only four started and the race was truly run in every particular.

Twinkippy was a fast pacesetter, with Hy-Cop and Attention in close pursuit, while Whirlaway brought up the rear. As they approached the top of the stretch, Attention ran into the lead. But Longden had gotten Whirlaway under way, and Field continues,

> . . . He came up on the outside of everything, and . . . had to go very wide indeed.
>
> Yet around everything he went, and then turned loose in

> earnest on the stretch drive for home. Good as Attention was, Whirlaway picked him up and scored going away.

What made Whirlaway's victory truly amazing was that a small stone had struck him in the eye at some stage of the race. This alone would have caused some more seasoned horses to bolt, but Whirly showed no signs of distress. Jimmy Jones was quoted later as saying Whirlaway won the race on "raw courage."

Thus Whirlaway came through in smashing fashion for his greatest victory as a two-year-old. He won the race in 1:18 flat for the six and one-half furlongs. In spite of ankle-deep mud, this was the fastest time for the race since Epithet had won in 1930 with a time of 1:17 3/5. It was truly a remarkable performance for a two-year-old.

Neville Dunn, reporting in Lexington's *The Herald-Leader*, expressed the joy of Whirlaway's home-town friends and neighbors with this postscript on the colt's victory:

> There was . . . rejoicing in Lexington . . . when Whirlaway won the Hopeful Stakes. . . . It is conceded by the majority of horse fans of this section that there is not a more deserving man in racing than Mr. Wright. He has done more for the sport and much for Lexington and Fayette County.

Whirlaway's eye injury became a major concern after the Saratoga race. It was so severe that Warren Wright called in a human eye specialist for consultation with veterinarians. There was considerable fear for some time thereafter that the colt might lose his eye. But at this point in his young career, another striking element of Whirly's character as a racehorse began to emerge — durability. The eye slowly responded to treatment, and in a few weeks he resumed his itinerary of racing for the final months of 1940.

Whirlaway returned to racing in late September, but evidently too soon after his injury to be in top condition. At Belmont Park in New York City, he finished fifth in the Futurity Trial on September 24 and third four days later in the Futurity. A mistake in the colt's preparation for the Futurity was made the day preceding that race when Whirlaway was allowed to blaze five furlongs down the track so fast that many

Whirlaway, trainer Jones, and jockey Longden in the winner's circle at Keeneland after the 1940 Breeders' Futurity.

feared he left his best effort on the turf. He was timed in better than one minute and five-eighths seconds, which was close to track-record time.

After the Belmont Futurity, Whirlaway was shipped to Lexington to prepare for the Breeders' Futurity at Keeneland Race Track, next door to the place of his birth. Evidently, a return to the home turf was exactly what the young colt needed. After all, the youngster hadn't seen his mother in over five months. On the first day of the Keeneland meet, October 8, Whirly won a prep race for two-year-olds by two lengths and appeared to be in top form for the feature race on October 19.

The Breeders' Futurity, a six-furlong race first run in 1910 on the old Association Course, then the oldest in America dating back to 1826, was held on the closing day of the meet. It shaped up as quite an attraction with high interest centered on three colts: Whirlaway, Our Boots, and Blue Pair.

Whirlaway trailed as usual in the first turn of the five-horse race, but by the time they reached the stretch, Whirlaway was closing in on Blue Pair. Then in a final burst of speed, he drew out in front to win by a length. Johnny Longden had predicted that Whirlaway would find the curved course at Keeneland more to his liking than the Belmont straightaway. The contours of Keeneland, Longden further stated, were made to order for Whirly's rapid turn into the stretch.

After the Breeders' Futurity at Keeneland, Calumet stable moved on to Baltimore and entered Whirlaway in the Pimlico Futurity on November 2. The distance was for a mile and a sixteenth, and Whirly hadn't raced beyond seven-eighths of a mile before. In his preparatory workouts for this distance, he had done so well that he was sent to the post as favorite.

Years later, Johnny Longden recalled what happened in the Pimlico Futurity. In the days preceding the race, heavy rains had created a dangerous mud hole near the final turn of the track, and Ben Jones had given Longden explicit orders to avoid taking Whirlaway through that particular spot on the course. But by post time for the race, the condition of that area of the track had improved markedly. Nevertheless, Jones still insisted that Johnny follow those previous orders. During the race, when the field of eight horses reached the designated danger zone of the track, all of the horses except for Whirlaway went through the terrain without a hitch. Johnny, riding as directed, took Whirly to the outside, lost considerable ground and speed, and finished third in the race. After the passage of 44 years, Johnny still maintains he could have won the race easily if he could have taken Whirlaway through the forbidden area on the run for the wire.

If Ben Jones showed great concern for what he perceived as a dangerous condition of the track in the Pimlico Futurity, he should have been appalled at the sea of mud at Pimlico for the Walden Stakes, also a mile-and-a-sixteenth race, on November 14. Track conditions on that day were considered to be the heaviest and toughest in years, compounded by a relentless rain. Johnny Longden, Whirly's rider in the last ten races, had just signed a contract with the John D. Hertz establishment for the remainder of the 1940 season and was not available for this race. George Woolf, rider of Seabiscuit in his victory over War Admiral in the match race of 1937, was engaged to ride Whirlaway in the 14th running of the Walden Stakes.

Neither the terrible condition of the track nor the sudden change of riders seemed to bother Whirlaway in this race. The veteran George Woolf let Whirlaway settle into his stride early in the race. The young colt showed no tendency to bear out and, after entering the backstretch, bounded to front in home lane, finishing four lengths ahead of his nearest contender, Magnificent.

Whirlaway's Walden Stakes victory enabled him to overtake his closest rival, Our Boots, and become leading money-winner of the 1940 two-year-olds with total earnings of $77,275. Thus Calumet Farm's first champion closed his first year of racing, a year in which he had endured an unusually heavy schedule of 16 races within a six-month span, by winning three of his last four starts. This handsome chestnut two-year-old had shown positive signs of stretch-running ability, flashes of great speed, courage, durability, and vigorous good health. For his noteworthy feats, Whirlaway received the decisive vote of turf writers as colt of the year.

During the timespan of Whirlaway's 1940 races, the war in Europe had gone badly for the Western democracies. France had surrendered to Nazi Germany. Following that debacle, England had been subjected to 12 weeks of merciless bombing by German planes during which 30,000 people in London had been killed. The day after Whirlaway's triumph in the Walden Stakes, the English cultural center of Coventry was leveled by the worst German air raid to date on England, with 1,000 casualties. The vengeful raid resulted in the destruction of three churches, including St. Michael's Cathedral. But the English showed remarkable courage during the ordeal, and at year's end they were braced for an expected invasion by German forces.

During the Christmas season of 1940, two speeches were delivered by radio on opposite sides of the Atlantic that exemplified contrasting philosophies of governments in fierce global conflict. Adolf Hitler, military dictator of Nazi Germany, stated in his radio address to German workers that the Nazi system was superior to that of the Western democracies and that he was the champion of the "have-nots." His rambling speech of 90 minutes left little doubt about his plans for world conquest, especially when he stated unequivocally that "the two systems of government cannot co-exist."

President Roosevelt broadcast his Christmas message to the nation from the White House in words foreign to Hitler's vocabulary:

> At this Christmas tide of 1940, it is well for all humanity to remind itself while this is in its name a Christian celebration, it is participated in reverently and happily by hundreds of millions of people who are members of other religions, or belong actively to no church at all.
>
> The reason is not far to seek. It is because the spirit of unselfish service personified by the life of Christ makes appeal to the inner conscience and hope of every man and every woman in every part of the earth. It transcends, in the ultimate, all lines of race, of habitat, of nation. It lives in the midst of war, of slavery, of conquest. It survives prohibitions and decrees and force. It is an unquenchable spring of promise to humanity.

And so it was as 1940 drew to a close.

Chapter
3

Whirlaway's Misfortunes

THE world began 1941 with a legacy from 1940 of immeasurable death, suffering, and destruction throughout Europe. Many held little hope for better days to come. In America, FDR was inaugurated as president for an unprecedented third time on January 20. And in sports, Bob Feller of the Cleveland Indians signed a contract for $30,000, the highest salary ever paid to a baseball pitcher to date.

Ben Jones had taken Whirlaway to Florida for three months of training, preparing the colt to start racing in early February with an eye toward the Kentucky Derby, set for the first Saturday in May. When Warren Wright had converted Calumet Farm to a thoroughbred racing establishment in 1931, he had had as his ultimate goal the development of a Derby winner. Finally, after ten years of all-out effort in that direction without any success, there was Whirlaway. Whirly had garnered Calumet its first trophy in the Saratoga Special on August 10, 1940, then quickly added three more trophies from important stakes races, including the great one for two-year-olds, the Hopeful Stakes at Saratoga on the 31st. As a result, Whirlaway had been chosen the juvenile champion and had gone to Florida picked by most as the favorite to win the Kentucky Derby.

But there were many other outstanding thoroughbreds starting their three-year-old campaigns in quest of the same prize. Our Boots had won the Belmont Futurity as a two-year-old; Blue Pair had won six straight races as a juvenile; and Dispose had started his three-year-old career by winning the Bahamas Handicap at Hialeah, doing seven furlongs in a record time of 1:22 2/5. With other Derby hopefuls on hand, such as Attention, Porter's Cap, King Cole, Market Wise, Little Beans, and Robert Morris, the 1941 racing season was shaping up as one of keen competition and thrilling races.

On February 8, Whirlaway made his first start of the winter season in Florida at Hialeah. His rider was lightweight Wendell Eads, 102 pounds, a new apprentice for Calumet Farm. The race was six furlongs and was billed as a prelude to the advertised feature, the Black Helen Handicap. But, as would be the case throughout his career, any time Whirly appeared on a track, he captured the immediate attention and interest of the crowd.

Whirly started slowly, so slowly that he seemed to have little chance to finish in the money. The other four horses ran away in a knot, forcing Whirlaway to go wide and lose ground in the stretch. After a quarter of a mile, though, the colt started gaining on the pack. Then at the head of the stretch, Whirly went wide as he had done in his early races as a two-year-old, losing ground in the process. But in a straight run down the middle of the track, he passed his rivals one by one in a rush and won by a head over Signator.

The magic of Whirlaway, with his long, flowing tail and glistening chestnut coat, was center stage once again. People rushed down to the winner's circle to congratulate Ben Jones and Warren Wright on the victory. Many remarked how beautiful a picture the colt made with his unclipped mane blowing in the breeze. Wright responded:

> Some plait the tail and braid the mane. We think Whirlaway has a nice mane and tail, and that they look best whipping in the breeze.

But something unexpected happened to Whirlaway in his next race, the Arcadia Purse, on February 18 at Hialeah. He finished third in this seven-furlong race preparatory to the Flamingo Stakes on February 22. What was most unusual was that the colt seemed sluggish and dispirited.

Ben Jones and son Jimmy were faced with a crucial decision. Warren Wright wanted that Flamingo trophy in the worst way, and he thought he had the horse that could win it. But he felt that the decision was better left to the discretion of his trainers. In later years, Jimmy Jones described the dilemma:

> We were satisfied not to enter Whirlaway in the Flamingo. He wasn't himself, but horses do those things. He wasn't holding his flesh, and he didn't seem to have his normal spirit and snap.

It was announced that Whirlaway had developed a little splint, a new bone formation located between the splint and shin bones. It was a common problem in yearlings and two-year-olds. Whirlaway didn't have a splint, but no one disputed it. Whirlaway didn't run in the Flamingo. Jones continued:

> I am convinced that had Whirlaway run in the Flamingo he would have lost his form entirely, and we would have had to start all over. . . . We might not have had enough time to do this before the Derby. . . . Maybe he wouldn't have been ready.

Rest appeared to be the best medicine for Whirlaway, and he was sidelined for a few weeks. The Flamingo Stakes race was won that year by a promising three-year-old named Dispose, with the second fastest time on record for the Flamingo.

Near the middle of March, Ben Jones noticed that Whirlaway was rapidly regaining his form. The colt was putting on weight and galloping stronger every morning. At that point, Jones decided Whirly would benefit more from an actual race than from workouts. It was hoped that this strategy would build up his form ahead of the schedule planned before reaching Kentucky for the Blue Grass Stakes.

With this decision made, Whirlaway was entered in a five-and-one-half furlong sprint at Tropical Park on March 28. Jimmy Jones explains a crisis that arose when Warren Wright read about Whirly's entry in the sprint in the morning paper.

> . . . Boy, was he upset!
>
> . . . He put ashore and headed for Miami. He reached Tropical Park . . . , went immediately to his box and confronted Ben Jones. He told Ben that Whirlaway must be scratched. . . .

But according to Jimmy, Ben said he would not scratch him because this was his way of training him. Both men sat down, still upset.

There was little doubt in Jimmy Jones's mind that if Whirlaway hadn't run well in that short race at Tropical Park, both he and his father would have been looking for jobs elsewhere. Interestingly enough, Whirlaway, who had not taken part in the confrontation between his trainer and owner, settled the whole issue by coming on the track, cranking up his speed machine, and winning the race with a fast finish.

Mr. Wright, at peace with the world after the race, smiled broadly and told Ben Jones he would never attempt to help train another horse. And, as was his trademark, the master of Calumet Farm kept his word and never again questioned his trainers. Tropical Park had enhanced Whirlaway's growing reputation and was proof of his ability to win crucial races — and in the process add luster to the lives and careers of those close to him.

After the March 28 race, Whirlaway was shipped home to Lexington where he would be entered in the Blue Grass Stakes, next door to his home. The Calumet colt had just turned three when he arrived at

Whirlaway at Calumet Farm.

Lexington's Keeneland Race Track in early April. His chestnut coat had developed a beautiful silken finish, and his golden tail extended almost to the ground. In the days ahead, his tail would become a mark of instant identification on the track.

Near-record crowds thronged to the Keeneland track just to watch Whirlaway in his workouts. In preparation for the Blue Grass Stakes, he was entered in a sprint of six furlongs at Keeneland on April 11. Apprentice Wendell Eads rode Whirly to victory in this short race by bringing him from far behind in the run for the wire. The colt continued to show improvement in the days following the short race and seemed to be in top form for the Blue Grass Stakes on April 24. But in that mile-and-an-eighth race, Eads allowed the colt to go wide on the turn for home and lost the race to Our Boots.

In a rare show of emotion after the race, Ben Jones expressed his displeasure with Eads for not riding Whirlaway according to instructions. Nevertheless, Jones showed his steadfast faith in Whirlaway by making this statement to the critics:

> The colt's all right and will prove it. This was his first race this year longer than seven furlongs and he just naturally tired at the end. He needs a strong boy to keep him straight and hard work to keep him fit.

The result of the Blue Grass Stakes race created considerable concern in thoroughbred racing circles regarding Whirlaway's future as a three-year-old. And it had demonstrated clearly that the young and inexperienced Eads lacked the strong hands needed to guide the willful colt on a straight course in the upcoming Kentucky Derby, now only nine days away.

Ben Jones conferred with Warren Wright concerning the problem. The name of Eddie Arcaro quickly emerged from the consultation as the best possible choice for a replacement. There was good reason for reaching such a decision. Arcaro had been riding thoroughbred racehorses for ten years in 8,000 races. He was recognized as a strong rider with a soft touch, a quality possessed by relatively few in the business. Jones recalled vividly that three years before, Eddie had ridden Lawrin to victory in the Derby.

The choice for a rider was clear, but that didn't solve the problem. Arcaro's availability on Saturday, May 3, was the determining factor. Eddie was under contract to Greentree Stable, and if that stable posted an entry on Derby Day, Whirlaway would not have him in the saddle for the "run for the roses."

In those days, most of the established racing farms had regular jockeys under contract. But Calumet Farm, being a relatively "new kid on the block," did not benefit from the services of an experienced rider on a regular basis. Consequently, in his short career, Whirlaway had been subjected to the riding styles of seven different jockeys. This frequent change of rider most assuredly contributed to the colt's inconsistent racing performances at that time.

Warren Wright began negotiations immediately after the Blue Grass Stakes race in an attempt to secure Arcaro for the Derby. In the meantime, Calumet Farm moved its stable down the road 60 miles to Louisville and Churchill Downs, the scene of the upcoming race.

While negotiations proceeded for Arcaro, Whirlaway was entered in the Derby Trial on April 29, just four days before the big event. With Eads still his rider, Whirlaway came from fifth place in a field of six, some nine lengths back, to look the pacesetters in the eye at the final turn for home. But at that point, Eads couldn't straighten Whirly out in the run for the wire. This resulted in the loss of at least eight lengths and allowed Blue Pair to beat Whirlaway by a nose at the finish.

The New York Times reported the result of the race:

> The Derby Trial race didn't prove a thing except that Whirlaway can come like the wind when steered on a straight road home.

Ben Jones remarked that Whirly would have *won* the race by eight lengths if Eads had ridden the colt correctly.

The distress of the loss was greatly alleviated by the announcement that Eddie Arcaro would ride Whirlaway in the Kentucky Derby. When contacted, Eddie was riding at the Jamaica Race Track in New York City. Warren Wright was elated to learn that the jockey was without a mount for the Derby and would be willing to ride Whirlaway. The only question left unanswered was whether or not there would there be time for Arcaro and Whirlaway to get acquainted by Saturday, just four days away.

Ben Jones was relieved to learn that Arcaro would be aboard Whirly in the Derby, but the trainer still had concerns. There were strategy considerations that had to be addressed, and time was minimal. Ben knew prime consideration had to be given the distance to be covered. The mile-and-one-fourth Kentucky Derby is the first trial for three-year-olds of that length.

Training was planned to familiarize Whirlaway with every aspect of the track. The patient trainer spent most of each day with him, riding alongside the colt on his own white pony. One day he would run Whirly as fast as possible. The next day he would walk him around the track, saddle and unsaddle him several times, allow him to nuzzle the inside rail, and keep him on grass awhile. The pre-race plan called for a comprehensive attempt to eliminate all possible obstacles that might encourage the colt to veer out in the stretch run, something that had caused the loss of his last two races.

Two parts of this plan were in place. The more experienced Arcaro would ride Whirlaway in the Derby, and the colt was fast becoming familiar with every foot of the track at Churchill Downs. To complete the plan, the trainer added a touch of creativity for insurance by providing Whirly with blinkers and cutting away the inside section, leaving broader vision out of the colt's left eye. Ben hoped this innovation would help draw the horse's attention to the inner part of the track.

This strategy was based on a sound understanding of equine visual perception. Horse psychologist R. H. Smythe clarifies this point in *The Mind of the Horse*. He explains that as a result of "semi-lateral or oblique eye positioning," the horse is able to view two separate pictures at the same time, one on either side of its body. Thus by restricting Whirlaway's field of vision to the inside of the track, it was hoped the horse would readily follow that course.

Arcaro finished his commitments at the Jamaica Race Track on Wednesday, April 30, 1941, and arrived at Churchill Downs on Friday, just one day before the race. With only a matter of hours left to prepare, Jones, Arcaro, and Whirlaway were on the track Friday morning, going over every detail of the race plan. From the moment Jones mounted his big gray lead pony and Arcaro threw his leg over Whirlaway for the first time, the rest of the racing strategy fell rapidly into place.

Jones took a position on his pony at the head of the stretch just a few feet from the rail. When Arcaro brought Whirly around the turn in the morning exercise session, the colt was compelled to drive through the four-foot opening between Jones's horse and the rail. The trainer explained to Arcaro where he wanted Whirlaway to be at each stage of the race. The substance of this rehearsal was to keep the colt off the early pace and not use his tremendous speed until he was straightened out for the stretch run to the finish line.

The objectives of the Friday morning workout seemed to be met without apparent difficulty. Arcaro told Jones he would execute what he had been told to do in the race. "Then we'll win, Eddie," replied the trainer.

Chapter
4

The 67th Kentucky Derby — Saturday, May 3, 1941

WHILE Whirlaway's race plan was being finalized late Friday afternoon, excitement and speculation surrounding the Kentucky Derby were mounting rapidly. All 11 horses entered in the 67th Derby were given a chance to win. There had never been a more formidable lineup. On May 1, Our Boots had been listed as an 8-5 favorite, having looked good in winning the Blue Grass Stakes a week before. On May 2, Porter's Cap from California, winner of the Santa Anita Derby and Chesapeake Stakes and current leading money-winner among three-year-olds, was made a co-favorite with Our Boots. Market Wise had recently won the Wood Memorial, thus qualifying as a serious contender. Blue Pair took the Derby Trial and, in so doing, showed good speed. Dispose had captured the Flamingo Stakes and had gone through an impressive workout over the mile-and-a-quarter Derby route on April 30. In a morning session on May 1, Robert Morris had appeared in top form as he caught up with Market Wise at the finish of a six-furlong workout. Other stables also expressed solid confidence in their entries on the eve of the Churchill Downs classic.

Colonel Matt J. Winn, 80-year-old president of Churchill Downs, had seen every Kentucky Derby since the classic had started in 1875. His chief goal since he had become head man in 1938 was to achieve an attendance of 100,000. Because of a strange phenomenon taking place in Louisville and throughout the nation, this cherished dream showed promising signs of fulfillment. The site of the Derby on the banks of Ohio River had become a mecca for thousands of racing fans. All places of lodging in Louisville and surrounding environs were filled and overflowing.

Forty special trains were arriving for the race. About half were overnight trains on which patrons slept aboard the night preceding the Derby. Other railroad cars brought a great influx from Chicago the morning of the race. Many other racing fans had journeyed to Louisville by automobile and, confronted with no available lodging, had slept overnight in their cars in the parking lot of Churchill Downs. In addition, thousands had journeyed from nearby Fort Knox and the mushrooming defense plants throughout Kentucky and adjacent states.

Every sector of American society was represented in the mosaic that was Churchill Downs on Derby Day 1941. A dozen governors and other high-echelon state and city government officials were identified in the huge crowd; 15 United States senators were on hand; and the movie industry was heavily represented with such stars as Bing Crosby, Don Ameche, Robert Young, Andy Devine, Joe E. Brown, Ole Olsen, Tony Martin, and Lana Turner.

Well-known figures in thoroughbred horse racing such as Samuel D. Riddle, owner of Man O' War, Charles Howard, owner of Seabiscuit and

Porter's Cap, John Hay Whitney, C. V. Whitney, Herbert Woolf, A. G. Vanderbilt, William DuPont, Jr., John Hertz, and Mr. and Mrs. Warren Wright were among those eagerly awaiting the start of the race.

Attendants manned the gateways of Churchill Downs at sunrise, and from that moment until late in the afternoon, continual lines of men, women, and children filed through the turnstiles to create what the *Daily Racing Form* reported as "the most cosmopolitan throng ever assembled in a race course."

Most of the early arrivals were prepared to stay in place for many hours. The general admission sections were bulging over seven hours before the race was run. Equally packed were the 50-cent bleacher seats constructed around the upper turn of the track. On a first-come basis, these seats were filled to capacity by noon, as described by Lexington's *The Herald-Leader*:

> The stands were a seething mass of moving color and the boys and girls trotted out their Sunday best under a brilliant sun. The infield stretch was packed so tightly one press box wag suggested squeezing lemons over the standees so they would feel more like sardines.

The terraced infield also drew heavily from the early incoming crowd, and long before the first preliminary race, an estimated 25,000 people occupied this standing-room area.

The scenes along the backstretch and the stable area were another story. Large parties and families, both black and white, who had presumably come in without paying front-gate prices, had lunches spread out. Some were drinking from bottles, some were asleep. Some lay on the grass and counted airplanes overhead. Inside the stable area, a black nanny goat munched grass, and a very small girl kept pointing at the goat and saying, "Horsie, horsie."

Several black boys had a piece of the fence apron pulled up and kept yelling at prospective buyers, "See the Kentucky Derby for only a dime."

Another group of white boys, a little farther down the enclosure, made a quieter appeal: "You can walk through our hole standing up for five cents."

Those with reserved seats, which had been sold out two months earlier, began arriving by 11 o'clock in large numbers. By one o'clock, every available space inside Churchill Downs was firmly occupied. But people were still arriving up to minutes before the "big race" began. These late arrivals dotted the rooftops of stables, adjoining buildings, and structures across the street from the racetrack.

What attracted such a vast gathering of humanity at Churchill Downs this Derby Day? Why would this Derby be the first to draw 100,000 fans and the largest crowd to witness a horse race on the North American continent? The answers to such questions were readily found in the excitement and interest generated by Whirlaway, the horse most turf experts had picked to finish third or fourth in the first crucial test for three-year-old thoroughbreds.

It was understandable why most experts were picking Whirlaway to finish out of the winner's circle. The colt had come in second in the previous Blue Grass Stakes and the Derby Trial. In addition, this horse had only met his Derby rider on Friday, the day before the race. There was also some reason to question even Eddie Arcaro's ability to bring Whirlaway around the final, sharp turn of the Churchill Downs track. Wendell Eads had been unable to steer the colt around the turn in the Derby Trial four days before without losing some 24 yards, and the race by a narrow margin of less than a length.

In spite of what the experts were predicting, unique factors were combining to establish Whirlaway as the Derby favorite. The chestnut colt with the long golden tail, smallest of the 11 entries, had already in his brief career fired the imagination of people from all walks of life as no horse had before in turf history.

Thousands had converged on Churchill Downs from all 48 states primarily to see Whirlaway race, and this was happening at a time in the nation's history when defense industry business and movement of troops in the Armed Forces made public transportation difficult to come by.

An illustration of Whirlaway's drawing power came to my attention while conducting research on Whirly's racing career during the summer of 1981. Visiting the National Museum of Racing Hall of Fame in Saratoga Springs, New York, I met a young lady serving as an attendant at the museum who proudly told me: "My father went to see Whirlaway race in the 1941 Kentucky Derby."

Many of these ardent Whirlaway fans had previously shown only a passing interest in horse racing. But on this day, they came in droves to show faith in what they believed was Whirlaway's true potential, which to this point was unclear even to those whose business it was to determine odds for the betting public.

The logic of this vast crowd that made Whirlaway the favorite by race time was perhaps best stated by Bill Corum, then sportswriter for the New York *Journal American* and the one responsible for characterizing the Kentucky Derby as the "run for the roses." On May 1, just two days before the race, Corum's column carried this headline: "IT'S MAY 1 AND MAY 1 BE WHIRLAWAY." The column read:

> You'll probably think I am foolish to pick Whirlaway the winner, but . . . I am not ashamed to have you know. It's based more on hope and stubbornness than logic. Hope that Warren Wright . . . will have a Derby winner. . . . Stubbornness because Whirlaway has been my Derby pick since last July.

For a couple of minutes at least, horse racing was not to be described merely as a "sport of kings." Instead, it was a sporting event in which one horse was made the favorite by the mass of people arriving at the track just hours, and even minutes, before the event was under way.

The weather forecast for Saturday, May 3, 1941, called for possible showers in Louisville, but instead the weather smiled on this huge gathering with sunshine and gentle breezes. Anticipating the big turnout, Colonel Winn had arranged for plenty of entertainment for the waiting crowd. Six bands played in relays on the infield, with the University of Indiana band and drill team receiving the most applause for spelling out D-I-X-I-E as the band played the tune. A popular vaudeville attraction was a silent act consisting of a dozen military figures going through a rifle drill.

To help police this extravaganza, there were on hand 440 state militiamen, 240 members of the Reserve Officers Training Corps, and 30 highway patrolmen. But in view of the fact that 100,000 people were packed in an enclosure where less than half that figure would have been considered very good, the record crowd displayed rare patience and decorum.

The interest in this particular Derby reached a level comparable to a presidential nominating convention. In order to ensure full coverage of

FINISH

Above and right, Whirlaway winning the Kentucky Derby.

the race, press credentials were issued to 600 reporters, 250 photographers, plus 50 radio announcers and technicians.

In the late afternoon, a few minutes past five o'clock, the vast multitude stood silently with heads uncovered as strains of "The Star-Spangled Banner" rang out over the expanse of Churchill Downs. This patriotic tradition was followed by the appearance of the 11 Derby candidates on the track and the parade to the post, highlighted by the playing of "My Old Kentucky Home." This series of events served as an emotional release, for the crowd, and the crescendo of cheers grew rapidly as the Derby hopefuls approached the starting gate.

Clem McCarthy, who had broadcast every Derby since its first transmission over the air in 1928 and was recognized as the best horse-race caller in broadcasting history, was at the microphone for the National Broadcasting Company. His usual rasping, staccato delivery would bring to listeners from coast to coast all the drama and excitement of the race.

Finally at 5:45.5 p.m., the seemingly endless waiting ceased, and the "run for the roses" began. Dispose took the early lead from Staretor, followed closely by Porter's Cap and Our Boots. At the half-mile pole, Dispose was still leading easily with Porter's Cap having taken over second place, followed by Blue Pair and Our Boots. Whirlaway was hardly in view at this point, being 14 lengths back in eighth place. At the three-quarter pole, Dispose was still in first place with Blue Pair having taken over second. Whirlaway had improved his position from eighth to sixth and was moving up fast.

At the mile pole, Dispose was still first followed by Porter's Cap and Blue Pair with Whirlaway fourth. At that point, the complexion of the race changed in a twinkling.

Clem McCarthy describes the action:

> And they're coming around the turn heading for home with Dispose in front by half a length over Porter's Cap and Blue Pair is right there in third. Whirlaway is coming on the inside and if he doesn't get blocked, he'll get in an awful drive.

Whirlaway did "get in an awful drive" in that final dash for home. Arthur Daley of *The New York Times*, calling him "jet propulsion in horseflesh," describes that part of the race:

> When Whirlaway started to come into focus, the viewers couldn't believe their eyes. . . . Whirly's ears were flattened down and his long tail fluttered in a flaming line behind him. The other colts seemed to be standing still. Only that copper blur was moving . . . inside some horses and outside others.

At a point in a mile-and-one-fourth race where horses begin to slow because of fatigue, Whirlaway was going faster with every stride. Arcaro did not have to urge him one bit. As a matter of fact, Eddie let him go at the last eighth pole and later remarked that he had the feeling of "flying" down that final stretch of the race.

With the huge crowd cheering him on, Whirlaway won the race by eight lengths, the largest margin by which the Derby has ever been won, and shared with only three other horses — Old Rosebud, Johnstown, and Assault. In so winning, Whirly set a Kentucky Derby record of two minutes, one and two-fifths seconds (2:01 2/5) for the mile-and-one-fourth distance, a record that stood for 21 years when Decidedly lowered it by a full second.

But the most impressive part of that remarkable record was the last two furlongs, or quarter-mile. Whirlaway ran that in 23 3/5 seconds, the fastest ever recorded to that date for a finish of the mile-and-a-quarter race. That part of the record stood for 32 years until Secretariat lowered it by only 2/5 of a second in 1973. The last eighth of a mile in the Derby was run by Whirlaway in 11 seconds, and that incredible time has never been matched or broken. Daley wrote that Whirlaway's final furlong of the 1941 Kentucky Derby was "the equine equivalent of nothing flat."

The cheering for Whirlaway did not wane at the end of the race. Seldom has a Derby victory brought such jubilation to the camp of the winner. Employees of the Calumet stable leaped into the air, shouting and slapping one another on the back. Warren Wright was so busy receiving congratulations that he was late arriving at the presentation ceremony.

The crowd formed a sea of colors and surged in waves, inching ever closer to their champion, while Whirlaway and Eddie Arcaro were escorted by Ben Jones to the winner's circle. Whirlaway, draped in a blanket of roses, stood quietly while Warren Wright proudly received the gold cup and congratulations from Governor Keen Johnson and Colonel

Whirlaway after the 1941 Kentucky Derby.

Matt J. Winn.

After the ceremony, Whirlaway was turned over to Pinkie Browne, the horse's exercise rider, who was completely ecstatic over the victory. Pinkie said,

> Whirlaway is one of the best horses in the world if he has the right rider. I told Mr. Wright before the race that he needn't worry — Whirlaway was a Derby winner.

Pinkie was in the process of "cooling down" Whirlaway after the race and trying to talk to a reporter at the same time. Unexpected help came from "Boogie," a spotted Dalmatian from the Calumet stable, who grabbed and held the trailing end of the horse's reins as they went around and around the long corridor encircling the stable. Whirlaway's canine pal seemed to want to be a part of Whirlaway's great victory as well.

Warren Wright was perhaps the happiest of the happy after the Derby victory. Whirlaway had won decisively the race that the owner of Calumet Farm had set as his ultimate goal ten years earlier when he had started rebuilding Calumet as a thoroughbred racing farm. After the race, Wright said of Whirlaway's victory:

> All the credit goes to Ben Jones and Eddie Arcaro. It was the greatest thrill in my life. I'd rather win the Derby than any race in the world.

Eddie Arcaro received his share of plaudits for his masterful ride of Whirlaway. Eddie noted:

> He's the "runningest" horse I ever rode. I never touched him once and he never bore out. The fact is I couldn't hold him back and I finally let him clear out an eighth of a mile from home.

But the one person who all agreed deserved the most credit for Whirlaway's accomplishment was his trainer, Ben Jones. His feat stands out as one of the greatest in the history of the American turf. He had taken what some critics had said was a horse with great potential, but one that

Warren Wright holding Whirlaway.

could never be trained not to run out on the final turn of the track, and made him into a champion. Some had even said that the horse was dumb and incorrigible. But Ben Jones never lost faith in Whirlaway. He was convinced the horse would be a great racer once the things bothering him were smoothed out. That process included long hours of work with the colt, gaining his confidence and understanding. Then, finally, the right rider for the horse was found. And the rest is history.

Those who saw Whirly perform in that memorable race of 1941 said that never before in the history of the Derby, or at least within the memory of those present, had any horse run so well. Many even went so far as to call it "the perfect race."

The Derby put to rest the earlier misconceptions about Whirly's racing style. Anita Brenner, writing in *The New York Times* magazine section, developed the concept that Whirlaway was a problem horse early in his career because he was an "equine genius" with a phenomenal burst of speed seldom if ever seen on the turf. It had taken some rare patience and ability on the part of Ben Jones to harness and control the horse's rare gift.

Jockey Eddie Arcaro said, after riding Whirlaway, that the horse's tendency to bear out on turns and thereby lose distance on the track was due to the fact that once Whirly

> . . . has put on speed he is going so fast it is hard for him to turn as sharply as he needs to, especially on the smaller and narrower tracks.

Eddie certainly proved Pinkie Browne's point about Whirlaway's need for the "right rider" when the jockey negotiated that treacherous final turn of Churchill Downs, and Whirlaway, to the amazement of many, stayed inside all the way around the turn.

Colonel E. R. Bradley, owner of four Kentucky Derby winners — more at that time than anyone else — agreed with the "right rider" assessment. Bradley had picked Whirlaway to win and remarked that

> . . . he is a great horse and superior to any of the current three-year-olds if he gets the proper ride.

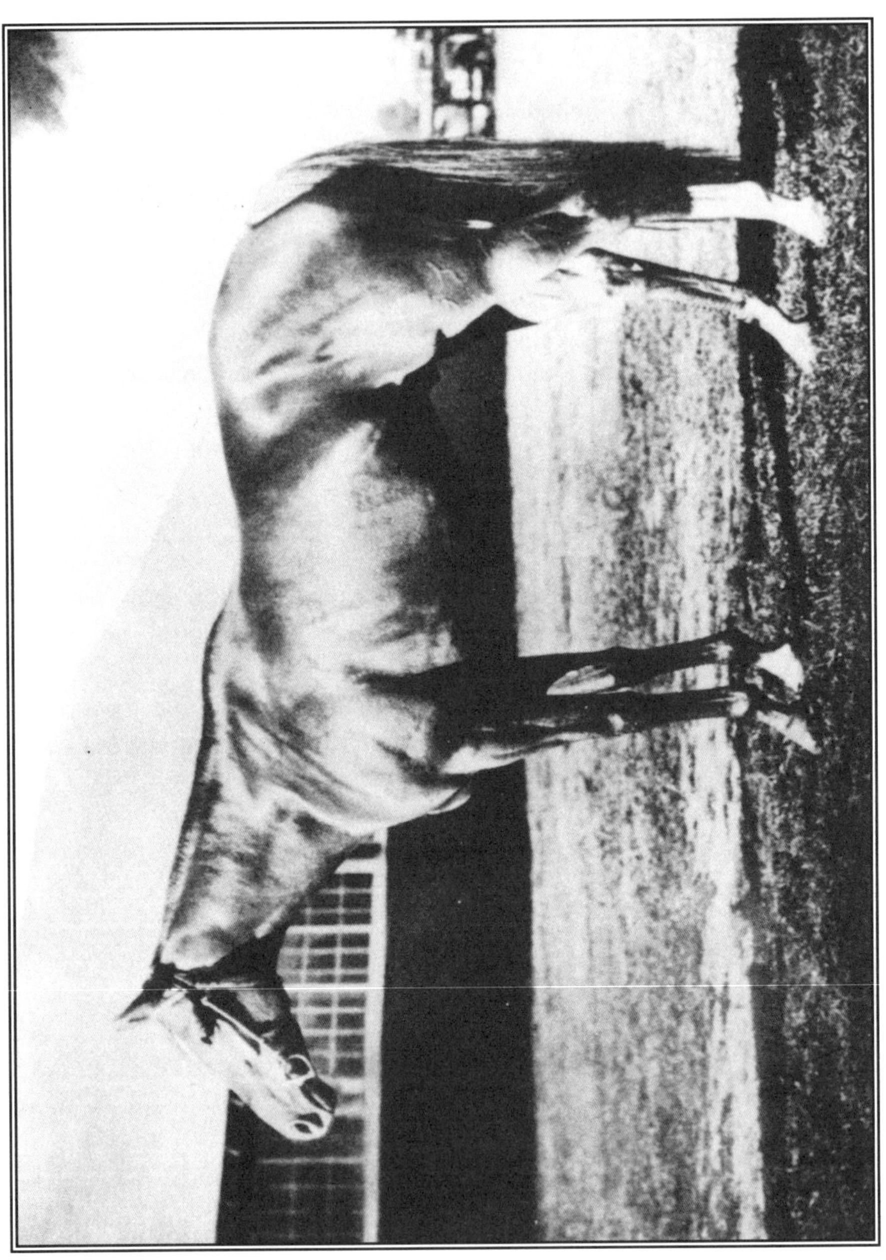

Whirlaway,
1941.

After the race, Ben Jones had few words to say about his great achievement. He was by nature a modest and unassuming person. He did offer this abbreviated statement:

> I knew Whirlaway had it in him and I thought Arcaro was just the boy to get it out.

Then Ben added something that must have struck fear in the minds and hearts of opposing owners and trainers contemplating future races against Whirlaway. He said in a somber tone,

> Whirlaway is just now getting good. He's not quite ready yet.

Colonel Winn, head man at Churchill Downs, was another very happy human being. Whirlaway had made his spectator attendance dream a reality with added flourish. The 67th Kentucky Derby, of 1941, proved to be "the largest, the fastest and the richest" to date.

D. J. Mahaney, business manager at Calumet Farm in 1941, stated that Whirlaway possibly received "more copy" than any other winner of the Kentucky Derby. This was certainly not an overstatement. The 600 reporters covering the event literally stumbled over one another trying to outdo each other in writing up this sports spectacular for their respective newspapers and periodicals.

Bill Corum, Whirlaway's number one fan among sportswriters, filed a story for the New York *Journal American*. In it he wrote,

> With those thousands of hysterically screaming fans . . . cheering Whirlaway on, the stocky chestnut with the long golden tail and mane made a show of the ten other starters when he turned on the blast furnace heat of his charge.

He went on to say that Whirly shot past the straining leaders so fast that "they probably did not know he had been there and gone."

In further tribute, he wrote,

> The chestnut, his long golden tail, which makes him look

almost like a show horse, catching the sun as he swung the bend, was coming for 'em now and one by one he made them lay the tired body down.

Jimmy Jones, son of Whirlaway's trainer, writing for the Louisville *Courier-Journal*, said,

> Whirlaway whirled down the stretch with a mighty and vengeful rush to win . . . and in the wake of the cyclonic chestnut's victory records disappeared like leaves caught in an autumn gale.

Jones felt that the biggest thing Whirlaway accomplished was vindication. He had been known as the "if" horse of the Derby and, Jones said, "generally regarded as a capable but erratic sort of colt." His victory over a fine field ended speculation about his greatness. Jones said,

> . . . From the moment he bounded to the front at the final-quarter pole, until he walked to the winner's circle to be draped with his chaplet of roses, there was no more doubting that Whirly was a great horse.

Grantland Rice's column in *The Boston Globe* noted:

> . . . Whirlaway didn't run out. The flying entry from Calumet Farm ran around, then over and then far away from the field to win . . . by at least eight open lengths. The amazing son of Blenheim II and Dustwhirl . . . wrecked the field with his killing spring down the stretch. . . .

John Wray, sports editor of the *St. Louis Post-Dispatch*, added:

> Whirlaway! They named him right. He whirled down the track at Churchill Downs . . . and almost dumbfounded . . . onlookers by winning in style and record time. . . .
>
> Boy, you never saw anything like the terrible blast

> Whirlaway turned loose. . . . In the language of the lamented Dizzy Dean "he poured it on."

Wray went on to say that Whirly had "completely sold himself as the horse of the year."

Paul Lowry of the *Los Angeles Times* said:

> Calumet Farm's Whirlaway usurped Twenty Grand's place in the thoroughbred's sun by winning the fastest and most spectacular Kentucky Derby in history. . . .

He goes on to explain that Whirlaway was in fourth place at the head of the stretch when Dispose passed the mile marker in 1:37 2/5. At the time, Porter's Cap was second with Blue Pair third. Then, as he saw it,

> The Calumet colt was two lengths off the leaders, and the manner in which he fairly flew over that final span of lightning fast strip can hardly be believed unless you . . . saw it.

Lowry suggested that Whirlaway might well be called

> . . . another Man O' War, Twenty Grand and a Johnstown all rolled in one, but for us he is a Whirlaway who belongs in a class by himself.

According to Walter Haight of the Washington *Post*:

> Seldom has a Derby horse looked so thoroughly beaten and then so definitely a winner.

John Rubbathen, in an editorial in *The Thoroughbred Record* wrote:

> It was Whirlaway's day from the start. He was cheered from the moment he appeared on the track coming from his barn until he entered the winner's circle to receive the collar of roses. . . .

> The tribute was genuine and spontaneous and deservedly so. . . .

Having seen over half of the 67 Derbies, he went on to say,

> . . . never have I witnessed anything as electrifying as Whirlaway's stretch drive. . . . He made his move in the stretch and the race was over as far as the others were concerned. . . . He seemed to be flying and . . . was so many lengths ahead of the rest, none was included in the picture.

The editorial ended with this tribute:

> . . . to one who loves a good horse and has the pleasure of seeing him victorious in a supreme effort, the memory of Whirlaway's Kentucky Derby will ever remain one of the highlights in this world-famous classic.

Charles Howard, owner of Porter's Cap and Seabiscuit, said after the race:

> There isn't a horse in the country that could have beaten Whirlaway in the Derby. Whirlaway is a great horse.

The environs of Churchill Downs were filled with celebration long after the race's finish, especially around the Calumet stable. After the presentation ceremony, Warren Wright, without audible objection from Whirlaway, gave the victor's roses to actor Don Ameche, for loyal support as Whirly's unofficial assistant trainer. Without further fanfare, Ben Jones led the Derby winner off to the stable, giving his protégé a well-deserved night off and a dinner that included extra portions of hay and oats.

At last the sun set on this sports spectacular that had begun in the early morning and lasted until late afternoon. But all those hours of entertainment, picnics, and recreation that preceded or followed the main event did not come close to matching the classic drama itself, the raw suspense and the high-decibel thrills that exploded in what Dan

Parker, columnist of the New York *Daily Mirror*, called "an imitation of a streak of lightning."

And Ben Jones had the audacity to say that Whirlaway was not quite ready yet.

Chapter
5

A Week Later — The Preakness

SINCE the full resumption of thoroughbred racing following World War II, a respite of two weeks has been given between the Derby and Preakness to afford more transition time for horses participating in both races. But in 1941, the Derby winner had only one week to travel from Louisville to Baltimore and prepare for the Preakness on the following Saturday. In those days, the trip was made by railway car instead of air cargo, to-

day's faster mode of travel. Thus, in 1941, Whirlaway had another race added to his agenda between the Triple Crown races, the race against the clock.

The long-tailed chestnut was boarded on an express railway car on Monday, some 36 hours following the Derby, and transported 600 miles to Pimlico Race Track outside Baltimore, Maryland, site of thoroughbred racing's second jewel in a Derby winner's quest for the Triple Crown. This would at most allow only three days of preparation for the Preakness.

As Whirlaway headed east to Baltimore where he would face another strong field of three-year-olds in the Preakness Stakes on May 10, some whispers abounded and rumors appeared in print about his incredible late burst of speed in the Derby. Dan Parker, New York *Daily Mirror* columnist, wrote on May 8 that this demonstration of speed "had set tongues wagging." One trainer apparently believed that Whirlaway had such a bad cold on Derby Day that he had been given a triple dose of medicine. He questioned whether the horse had been given a saliva test.

This brought immediate reaction from sportswriter Bill Corum with a verse of satire in his New York *Journal American* column on May 9:

> No, Dan, it wasn't the cough medicine
> that carried them off;
> It was the coffin they should have
> carried the rest of the horses in,
> When he left them for dead at the
> head of the stretch.

Even the gentle Missourian, Ben Jones, had his adrenaline increased by the ugly rumor. He said that if Mr. Wright would approve it, he would match Whirlaway against any three-year-old horse anywhere and

> . . . bring Whirlaway out of the stable at midnight, high noon, or anytime, and without any notice whatsoever throw a saddle and rider on him and let him show you what he can do to any horse of his age at any distance and under any conditions.

Parker, obviously realizing his mistake, recanted his story in the following day's column. He further reported that he had received word from Louis F. Neely, sportswriter for *The Louisville Times*, that Whirlaway had been given the saliva test after the Derby under proper conditions and controls and that the results were negative.

But fame doesn't come easily, even for a racehorse. There were other attempts to discredit Whirlaway's stunning Derby victory. One such tale rumored that the track at Churchill Downs had been deliberately rolled and packed to ensure a fast time for the benefit of the huge crowd. Another bit of fantasy suggested that Whirly's long tail had prevented trailing horses from closing in on him in the stretch run. Whoever contrived that wild story about the 1941 Derby stretch run forgot to mention it would have been utterly impossible for Whirly's tail to distract the other ten horses in the final furlong of that race, since both his body and accompanying tail were disappearing over the horizon after hitting the finish line some 24 yards ahead of the pack.

Although these fabrications were fully discredited, the stories still gave added drama to the upcoming Preakness. The race would serve as a litmus test for Whirlaway's burst of speed — was it real or just a freakish happening in the passing parade of thoroughbred racing?

There were other factors generating excitement and interest in the second test leading to racing's Triple Crown as well. Whirlaway's possible problems in the running of the Preakness were giving Calumet stable some definite concerns. Pimlico is a smaller track than the one at Churchill Downs, narrower with sharper turns, a sixteenth of a mile less than the Derby distance. Furthermore, Whirlaway had experienced some difficulty making the final turn of the Pimlico course as a two-year-old.

Another concern was the matter of Eddie Arcaro's services with his contracted employer, Mrs. Payne Whitney's Greentree Stable. If one of Greentree's eligibles should run in the Preakness, Eddie would be required to ride that horse instead of Calumet's Whirlaway. Also, even if there were no Greentree starter in the Preakness, Arcaro might have to ride that stable's color-bearer in a stake race in New York on Preakness Day.

Ben Jones was undaunted by these possible problems. He felt the strain was off after winning the "big race" in Louisville. The plan of familiarizing his entry with the track was used in preparing Whirlaway for the Preakness, the same routine that had been used in readying the colt the previous week for the Derby. J. Fred Colwill, chief steward at Pimlico and long-time friend of Ben Jones, recalls how the trainer would take Whirlaway out at daybreak for practice and walk his steed over all its contours, which Ben believed would give the horse a secure feeling at each sharp turn of the narrow track.

As Preakness Day approached, concern lessened for Calumet Farm with the welcome announcement that Arcaro would ride Whirlaway in the Maryland classic. Good weather loomed ahead for the race in spite of rains the previous two days. A warm southerly wind swept across the racing strip Saturday morning, drying it out considerably before post time.

Once again Whirlaway's drawing power at the gate was in full bloom. The crowd started gathering eight hours before the race; people soon filled the stands, covered the infield, lined the streets surrounding the enclosure, and dotted rooftops of nearby homes. The multitude at last reached 42,000, said by track officials to be the largest crowd in the history of Pimlico as well as tops for a horse race in the state of Maryland.

The cosmopolitan complexion of this human gathering was similar to that of the previous week in Kentucky. Hollywood was out in full force with Don Ameche and Robert Young again on hand. Representatives from the nation's capital included Stephen Early, President Roosevelt's secretary; senators Alben Barkley and A. B. Chandler; and one of the President's sons, Elliott. Other dignitaries present included ambassadors, federal officials, and other dignitaries, with Governor Herbert O'Conner of Maryland heading the list.

In this vast crowd, for that day, every rung of society's ladder was represented — the Vanderbilts and DuPonts, military personnel, defense workers, public service officials, high school and college students, plus whole families including some with young children. Another notable in the crowd was Earl Sande, considered one of the greatest jockeys of his time and rider of Gallant Fox, the 1930 Triple Crown winner. Sande was to be guest of honor at the traditional Preakness Night dinner following the race.

The Preakness competition, as it turned out, would differ from the Derby field. Horses who had raced in the Derby — Our Boots, Dispose, and Porter's Cap — were being given a better chance against Whirlaway over the shorter-distance run. Horses entered in the Preakness who were not at the post for the Derby were King Cole, Kansas, Curious Coin, and Ocean Blue, with King Cole considered best of that lot.

Staretor and Market Wise, second- and third-place finishers in the Derby, would not be present. Even today, with a two-week interval between these races, many owners harbor fears concerning possible injury or burnout of their horses from running them in both races. Sam Riddle, of Glen Riddle, Maryland, owner of Man O' War, would not enter Big Red in the Kentucky Derby of 1920, saying he was not about to risk sending his horse "way out west" for the Derby. By making that decision, Riddle denied Man O' War a chance to become a Triple Crown winner, because the great colt did run in the Preakness and Belmont Stakes and won both races easily.

Finally, at 5:50 p.m. on Saturday, May 10, 1941, the 51st running of the Preakness was under way. Seven of the eight horses started the race in a bunch with King Cole taking an early lead. Whirlaway was dead last leaving the gate. Ed Thorgerson of Fox Movietone News commented, "Whirlaway walks out of the gate counting the house." King Cole and Dispose set the early pace, followed by Our Boots and Curious Coin. Whirlaway, according to Grantland Rice's account in *The Baltimore Sun*, "looked as if he had started in another race." The Derby winner was at least ten lengths behind and still losing ground as the other horses ran by the stands. At the first turn, Whirlaway looked to be completely out of the race. As the field headed for the far turn of the track, King Cole and Dispose were 20 lengths beyond the Calumet racer.

At that point, Thorgerson, calling the action for "Fox Movietone Newsreel," described the dramatic change taking place as Whirlaway came into the picture near the mile pole:

> . . . Arcaro takes him wide . . . [and] calls . . . for all he's got. He's moving, coming fast. Look at him come. He's traveling wide open. . . . Whirlaway is now running fourth; he's third; he's second; he's closing in on King Cole; he's looking him in the eye. Whirlaway is now out in front.

Once in front, Whirlaway continued running faster and faster as if he would never slow down. He went on to win the race by at least five lengths of open space. The proponent of "instant speed" had picked up

25 lengths (75 yards) in the last three-quarters — 20 from behind to five in front.

Grantland Rice called this "an almost incredible performance of speed and stamina."

Whirly's time for the mile-and-three-sixteenths was 1:58 4/5, which was exceptionally good over a track that looked faster than it was. The thin coating of topsoil covered heavier footing underneath. The finishing speed again was the major factor. The "Calumet Comet" ran the last three-sixteenths in 18 seconds. Eddie Arcaro, commenting on the fast finish, stated:

> There's many a horse you couldn't drive to that anywhere. And I never laid a whip on him in the last two races.

Eddie told Grantland Rice after the race:

> I never rode such a horse in my racing life. We were practically last at the post. Around the first turn the field leaders seemed to be at least a mile away. I didn't dare start moving Whirlaway too soon and I had to gamble on his finishing speed. . . .

Arcaro said he couldn't tell whether he was in a running mood or not, but found out after he had turned him loose and told him to go. He said,

> . . . I thought then I was riding a blinding tornado. As I passed King Cole I yelled "good-bye" to Johnny Gilbert. And Johnny said "good-bye" back.
>
> . . . Not even a cyclone could head us off. . . . I might as well have been shot from a gun. What a horse — what a horse!

Ben Jones was modest as usual in meeting with reporters after the race. "All I do is train Whirlaway. He runs his own race," said the trainer. But, he added, "I tell you no horse can run with him when he wants to run and when he is ridden in the right way."

Warren Wright, who saw his star three-year-old win one of the most

Whirlaway in Preakness Winner's Circle at Pimlico, May 10, 1941, with Eddie Arcaro aboard.

sparkling victories ever seen in the Preakness, was nearly swamped by friends and admirers of Whirlaway when he came down out of the stands to give his horse a loving pat. Standing by Wright in the winner's circle when they folded the victory blanket of black-eyed Susans over the Preakness winner were actors Don Ameche and Robert Young. After the presentation ceremony, Ameche tried to save as many of the blossoms as possible for admirers wanting boutonnieres from the blanket.

After the ceremony, proud owner Wright had these words of praise for his horse:

> This race adds a lot to Whirlaway's prestige and shows his Derby victory was no fluke.

There were glowing accounts of Whirlaway's great Preakness win in newspapers and periodicals throughout the country, written by some of the greatest sportswriters in history. After Whirly's Derby victory of a week before, some writers had had reservations about the horse's ability to win in Baltimore. But when Whirlaway gave a repeat performance of the Derby, with added thrills, dissenters joined in the chorus proclaiming him the champion three-year-old of the year.

Clem McCarthy, legendary broadcaster of horse races, said he could recall only a few races in his career in which horses ran the last quarter in such spectacular fashion as Whirlaway's Derby finish, and added,

> I know of no horse repeating that dashing last quarter as did Whirlaway in the Preakness.

Grantland Rice's column in *The Baltimore Sun*, May 11 noted:

> The chestnut comet did it again. Coming from far behind . . . , the flying Whirlaway added the Preakness to his Kentucky Derby with a margin of five lengths over King Cole. . . .
>
> As Arcaro started his move . . . and Whirlaway responded with his blinding speed, a terrific racket broke from 42,000 throats. . . .

He went on to say,

> . . . the rest of the field looked as if it were standing still, marking time against the rush of the wind. Whirlaway came on and on. . . . [He] opened up, increasing daylight as he flashed along the Preakness distance. Under Arcaro's perfect handling [he] ran as true as an arrow and almost as fast.

Rice concluded by saying,

> . . . And apparently now there is nothing to stop this "small brown bounding beggar, this Indian Rubber Idiot on a spree." . . . There is no longer any doubt about Whirlaway's place among the 3-year-olds of 1941. The Chestnut Comet stands alone with no one in sight.

"On The Line" with Bob Considine in the Washington *Post* added:

> It's trite to pour another bowl of adjective soup down your back . . . but . . . there hasn't been an easier running horse . . . for a raccoon's age.
>
> That sucker just rolls along. There's no whipping him, no wild whistling through distended nostrils, no creaking of his bone and tissue. He just rolls.

Commenting that Whirlaway not only made up 25 lengths to win the Preakness, but that he had also won by five lengths, Considine said he made up most of them with what he called

> . . . a stunning smooth rush of power. . . . He seemed to be running right over them. Actually he ran through them . . . and past them as if they were rooted there, graven, and he was a sweeping, swinging ghost horse.

Joe Palmer, writing in *The Blood-Horse*, warned that Rule 30 says that after June 30 of each year, there can be no race at less than five furlongs. He thought Whirlaway was in danger of violating that rule if he ran in the Travers Stakes like he ran in the Preakness, for it was strictly a two-furlong race!

Palmer said that until late on the afternoon of May 10, he had admired Whirlaway "with some reservations," but that they were "left *en bloc* on the roof of the Pimlico grandstand a little later, and . . . are beyond recovery."

According to Palmer,

> . . . If a race were ridden with greater confidence, the jockey would have to take his feet out of the stirrups and jog. When the field came by the first time, Whirlaway was so far last that he wasn't bothered by the dust . . . others were raising.

Palmer also said somebody suggested afterward that maybe the other horses didn't even see him go past because of what he saw as

> . . . the deadliest weapon a thoroughbred can have — an annihilating burst of speed which he can turn on at any stage of the race.

After the race, Eddie Arcaro reflected what other sportswriters throughout the country were saying in their columns concerning Whirlaway's incredible Preakness victory. To Lewis Burton of the New York *Journal American*, he said Whirlaway

> . . . is the greatest racehorse I have ever seen. He could carry you and me and beat a horse like War Admiral. I have never seen a horse you could compare him to, outside of maybe Cavalcade. A jockey gets to ride a horse like Whirlaway only once in a lifetime.

Perhaps the ultimate statement about Whirlaway's performance in the Preakness was made by Walter Haight in the Washington *Post*. He described Whirly's stretch run as giving the appearance of a "bronze bullet" in flight.

Turf writers who saw Whirlaway run in both the Kentucky Derby and the Preakness must have had their vocabularies completely drained of metaphors and hyperboles in describing those blockbusters. After watching the chestnut "Pegasus" fly down the stretch of Churchill Downs, few "hardboots" believed Whirlaway could even come close to matching that demonstration in the Preakness. But many veteran observers of the racing scene like Grantland Rice considered Whirly's "almost incredible" run around the Pimlico course to be even more spectacular than his Derby scenario.

Whirlaway's Preakness, by unanimous vote of all sports analysts of that day, was beyond reasonable doubt the most thrilling edition of the Maryland classic in its previous half-century of existence. But a logical question quickly arises from the wake of this lofty evaluation: How does Whirlaway's Preakness performance compare with the 49 subsequent triumphs in Triple Crown's second jewel? Finding a plausible answer to that interesting query presented a formidable research challenge.

Fifty-plus years have come and gone since the running of the 1941 Preakness, and finding individuals with the credentials necessary for making a valid comparison of Whirlaway and other Triple Crown winners would be difficult — they had to have been there.

After some three years of research on the subject, light finally appeared at the end of the tunnel when I obtained a 1982 edition of *Preakness at Pimlico*. The first chapter of this attractive publication is appropriately dedicated to the memory of Red Smith, beloved Pulitzer Prize winner for sportswriting, who had passed away on January 15, 1982. Red earned and held the highest esteem his profession could bestow upon him. His writing quality is shown even in a statement he made concerning his approaching death: "Dying is no big deal; the least of us will manage that. Living is the trick."

Horse racing was the sport Red Smith loved the most. Red's chapter in the 1982 Pimlico press book contains his thoughts about the Preakness Stakes, of which he was as much a part as the horses, owners, trainers, and jockeys. His last column for *The New York Times,* written shortly before his death, had contained these thoughts. Red wrote that he had seen such thrilling Preakness winners as Native Dancer in 1953 and Secretariat in 1973. He saw the exciting stretch duels between Ridan and Greek Money in 1962 and Codex and Genuine Risk in 1980. The last Preakness witnessed by Red was Pleasant Colony's impressive victory in 1981.

In evaluating some 40 Preakness runnings since 1941, this titan among sports analysts for over 50 years wrote:

> Of them all, though, Whirlaway's Preakness will always be the most vivid in memory. When he turned on the heat, you could hear a frying sound.

Another notable figure of the thoroughbred racing world who had intimate knowledge about Whirlaway's Preakness spectacular was Johnny Cothorn, better known as "Johnny the Clocker," who had been timing thoroughbred racehorses at Pimlico for many years. It was quite by accident that I was able to interview him.

During my stay in Baltimore, I visited a downtown bookstore looking for rare books on thoroughbred racing, the Preakness, and Whirlaway. When informed by the attendant that no such books were presently in stock, I started to leave, when he stopped me with this question: "Are you going out to Pimlico Race Course while in town?" I replied that a visit to Pimlico was planned for the following day, and he told me to contact Johnny Cothorn, who had probably clocked Whirlaway in the 1941 Preakness.

At that moment I felt like a newspaper reporter having just gotten wind of an important story. I lost no time in contacting Pimlico Race Course by phone and finally reached Johnny. I informed him of my interest in seeing him, and much to my surprise and joy, he told me that he had indeed clocked Whirlaway in the 1941 Preakness. He agreed to meet with me the following morning, and said he would be clocking horses early and that we could talk during breaks in the action.

I arrived at Pimlico the next day around 7:00 a.m. I was met at the gate by Frank Rock, one of Johnny's associates, who directed me to a section of the grandstand adjacent to the finish line. It was there that Johnny and another associate were clocking a group of thoroughbreds making their morning practice runs. After introductions were made, I asked Johnny if I might watch him clock a few horses before starting the interview. He graciously consented.

What I witnessed for the next 10 or 15 minutes was a master craftsman at work. Employed as a clocker for the *Daily Racing Form*, official publication for thoroughbred racing, Johnny kept voluminous log books containing clockings of horses preparing for races at Pimlico. As each horse lined up, Johnny knew that horse's name on sight and the distance for which the horse was to be timed. I observed in amazement as he clocked one horse after another without a hitch. At the same time this wizard of the stopwatch was clocking horses, he was instructing his friend, Myer Pruce, in the basics of the art. It was a performance of excellence and a rare level of skill.

Finding myself engrossed in Johnny's work, I was reluctant to start the interview. But not wishing to impose on my genial host any longer than necessary, I proceeded with the business at hand. My meeting with Johnny that early summer's morning at Pimlico had already rewarded me with an unexpected benefit — a brilliant seminar on the finer points of clocking thoroughbred racehorses.

My initial interview questions were the usual ones on background and experience. Johnny Cothorn had enjoyed a rich life of satisfying experiences, and at 76 he looked more like a man of 55. This charismatic human being has had two successful careers. He was with the Baltimore Public Schools for 36 years, 23 as a teacher and 13 as a principal, before retiring from education in 1971. But from an early age, Johnny's first love had been thoroughbred racehorses. He had witnessed his first Preakness in 1927, while still a teenager. In 1934, Johnny did what many school teachers have been forced to do out of economic necessity, hold down two jobs. He started working as a clocker for Joseph Williams and the *Daily Racing Form* at Pimlico. He was a teacher for nine months, and a clocker on weekends during the school year and full-time during the summer racing season. Following his retirement in 1971, he took a year off for a well-deserved vacation.

But in 1972, the *Daily Racing Form* coaxed the clocker into returning to Pimlico, where he had started timing thoroughbreds some 38 years before.

After this interesting foray into Cothorn's past, I inquired about the more specific aspects of thoroughbred racing. There was no doubt in my mind that I was the recipient of information from one of the best authorities on the sport over the last 50 years.

Johnny knew my chief interest at the moment was Whirlaway's Preakness victory, and thus recounted what he termed a "vivid" recollection of Whirlaway's thrilling performance in that 1941 race.

> Until the horses neared the mile pole at the turn into the stretch, I thought Whirlaway was hopelessly out of the race. I was focusing on the leaders at the time. When Whirlaway disappeared in the pack and came out in front at the head of the stretch in a matter of a few seconds, I found it difficult to believe what I was seeing. But my amazement didn't stop there. Whirlaway kept coming faster and faster with every stride and won the race by a wide margin. I had never witnessed a stretch run in the Preakness like that one before. It was simply unbelievable.

I was convinced that Johnny had "vividly" remembered Whirlaway's Preakness performance, for he had described the action as if the race had been run only moments before, instead of 40 years earlier. This keeper of time at Pimlico continued his recollections of Whirlaway. He directed my attention to a horse on the track. "That horse," said Johnny, "has a long tail, but Whirlaway's was longer." And he remembered Ben Jones as a great trainer and Pinkie Browne, Whirly's exercise rider, as someone who idolized the little horse with the big tail.

I asked Cothorn to compare conditions of thoroughbred racing in Whirlaway's day with those of recent years. He stated that racetracks since World War II have been carefully developed and conditioned by engineers; in Whirlaway's day they were left more to chance, thus increasing the risk of serious injury to both horses and riders. He explained,

> . . . tracks today are prepared for maximum speed, especially for such races as the Preakness, with the hope a new track record will be set in the presence of a large crowd.

In comparing jockeys of more recent times with those of 1941, this long-time turf observer expressed the opinion that most riders in the earlier period had to undergo a tougher apprenticeship than those of recent vintage. Johnny explained it this way:

> Today, too many would-be jockeys do not possess the strong hands and savvy necessary to control an 1,100-pound

> racehorse, especially on the sharp turns of the track. . . . A racehorse will instinctively run to the outside part of the track unless his rider has the strength and ability to prevent the move.

At this point in the conversation, I asked Johnny to give me an estimate of how many racehorses he had witnessed or clocked in his career spanning nearly half a century. He said he had never given any thought to such a total, but after some basic calculations, he came up with a ballpark — "racetrack" — figure. Johnny estimated that he clocks an average of 50 horses a day, 6 days a week, for 16 weeks during most calendar years. Deducting time for schooling, time away during World War II, and other career-related interruptions, the veteran clocker has easily given 35 years to clocking. This means that Johnny Cothorn has timed well over 150,000 thoroughbred racehorses in his illustrious career.

I anticipated that my final question would be the most difficult for Johnny to answer definitively:

> Of all the great or near-great thoroughbreds you have clocked in the many races at Pimlico for almost fifty years, which horse in your memory stands out from the rest?

Without even a slight pause for reflection, Cothorn replied:

> Whirlaway's Preakness run to victory in 1941 clearly is the most impressive display of speed I have ever seen on the racetrack. When a horse can come from that far behind and pass all the other horses, the cream of the crop for that year, almost as if they were standing still, and continue running at full speed, then, that horse has got to be something special.

I was about to finish the interview when Johnny suggested I talk with Myer Pruce, his friend and associate, whom he said had also seen Whirlaway run in the 1941 Preakness. At that moment I knew I had uncovered some more hidden treasure along the research trail of Whirlaway's amazing racing career.

Myer Pruce had indeed watched Whirlaway run in the 1941 Preakness and seemed eager to recount the experience. He was a high school student at the time. Myer said Whirlaway was the "sports hero" of teenagers in those days — a surprising statement, for I had never before read or heard of a racehorse being a sports hero for a teenage generation.

Pruce said he had gained admission to the 1941 Preakness through the courtesy of a photographer friend sent to cover the race. This stroke of luck allowed Myer to view the contest from a good vantage point at the far side of the track's infield.

Pruce gave his account of the 1941 Preakness:

> As the horses came by the photographer's stand and headed toward the distant turn of the backstretch, Whirlaway was so far behind it seemed he never had the slightest chance of winning. He stayed last until he neared the mile pole, but at that point he started gaining fast. It was unbelievable the way he picked up speed so quickly. He seemed to fly by the other horses and galloped home an easy winner.
>
> I shall never forget the thrill of that day when Whirlaway turned on his speed at the mile pole.

Following my conversations with Cothorn and Pruce at Pimlico in the early summer of 1981, I felt confident in proceeding with the writing of a substantive chapter on the 1941 Preakness as it related to Whirlaway's racing career. As I continued the research on the Whirlaway story during the next four years, I never located written accounts or personal contacts that would surpass these eyewitness accounts.

One thing I have learned, though, from these years of research on Whirlaway, is to be on the alert for the unexpected. Sportswriters seldom mention Whirlaway or any of his great races, and thus I was surprised in 1985 when I actually did see his name in print. On May 21 of that year, while perusing the sports pages of the Los Angeles *Herald Examiner*, my attention was drawn to a story on the 110th running of the Preakness at Pimlico on the previous Saturday, which had been written by Bill Tanton, sports columnist for *The Baltimore Evening Sun*. Tanton's commentary dealt primarily with the dilemma created for Pimlico Race Course and its Triple Crown race by the absence from the Preakness of Spend A Buck, the 1985 Kentucky Derby winner. Dennis Diaz, Spend

A Buck's owner, opted instead to run his horse in the Jersey Derby at Garden State on Memorial Day. By winning that race, Spend A Buck collected a record purse of $2.6 million.

What did this seemingly unrelated dialogue have to do with the 1941 Preakness and Whirlaway? Actually it was only a short sentence contained in the introductory part of Tanton's article that prompted me to delve further into the piece. The columnist wrote that as a child his parents had taken him to see Whirlaway run in the Preakness. The thought struck me that this childhood experience could be a priceless addition to the more mature eyewitness accounts of the race already incorporated in the Whirlaway story.

A couple of days after reading Bill Tanton's Preakness story, I contacted him in Baltimore by telephone. I explained my reason for calling and asked if he would mind sharing with me more details about his experience at the 1941 Preakness and whether he would grant permission for me to use the account in the Whirlaway story. He graciously consented to both, and the following are his recollections of that day at Pimlico over 44 years earlier:

> In 1941, I was ten years old when my parents took me to see the Preakness. Of course, they had no problem with waking me early on the day of the race. We were up at 5:30 that morning and were on our way to Pimlico as soon as possible, in order to avoid the rush of the large crowd expected to file into the concourse for the race.
>
> From the time we passed through the turnstiles of the racetrack until post time for the Preakness, my father [told] . . . me how important this race had come to be for Baltimore, Pimlico, and thoroughbred racing. My parents were typical of most horse racing fans of that day. They never bet much on the horses but dearly loved to see a great race like the Preakness.
>
> My father really prepared me for enjoying the race. He told me Whirlaway had won the Kentucky Derby just a week before and that if he should win the Preakness today would undoubtedly be widely recognized as the greatest racehorse in the country. He said this year's race promised to be very excit-

> ing and that I would remember this event as one of the great sports highlights of my life.
>
> One of the first things we did that morning at Pimlico was to go to the barn area where the horses were quartered. Of course we couldn't get very close to the stables because of security restrictions, but we could see the horses moving around in the area and knew Whirlaway must be somewhere among them.
>
> Time passed slowly after our visit to the stable area. By then I had already decided Whirlaway was going to win the Preakness and was eager for the race to start.
>
> In order to provide me with a better view of the race, my father secured for us a location along the rail of the track. At the time I thought my vantage point would make it easy for me to identify the front-running horses at different stages of the race, but soon after the horses and riders left the post and went into the backstretch, my preconceived notion was lost in the noise and movement generated by the overflow crowd of spectators present for the race.
>
> This distraction did not dampen my enthusiasm one bit. I cheered for Whirlaway from beginning to end and when he crossed the finish line out in front, I really believed my vocal support helped him all the way to that victory.

All the testimonials on Whirlaway's dramatic victory in the 1941 Preakness express the same feeling of wonder and disbelief at witnessing such suspense, thrills, and excitement, all compressed into less than two minutes of racing.

What made Whirlaway's Preakness performance even more remarkable was that it followed by only one week his equally amazing victory in the Kentucky Derby. Arthur Daley, writing for *The New York Times*, said that Whirly's double feature "defied credulity."

Chapter
6

The Belmont Stakes — "Test of a Champion"

THE Preakness marked the completion of Whirlaway's fourth race with a span of only 16 days and the ninth time he had gone to the post since starting his three-year-old campaign in Florida on February 8. The two horses preceding Whirlaway to win both the Derby and Preakness had been War Admiral and Omaha, and they had raced only eight and nine times, respectively, in their entire three-year-old careers. Man O' War hadn't started his three-year-old campaign until May 18, 1920, when he won the Preakness, not having been entered in the Kentucky Derby that year.

For a couple of days after the 1941 Preakness, throngs of admirers came to Pimlico to catch a glimpse of Whirlaway. After witnessing him literally fly down the stretch in the Preakness, many probably suspected there were hidden wings somewhere in that long, bushy tail. Nevertheless, Ben Jones and friend Don Ameche willingly obliged by showing Whirly off to the visitors. Then it was off to New York to make ready for the colt's entry in the last race of the "big three," the Belmont Stakes.

Meanwhile, a surprising thing happened to Whirlaway on his way to the Belmont. Plain Ben suddenly took on the facade of "Fearless Ben" and startled many turf observers by announcing he was going to enter the Triple Crown hopeful in the Henry of Navarre Purse, a Belmont Park Race for three-year-olds and up, on May 20, some two weeks before the Belmont Stakes. Fans probably thought the usually placid Missourian had been overcome by all the excitement and hyperactivity generated by Whirlaway's Derby and Preakness victories. Didn't Ben realize that Whirly might somehow be seriously injured in this rather meaningless race and thus not be able to answer the bugle call for the all-important Belmont?

Warren Wright, Whirly's owner, remained poised and eager to accept thoroughbred racing's highest honor after ten years of seemingly endless waiting for the coveted prize; this rare achievement now seemed within his grasp.

Most turf columnists had already phoned in their estimates on how many light years Whirlaway would be in front at the finish line of Triple Crown's coronation race. Surely Ben Jones would reconsider and not risk a possible disaster for Whirlaway and the Calumet Farm family at this crucial time in the horse's career.

Ben quickly tried to allay the fears of worried Whirlaway fans by explaining that he merely wanted to see what Whirly could do running against older horses. But perhaps there was another reason for saddling Whirlaway for an extra race at this time. Ben might have harbored a fear that a prolonged layoff would cause Whirlaway to lose his racing form. After all, he had won the Derby and Preakness within a week's time. He had completely overwhelmed his three-year-old opponents in those races and seemed to thrive on a constant diet of racing since he had started his track career 11 months and 25 races earlier.

Actually, most turf fans welcomed any opportunity to see Whirlaway race, but after the theatrics displayed in the Derby and the Preakness, what else could this horse do to thrill them? Perhaps he might do a few cartwheels as a final act to his usual stretch drive! Those witnessing the Preakness had already been drained of their last drop of adrenaline by Whirlaway's unbelievable come-from-behind win; maybe they wouldn't expect quite that much excitement from his run in this tune-up race for the Belmont Stakes. Nevertheless, these same enthusiasts had been programmed to look for something more than a ho-hum performance from Whirlaway whenever he left his stall, be it for a workout or for a race. They knew Whirly would come up with something special for the Henry of Navarre race.

Whirlaway's unexpected appearance in the race, even on short notice, attracted an off-day record attendance of over 16,000. And for the surprise element, the script suddenly changed with the announcement that Eddie Arcaro would not be riding Whirlaway.

This unexpected turn of events resulted from the entry of a Greentree Stable horse named Hash. Because Greentree was Arcaro's contracted employer, Eddie would leave the starting gate aboard Hash, opposing the horse he had ridden so convincingly to victory in the Derby and the Preakness. The loss of Arcaro as Whirlaway's rider at that point in the quest for the Triple Crown, even for a relatively unimportant trial race, was cause for considerable concern in the Calumet camp. In their first two races together, Eddie and Whirly had already created an aura of invincibility, and many turf observers believed that Arcaro was the only jockey alive capable of managing the colt's explosive speed on the sharp turns of a racetrack. Calumet Farm had been fortunate indeed that Greentree Stable hadn't had one of their horses running in either the Derby or the Preakness. Much space could be given to speculation about how well Whirlaway might have fared without Arcaro as his mount in those races.

Suddenly Ben Jones was confronted with the same problem he had agonized over just before the Kentucky Derby, finding the right rider for Whirlaway. Arcaro had replaced Calumet's apprentice rider Wendell Eads because the lightweight jockey had been unable to guide Whirly in a straight direction in the two races preceding the Derby. But on such notice, it was impossible to find a rider of Arcaro's caliber for the Henry of Navarre race. Either Eads would occupy the saddle, or the horse would have to be scratched. Of course, welshing on running in a race to which he had been committed was unthinkable. This horse had 25 straight successful races on his ledger.

There never was, and never would be, such a phenomenon as an "ordinary" Whirlaway race. The Henry of Navarre Purse, which had started out as a friendly workout session for "Mr. Excitement" was now beyond the realm of that category. A new level of interest in the race was reached with the announcement that Mioland would be a starter in the May 20 race.

Who was Mioland? This equine creature was certainly more than an ordinary, garden-variety racehorse. At that time in turf history, Mioland was hailed on the Pacific Coast and elsewhere as leader of the handicap division and had been rated by many in 1940 as the best three-year-old.

All possible sources for drumming up interest in the Henry of Navarre race were completely exhausted as post time finally arrived. Arcaro was riding Hash and Eads was aboard Whirlaway — the leading three-year-old was pitted against the top four-year-old.

In spite of all the fanfare and suspense that had descended on the race, it turned out to be a rather typical afternoon at the track for Whirlaway. In the early part of the race, he took up his usual rear-guard position. But at the far turn, Arcaro began to move up with Hash, and Eads did likewise with Whirlaway. In the run around the last turn, the field came together. This time Eads managed to keep Whirly inside, and, at the head of the stretch, he broke in front of Mioland and Hash. Later the young rider did allow Whirlaway to bear out, but by then they were on their way to the finish line, in front by three lengths with plenty of power in reserve. Mioland finished second by a narrow margin ahead of Hash.

Bryan Field gave this appraisal of the race in his *New York Times* column:

> The enthusiasm of the 16,264 present at Belmont was boundless and now the impression prevails everywhere that the Calumet Farm colt is just about the keenest racing machine seen on American tracks in years.

Lexington's *Herald-Leader* gave this editorial comment on the race:

> Whirlaway wiped out any lingering doubts of his greatness in the Henry of Navarre race.

A couple of days after the race, a blessed event was announced by Calumet Farm in Lexington and heralded throughout the land. The local paper reported that a baby sister had been born to Whirlaway, "the most talked about racehorse on the American turf today." It seemed that simply by being Whirlaway's sister, the newborn had become famous upon arrival.

During the break between the Henry of Navarre race and the Belmont Stakes, Dr. Charles H. Strub, chief executive of the Santa Anita track in California, was a visitor at Belmont Park. While there, he proclaimed that he was one of the "original Whirlaway rooters." The main purpose of his visit was not disclosed at the time, but Strub was actually in the process of negotiating with Warren Wright for Whirlaway's entry in what was being billed as the richest horse race in the world — the Santa Anita Handicap. The eighth running of the mile-and-a-quarter winter classic had been set for March 7, 1942, and the head man at Santa Anita wanted Whirly as a magnet to ensure a record attendance for the meet's $100,000 purse.

Even after soundly defeating Mioland, the leading four-year-old horse of the day, trainer Jones still felt uncomfortable about Whirlaway loafing around the stall for two weeks. At this stage of his career, Whirly must have been a little confused about his role in life. Was he a racehorse or a workhorse? After all, he had run his last four races in just 26 days.

But Ben certainly didn't slacken up on Whirlaway's training in the days preceding the Belmont Stakes. In a workout the weekend before the race, Whirly ran a mile in the impressive time of 1:38 2/5. Then on June 3, just four days before the "big race," he reeled off a mile-and-a-quarter in 2:02 2/5. That's faster than most horses win races even today at that distance. As a matter of fact, Whirlaway's "breeze" on that day in 1941, run on the main track at Belmont while a light rain was falling, matches Spectacular Bid's winning time over the same distance on a fast track in the 1979 Kentucky Derby. It is also the same time by which

Swale won the Derby in 1984.

With such a display of speed by Whirlaway that close to the capstone Triple Crown race, many turf observers feared that Whirlaway had burned himself out for the Belmont, for that race would be over a distance of one mile and a half. Sportswriters devoted much space in their columns to Whirly's amazing run. Jack Guenther gave the breakdown of the speedy colt's feat in his *Herald-Leader* column of June 3: at the half-mile marker, 46 4/5; one mile, 1:36 2/5; and a finish of 2:02 2/5 for the mile and a quarter. Guenther wrote:

> When Whirlaway stopped running all the clockers on the grounds hustled off to the nearest jeweler to be reassured that their stopwatches hadn't gone completely wild.

John Kieran, in his *New York Times* column, dramatized Whirlaway's running just for practice in a humorous vein, saying that clockers on hand were making remarks to one another as Whirlaway passed the markers along the rail. He said,

> . . . one timer gave his stopwatch a nasty shake and remarked: "Drat this thing! There must be sand in the works."

Another had stared at his watch and thrown it right out on the track. Horses didn't run *that* fast, so the watch was wrong. He chucked it. Then a third clocker,

> . . . after studying the time shown by his watch . . . repeated the ancient wheeze supposed to have been made by the rustic seeing a giraffe for the first time: "There ain't no sech animal!"

Whirlaway's stunning performance brought high praise from his trainer. Ben confidently stated that Whirlaway was better now than at any stage in his career and he believed that the colt would win easily in the Belmont Stakes.

The recent victories of Whirlaway proved so disheartening to his rivals that out of an eligibility list of 27 three-year-olds, only four were entered in the Belmont Stakes — Robert Morris, Itabo, Yankee Chance, and Whirlaway. Since Greentree Stable had no entry, Eddie Arcaro was free to ride Whirlaway. According to most predictions, Whirlaway's victory seemed assured; but in the long history of the Belmont Stakes dating from 1877, nine starters in the Belmont having won the Kentucky Derby and the Preakness failed to capture the Triple Crown by losing the capstone third race. It is the first race for three-year-olds over the mile-and-a-half span, and the problem facing Arcaro was how to manage Whirlaway's explosive speed with a sufficient reserve to reach the finish line ahead of the field.

In spite of the small field of entries, a large crowd of 30,801 jammed Belmont Park on June 7, 1941 to see Whirlaway try for the third jewel of the Triple Crown. The track was fast when the race started at 4:57 p.m.

Bryan Field of *The New York Times* commented on Arcaro's reversal of riding tactics by suddenly sending Whirlaway dashing to the front. It was particularly revolutionary considering that he had waiting orders from Trainer Ben Jones. Field wrote,

> Whirlaway dashed far ahead in a twinkling. . . .
>
> The big challenge . . . came from the far turn to the head of the stretch. There Alfred Robertson moved forward . . . and cut that big lead, but he never made Arcaro go to the drive nor did Eddie ever make use of the whip. . . .

In fact, he said Whirly ran so easily down the stretch

> . . . that he had his ears pricking, and he also had that mightiest triple crown tilted jauntily on his handsome forelock. He just was so good he made ducks and drakes of his opposition.

The outcome of the race was not the big surprise, because Whirlaway was a heavy favorite. The main topic of conversation after the race was his early rush to the front and lead in the race for a full mile. Arcaro explained what happened:

> I was last with Whirlaway going away and I was going to

> stay last for a while. But the pace was too slow to suit us. . . . So I yelled to the other jockeys, "I'm leaving." I just leaned over and told Whirly, "Let's get running." That's what he did. . . .

As Arcaro said, "That's about all you can ask of any horse."

Warren Wright was not present to congratulate Whirlaway on becoming only the fifth horse in history to win the Triple Crown. He was in Colorado attending his son's graduation from the University of Denver; but, in a sense, both his sons — Warren, Jr., and Whirlaway — graduated on the same weekend. Owner Wright spoke to reporters after the broadcast and quickly gave credit to Ben Jones for the astute training of the champion. He gave this perceptive analysis of what Jones had done:

> One doesn't employ a system in raising an unusual child. One studies the child, watches nervous reactions, follows awakening interests, or, in other words, carefully bends the twig.

After the race, Ben Jones stood proudly with Whirlaway and Eddie Arcaro in the winner's circle. Again the winner was draped with flowers, this time gardenias. Ben had just become the fourth trainer ever to have a Triple Crown winner. But, as reported in Louisville's *Courier-Journal* of June 8, Jones seemed more elated that Whirlaway had been so nonchalant about the "big race." Just before the start of the race, the soon-to-be-crowned champion had almost fallen asleep in his paddock while being saddled.

The capturing of thoroughbred racing's Triple Crown by Whirlaway brought forth another outpouring of public acclaim.

Lexington's *Herald-Leader* noted that Whirlaway had run around them in the Derby and through them in the Preakness, but that he

> . . . tried a new way in the Belmont Stakes today — and won just as easily. The chestnut cannonball from the Bluegrass completed his "Triple Crown" conquest by running from the front end of the field . . . , and still bounced home three lengths to the good without even "mussing his hair."

John Kieran, in *The New York Times*, added:

> There was really nothing to the Belmont Stakes. The Calumet colt took the lead after rounding the lower turn, went way out ahead, coasted most of the way and romped in a winner.

The Boston Globe carried the headline: "Whirly Dons Triple Crown, Romps in Belmont Stakes."

And *Newsweek* magazine said, "Whirlaway the Great — Straight and true atop the fuzzy, brown unwrinkled brow of Whirlaway sat the Triple Crown of racing."

From coast to coast headlines hailed Whirlaway as the Triple Crown champion, a term minted several years earlier by Charlie Hatton, long-time distinguished columnist for the *Daily Racing Form*. Thus, in 1941, when Whirlaway swept these three classic races, Hatton's rhetorical term had the parentheses removed forever.

To this point in his short but dramatic career, Whirlaway had attracted a great host of fans and admirers. As the crowd favorite in each of the Triple Crown races, he was largely responsible for the landmark record attendance at the 1941 Derby and for the largest crowd to that date for the Preakness and the state of Maryland. His appearance in the Belmont had contributed heavily to its record-breaking attendance of 1941.

Opposite: Belmont Stakes Winner's Circle, Belmont Park, June 7, 1941, Whirlaway, with Eddie Arcaro aboard, B. A. Jones, trainer, and Warren Wright, owner.

Chapter 7

The Long Summer Campaign

WINNING the Triple Crown, thoroughbred racing's highest honor, usually afforded the winning horse at least a short respite from track activities, but for Whirlaway there would be no time for relaxation. Two weeks after the coronation, the king of three-year-olds was off and running at New York's Aqueduct in the Dwyer Stakes. The Dwyer is best remembered for its 1920 running, one furlong shorter then, which Man O' War won by staving off John P. Grier in a thrilling stretch run. In the 1941 mile-and-a-quarter edition of the race, the winning combination of Eddie Arcaro and Whirlaway spotted the opposing three-year-olds from four to ten pounds and still won with relative ease, beating Market Wise to the wire and setting a new stakes record in the process.

Just hours after Whirlaway's victory in the Dwyer Stakes, the war in Europe took a sudden and ominous turn eastward. At 3:15 a.m. on Sunday, June 22, 1941, Hitler gave the word to start the invasion of Russia, Operation "Barbarossa," with what he termed the "greatest force in history."

Meanwhile, back in the United States, the Whirlaway "road show," which had been launched six months before in Florida, continued at a pace akin to barnstorming. After the Dwyer Stakes, the Calumet champion was shipped by railway car to Chicago to begin preparation for the Arlington Classic set for July 26. Ben Jones had planned on using Eddie Arcaro as Whirly's rider in the race, but upon arrival in the windy city, he learned that Eddie would not be available. A few days before, in a race at Empire City in New York, the jockey had received a 30-day suspension from racing for rough riding tactics.

This disappointing news presented Calumet stable again the problem of finding a rider for Whirly. With little time left to fill the void, most turf observers figured Wendell Eads, Calumet's apprentice jockey, would occupy the empty saddle. But when Eads rode Whirlaway in a mile-and-an-eighth allowance race several days before the feature attraction, he had considerable difficulty rounding the final turn of the track into the stretch. Whirly won the race in spite of the misadventure, but trainer Jones had seen enough to be convinced that the horse needed a more experienced rider for the mile-and-a-quarter Classic.

Ben Jones had faced this problem before, eight times to be exact, and so the search got under way, and with only a few days to spare before the race, something unexpected happened. One morning, a free-lance jockey named Alfred Shelhammer received word that Calumet stable had a mount for him to work that day, but the horse's name was not divulged in the request. Shelhammer had picked up a few Calumet mounts during the current Arlington meet, and, therefore, he was not overly surprised at the latest job offer. However, he did retain a certain amount of curiosity about which horse was in the offing for this workout — and the possibility that the horse in question might be Whirlaway did cross his mind. On arriving at Calumet's headquarters, that nucleus of a thought suddenly became reality. It was Whirlaway.

After receiving instructions for the session, Shelhammer climbed aboard Whirlaway for the first time and the two hitherto strangers took off on a mile-and-an-eighth run, covering the distance in the respectable time of 1:52 and encountering no major problems. At the conclusion of the workout, Pinkie Browne, Whirly's regular exercise rider, walked the colt back under the grandstand where he could cool down and graze leisurely on the paddock grass. By then, a group of reporters had gathered to catch a glimpse of their turf favorite and to learn the latest news on the search for the new rider. It was in this paddock setting that Shelhammer first learned that he would ride Whirlaway in the upcoming Arlington Classic.

A once-in-a-lifetime opportunity had at last come to Alfred Shelhammer; but in that brief moment of elation, little could he imagine the awesome challenge that awaited him at the starting gate on July 26, 1941. Going into the Classic, Whirlaway had won six straight, including the Triple Crown and Dwyer Stakes races; add to that the immense pressure that was certain to be generated by a huge crowd of 50,000, mostly ardent Whirlaway fans, cheering the turf star on to what was expected to be yet another come-from-behind victory.

When the bugle signaled post time for the Midwest attraction, six three-year-old thoroughbreds were listed on the track's tote board, including two of Whirlaway's strongest foes from past races — Attention and Our Boots. Despite the absence of Eddie Arcaro as Whirly's rider, the Calumet entry was installed as a heavy favorite at 2-5 odds. Actually, by July 1941, some racing enthusiasts held the belief that this horse could win running backwards without a rider. He had already established his supremacy as a three-year-old, but in addition to his ability to win races, he was a stunning chestnut animal with an exciting racing style. In addition, this Triple Crown champion was quickly establishing himself as the most reliable competitor in turf history — something that formed an even stronger bond with his fans than his beauty. It appeared as if Whirlaway had entered into what amounted to an irrevocable loyalty contract with his fans, with no exclusionary clauses:

> I, Whirlaway, promise to appear and compete in any race to

which I have been committed.

The Arlington Classic about to get under way would be race number 30 for Whirlaway. He had not been scratched from a single one in his career thus far, had accommodated the riding styles of eight jockeys before Shelhammer appeared in line, had raced on treacherous turf with wind and rain flowing through his mane and tail, had survived the imposition of extra weight and being hit in the eye with a flying rock — yet when post time for the next race was announced, there he was.

With little time for strategy to prepare for the race at hand, Ben Jones devised an abbreviated plan for Shelhammer to use in his ride on Whirlaway. Among other things, he told the jockey not to take hold of the horse when he started picking up speed. The veteran trainer evidently feared that a sudden slowing of the speedster's pace by his new rider would cause him to head for the track's outer rim, thereby losing precious ground. Ben probably based his reasoning on two major considerations — Whirlaway's soft mouth and Shelhammer's lack of experience in controlling the colt's explosive acceleration. Arcaro's phenomenal success in handling Whirlaway had been attributed in large part to his "strong hands and soft touch." In four consecutive races, Eddie had skillfully managed Whirly's tremendous speed to maximum advantage. Would Whirlaway respond to Shelhammer's touch in like manner? That question was about to be answered.

At the start of the Arlington race, everything went according to plan with Whirlaway in solid control of last place. Our Boots took the lead soon after the start and was ahead by a length and a half at the quarter. Going into the mile, Our Boots began to tire and Attention took the lead. United Press gave this account:

> . . . Whirlaway opened up his bid and set sail for the new leader as he spun around the curve. All over the big plant the chant went up, "Here he comes, Here he comes." . . . Right here his new jockey, Al Shelhammer . . . gave him the whip — but he couldn't quite pull away.

Down the strip known as "heartbreak highway," Whirlaway and Attention battled, as Our Boots kept on coming. The crowd expected

Whirlaway to make his customary late drive any moment, but this time he didn't have it in him.

Attention continued in front and reached the wire a length and a half ahead of Whirlaway. Naturally, Whirlaway fans were disappointed with the outcome. Nevertheless, they realized that Whirlaway's heavy racing schedule of the past seven months had eventually taken its toll. But they had never before witnessed the Triple Crown champion fall behind in the stretch after once catching the front-running horse. It hadn't happened in Whirlaway's string of six victories preceding the Classic. In each of those races, whenever he had caught the leader, regardless of where this occurred, he had moved ahead and remained there to the finish line. Whirlaway and Attention had previously engaged in two close races as two-year-olds, so most turf observers accepted the consensus, though reluctantly, that Whirlaway simply wasn't up to top form for this race.

One possible source for a more plausible explanation of Whirlaway's atypical performance was not carried anywhere in the United Press release on the race. Not one of the reporters at the track that day bothered to ask Shelhammer for his version of the stunning turf upset. Eddie Arcaro had been quoted in newspaper columns from coast to coast following each of his four triumphs on Whirlaway. So it seems logical to ask, why didn't someone with pencil in hand question Eddie's replacement about his ride on this horse?

Because Shelhammer's account never appeared in print at any time since the 1941 running of the Classic, and five years of this research never disclosed the whereabouts of the jockey or what had happened to him since that time, no account could be rendered. Months and years drifted on, and by the summer of 1984, my basic research on the Whirlaway story was complete. Throughout that period, I had maintained an open-ended pursuit for information needed to meet my goals for writing the story. I realized that several revisions of the manuscript's first draft loomed ahead, but I confidently believed my data bank reserve was at last adequate to satisfy those demands, come as they would.

The following weeks were devoted to the task of organizing the story's content. It was during this that something quite unexpected developed. One day in November 1984, I was casually scanning the sports section of the *Los Angeles Times* when I finally settled down to read an account of the Breeders' Cup race, which had been run the day before at Hollywood Park. In that feature race, two interference calls were made on horses, drastically altering their positions at the finish line. Much space was given in the column to a discussion of those inquiries. My interest in the story became locked in place when I read that a person named Shelhammer was one of the racing stewards involved in rendering decisions on those costly infractions. Could this be the same Shelhammer who had ridden Whirlaway back in 1941? Without further ado, the research file on that Chicago race of 44 years earlier was about to be reopened.

As I hurried to make contact with Hollywood Park and Shelhammer, I recalled other times and places along the research trail when it had seemed that the well of additional information had gone dry and the end of the road had been reached. Could it be that yet another access route remained uncharted? The person at the other end of the telephone connection was Alfred Shelhammer, now racing steward for both Hollywood and Santa Anita parks, the same Alfred Shelhammer who had ridden Whirlaway in the 1941 Arlington Classic.

After stating my reason for calling, I asked the former jockey if we might get together sometime soon, at his convenience, and discuss his ill-fated ride on Whirlaway. He graciously consented, but suggested we wait until after the upcoming holidays when he would be working in the winter racing meet at Santa Anita and would have more time to spend with me.

On January 8, 1985, we finally met in Shelhammer's office at Santa Anita. Participating in that same interview session were two other jockeys from the Whirlaway era: Johnny Longden, who had ridden Whirlaway in several races during the colt's two-year-old season, and Johnny Adams, rider of Daily Trouble, another entry in that same Arlington Park race in which Shelhammer and Whirlaway had participated. At the outset of this rare gathering of authentic voices from an almost forgotten era of thoroughbred racing, it was rather obvious to me that considerably more was in store than just filling in some missing details of Shelhammer's ride.

From the introduction on through the parting remarks of the nostalgic session, I was to become privy to several aspects of the inner workings of horse racing as it was practiced in those days that my previous research on the subject had failed to disclose. Shelhammer described his trip aboard Whirlaway in the 1941 Arlington Classic. He said that in those days there were no film patrols to monitor races, and that many jockeys got away with interference tactics that today's cameras would easily detect. He felt that he had to move early on Whirlaway. When he reached the first turn, one jockey was staying way out in the middle of the track as another weaved back and forth between the other entries. As he tried to go inside, he ran up into the pack of horses. They were weaving back and forth, and he couldn't break through. He was afraid of going down because Whirlaway was getting stronger and stronger. But his instructions had been that once he moved on Whirly, don't take hold of him or he'll bolt. He finally broke through the pack. But in doing so, he had covered the fourth quarter in 23 1/5 seconds, losing a lot of speed needed for the last quarter. In the stretch, he took after Attention. His jockey was shaking his whip. At some time during the race, Whirlaway had been hit in the eye with a rock, a clod, or something. Whirlaway stayed with Attention for about one-sixteenth of a mile, but he had used up too much speed in that frustrating fourth quarter. So, in the last 100 yards he slowly fell behind. Following the race, when Whirlaway's eye was examined by Calumet stable, it was feared the colt might lose it. Shelhammer was upset to learn later that a jockey had told people the way he beaten Whirlaway was by hitting him in the eye with his whip. He was sure that hadn't happened, however. Shelhammer feels that the strict orders he was given caused him to lose the race, and that if he had been given some leeway when the occasion called for it, he would have broken through the pack of horses sooner, established an inside position, and won the race by several lengths.

Before the unexpected meeting with Shelhammer, there had been little reason to believe that his account of the 1941 Arlington Classic would portray such a different picture of Whirlaway's performance in that race from the one painted by the United Press story of the event. I had assumed his version would merely complement the consensus reached by most on-the-scene observers — that either Whirlaway was not in top form that day or that Shelhammer hadn't been able to handle the horse according to the strict riding orders given him by Ben Jones preceding the race.

I could only wonder at how fortunate both he and Whirlaway were to finish the race — and in second place at that. Shelhammer was probably right in stating that he should have taken Whirlaway through the pack of horses earlier in the race. Eddie Arcaro was confronted with almost the same problem in the Belmont Stakes. In that mile-and-a-half contest, with the Triple Crown on the line, Eddie had shocked the huge crowd by doing the unthinkable and taking Whirlaway into the lead before reaching the half-mile pole. The slow pace that the other horses had set would prevent Whirlaway from taking an early lead. It was at this point that Arcaro decided to change his racing orders. He immediately took Whirlaway out in front and stayed there for a full mile, finishing the long race well ahead of the other horses, without once using the whip.

Considering the many obstacles thrown at him in his ride on Whirlaway and the strict orders under which he was forced to operate, Shelhammer did a masterful job of handling Whirlaway throughout the race.

After narrowly escaping more serious injury from participation at Arlington Park, Whirlaway was hurriedly shipped by railway car back East to Saratoga Springs in upstate New York to begin preparation for entry in the prestigious Travers Stakes set for August 16. Once on site at Saratoga, Ben Jones decided to enter the tireless competitor in the Saranac Special on August 6. But with Arcaro still under suspension, Calumet stable was once again plagued with the recurrent task of locating a rider.

This latest dilemma further underscored one of the most amazing and unique aspects of Whirlaway's racing career. No Triple Crown champion in the long history of the turf has ever been subjected to such a continuous change of jockeys. The scenario in which Whirlaway found himself could be compared to a football team lining up with a different quarterback calling signals every other game during the season. Timing and execution are surely as important for success in horse racing as for any other sport's competition.

But the business of employing a new jockey for Whirlaway had long since become routine for Ben Jones. Some turf writers have conjectured that Plain Ben's difficulty in keeping a suitable rider for Whirlaway stemmed from the colt's willful temperament and incorrigible habit of drifting to the outer rim of the track during the race. Of course, we know now that simply wasn't true.

Eddie Arcaro was still under suspension and would be until after the running of the Saranac Special. Would Calumet stable be able to find another experienced jockey on such short notice? Fortunately, there happened to be such a rider available, the blond, pleasant-faced jockey named Alfred Robertson. This was the same Robertson who had ridden Our Boots in the Arlington Classic, the race in which another Alfred and Whirlaway appeared to have been "headed off at the pass." Naturally, the Saratoga Alfred was also pleased at the prospect of riding the current Triple Crown champion, and having been a participant in the Arlington race, he would know how to steer Whirly clear of such circumstances in the Saranac.

As if changing riders of Whirlaway in each of his last four races were not enough to cause the champion to give up his crown and pursue a different career, the Saranac Special would be a mile race, a distance for which the colt had not been trained. And he would be pitted against War Relic, a son of Man O' War, who had recently won the Massachusetts Handicap while breaking Seabiscuit's old track record in the process. Then, in what appeared to be an obvious attempt to preclude any possible chance of Whirlaway winning the race, he would be required to lug 130 pounds over the course, 13 to 20 pounds more than his opponents and the most he had ever carried in his racing life.

John Lardner, sports columnist for *Newsweek* magazine, gave this summary of the Saranac Special:

> Whirlaway broke slowly, as usual, trailed the field to the far turn, came around his enemies like a runaway locomotive, ran wide into the stretch, drifted out and won by a beestung nose well out beyond the middle of the track. The other antelopes were bunched along the rail. . . .

Those watching the thrilling race were amazed that Whirlaway managed to win, considering he had been trained exclusively for races of over a mile in duration, and, at least from a spectator's view, it appeared that Robertson was having some difficulty in controlling his mount. But in talking with reporters after the race, the jockey offered no apology for Whirlaway's wide run. When asked by Lardner about the matter, he said,

> I took him around the field because I had to, and then he

> started to drift. If I checked him and pulled him in, we might have lost the race. . . . You can't rough a horse. I figured we had room and speed enough to win anyway, and we did.

Well, it's difficult to argue with success. Robertson evidently reasoned that he could not afford the loss of time that would be required in attempting a breakthrough of the solid line formed by his enemies across the inner half of the track. After all, this jockey remembered to the smallest detail exactly how a similar circumstance had deprived Shelhammer and Whirlaway of victory in that recent Chicago race. Anyway, Ben Jones must have been pleased with Robertson's ride on Whirlaway. Immediately following the race, Alfred was hired to pilot the Triple Crown champion for the remainder of the 1941 racing season. As the agreement was finalized, Whirlaway was heard to have whinnied his approval.

Unfortunately, there was at least one person in the stands that day who was not very happy about the outcome of the race. Sam Riddle, owner of War Relic and the legendary Man O' War, wasted no time in venting his anger over the stewards' verdict of the photo finish awarding Whirlaway the victory over War Relic. With his blood pressure apparently nearing an apoplectic level, venerable Sam stood up in his box, waved his cane, and declared himself to the officials. Everyone in the immediate vicinity scurried right and left, and Riddle managed to calm down, but he announced later he would not enter War Relic in the Travers Stakes. Because of his displeasure with the Saratoga track officials, he declared he was shipping War Relic on to race in the Narragansett Park meet, saying he'd be treated more fairly there.

Of course, Sam Riddle wasn't the first, or last, owner to protest a photo-finish verdict in which one of his horses was involved. But it may be stated that a camera has never been convicted of perjury. John Kieran, noted sportswriter for *The New York Times* in those days, discussed the close finish of the Saranac Special in his column:

> The cameras were tested and proved scientifically accurate. Who criticizes them? Why, fellows who think they are better with their naked eyes. Tut! Tut! Think how magicians make their living. Eyes are easy to fool. Especially when the mind

The Travers at Saratoga, August 16, 1941, 1st Whirlaway, 2nd Fairymant, 3rd Lord Kitchener.

> behind them starts out with a prejudice. . . . The camera isn't prejudiced.

Whirlaway's amazing performance in the Saranac Special proved he still retained an abundance of stretch-running speed, even after completing 15 consecutive races since the beginning of his 1941 season. The mile race also gained for Whirly a regular traveling companion, a rare accomplishment for him in its own right. And Ben Jones could at last approach the next race without spending time frantically beating the bushes in search of an unclaimed jockey for Whirlaway.

The next race on the agenda for the newly formed racing duo was the prestigious Travers Stakes, Saratoga's traditional classic for three-year-olds. The 1941 version would mark the 72nd year of its running. This mile-and-a-quarter classic is the oldest and most historic of American races, first run in 1864, a year before Lee and Grant met at Appomattox Court House and ended the Civil War. It is appropriately called the "Midsummer Derby" and is considered the next most important race for three-year-olds after the Triple Crown contests.

The sky was heavily overcast the day of the Travers, and because of recent rains, the Saratoga track was in horrible condition, a veritable sea of mud. On a day when it appeared that flood warnings might have to be posted on the roads leading to Saratoga Springs, track officials must have been ecstatic as they watched throngs of people streaming through the turnstiles at the concourse, until the stands were filled by an all-time record crowd of 24,131. Why would that many human beings show up for a horse race under such inclement weather conditions? Didn't those fans, most of them Whirlaway supporters, know there was a strong possibility their favorite might be scratched because of the track's dangerous footing? Whirlaway fans never bothered checking the weather report for the day set for one of his races. They knew if he had been entered in the race, he'd be there.

Whirlaway was indeed on hand at post time, despite all the fuss about the weather, track conditions, and carrying 130 pounds over the mile-and-a-quarter course. Under the best of racing conditions, toting 18 pounds more than his rivals that far over uncertain real estate should have slowed Whirlaway considerably, perhaps even ensured his defeat. On this day, the cards were really stacked against him. But this unique equine always ran to the beat of a different drummer than the average thoroughbred. So, what happened?

Sid Feder, reporting for Lexington's *Herald-Leader*, gave this description of the 1941 Travers:

> While Fairymant and Lord Kitchener took off with a rush, . . . Robertson just stayed back and let 'em go. At the mile mark Whirly was still nine lengths out of it . . . [when] Robbie gave him the word.
>
> He was a mud-covered lightning streak . . . and won . . . by three lengths in a gallop. . . .

Cornelia Prime, writer for *The Thoroughbred Record*, made this assessment of Whirlaway's Travers victory:

> After the race, many seasoned horsemen stated they considered the Travers to be Whirlaway's best race.

When compared to his thrilling performances in the Derby and the Preakness, it is highly debatable whether Whirlaway's Travers win should be judged his best. Nevertheless, in over 100 runnings of the "Midsummer Derby," few thoroughbred champions have won it or, for that matter, any Saratoga race in which they were participants.

In 1930, Gallant Fox won the Triple Crown but lost the Travers to Jim Dandy, a 100-1 entry. Affirmed, the 1978 Triple Crown winner, came close to winning the Travers but lost to Alydar on a stewards' disqualification. Other turf greats have also suffered unexpected defeat at Saratoga. The ultimate in turf upsets took place on the health spa track in the 1919 Sanford Stakes, when a horse appropriately named Upset handed Man O' War the only defeat of his career. Another shocker of equal magnitude happened at Saratoga in the 1973 Whitney Stakes when Onion, a four-year-old gelding who had never won a stakes race and was a lightly regarded 6-1 choice, administered a masterful defeat to the 10-1 favored Triple Crown champion Secretariat. Pleasant Colony, winner of the Kentucky Derby and Preakness, lost the 1981 Travers to 24-1 long shot Willow Hour. And in the 1982 Travers, three Triple Crown race winners — Kentucky Derby champion Gato Del Sol, Preakness victor

Aloma's Ruler, and Belmont winner Conquistador Cielo — competed against each other, with none of them finishing as the winner. That year the laurels went to another unknown named Runaway Groom.

Through the years, Saratoga has earned the reputation of being a "graveyard of favorites." Of all the turf champions who have competed in races at Saratoga, only Whirlaway was able to overcome the track's perennial "curse." Whirly won four races there during the 1940 and 1941 seasons, including the Hopeful Stakes and the Travers. "Mr. Longtail" is the only Triple Crown champion ever to win the Travers, and the impressive manner in which he achieved his victories on America's oldest racetrack far transcends the number of races he won there.

By late summer, racing campaigns of leading three-year-olds usually start winding down, but the torrid pace of Whirlaway's 1941 campaign had shown no signs of slackening since its beginning back in February. Instead, the time lapse between races had continually been narrowed, and all of this running around the oval had transpired on nine different tracks. No other Triple Crown champion had ever been subjected to such a heavy schedule, and Whirlaway still had races to run before reaching the final finish line of his three-year-old campaign. Two days after running in the Travers in upstate New York, Whirlaway was on his way by rail car to Chicago to enter in Washington Park's American Derby set for August 23, only six days away.

At that point in his racing career, Whirlaway had begun to take on the demeanor of his trainer — nothing upset him anymore. After having a quick shower and removing all that mud he had picked up from the Saratoga "mud wrestle," Whirlaway probably decided to follow a plan of action that went something like this: Throw a few necessities in an oat bag today (Monday), take a cab to the Union Station, catch the first train going west, and hope to arrive in Chicago early enough Saturday to be at the track on time for the American Derby, scheduled for late afternoon.

No doubt a few changes had to be made in the first draft, but whatever the final travel itinerary, it worked. Whirlaway was quickly entrained and shipped to Chicago with Jimmy Jones in charge, while the horse's trainer booked passage by air in order to make advance arrangements for the race. When the Whirlaway "caravan" arrived in Chicago, Howard Barry, sportswriter for the *Chicago Tribune*, asked Jimmy Jones about preparing Whirlaway for the upcoming race on such short notice. Jimmy had a ready answer for that query:

> Whirlaway doesn't need any serious workouts now. He just races and travels.

The Calumet champion somehow managed to survive the arduous railway trip without mishap and answered the bugle call for the 17th consecutive time in 1941, the 33rd of his career, and never once during that time had he been scratched from a race in which he was entered. On hand were 35,000 fans to witness the American Derby that day. The fans had backed Whirlaway down to odds of 1-5, making him the shortest-priced favorite in the long history of the race, dating back to 1884. This strong show of support was but another indication that most turf enthusiasts had come to the track primarily to see Whirlaway run, for a wager on him to win would net but a paltry sum.

The Triple Crown champion seemed no worse for wear. He ran as smoothly as a machine throughout the race and crossed the finish line two-and-three-quarter lengths ahead of his nearest pursuer, Bushwhacker. He ran the mile-and-a-quarter in 2:04, equaling Cavalcade's record set in 1934. Jockey Robertson, who had by then ridden Whirlaway in his last three races, described his ride to reporters after the race:

> Whirlaway was full of run today, and I had to restrain him from going to the top too early. He responded when I called on him and was running easily at the finish. Whirlaway was in grand shape. . . .

Barry, in the *Chicago Tribune*, also gave Whirly's performance a high rating:

> Whirlaway's victory in the American Derby climaxed a campaign unparalleled by any other three-year-old in the history of the American turf.

Whirlaway had fared much better in Chicago this time than he had a month earlier at Arlington Park. So why did Ben Jones make a hasty decision to leave town immediately this time? Shortly after the Washington Park race, he announced that Whirlaway was being shipped back to New York, where his next start would probably be in the mile-and-five-furlong Lawrence Realization Stakes, another of those traditional, prestigious races for three-year-olds. But that race wouldn't be run for another month.

For whatever reason, it was back to the rail car and on to New York for Whirlaway. The relentless equine campaigner must have been thoroughly confused by all this hubbub surrounding his life. He was making his second return trip to the East Coast within the past month. Perhaps Jimmy Jones had stated Whirly's case perfectly when he said, "He just races and travels."

After Calumet stable had reached its destination in New York City and had settled in at Belmont Park to await the Lawrence Realization Stakes set for September 20, owner Wright and trainer Jones decided to enter their much-traveled champion in the Narragansett Special up the coast about 200 miles at Pawtuckett, Rhode Island. That race was set for September 13, and Whirly's decision-makers figured they would still have time to transport him back to New York and enter him in the Belmont race. But the Lawrence Realization race was the only major contest for three-year-olds left on the 1941 racing calendar, so why enter Whirlaway in a race of lesser importance that late in the year?

The Calumet "brain trust" had a different motive for deciding to enter Whirlaway in the Narragansett race. By adding the American Derby first-place money of $44,975, the Triple Crown champion's earnings would come to $320,611, thus making him a serious threat to break Seabiscuit's all-time record of $437,730. Just in the last four months of racing, Whirlaway had already accomplished far more than Warren Wright had ever hoped for as an owner of thoroughbred racehorses. In fact, the money-winning title was the only turf laurel that had escaped his path of triumph during that time.

When the news broke that Whirlaway would be running in the Narragansett Special, people throughout the New England area were pleased. When Whirly appeared on the track, he was given a standing ovation by an all-time record crowd of 48,000, which had filled the stands and overflowed the infield. This Narragansett record attendance was typical of what happened every time Whirlaway was in town, any

Belmont Park, Lawrence Realization Stakes, September 20, 1941, 1st Whirlaway, 2nd Alaking, and 3rd Time Counts.

town, for a race. He had already attracted over 500,000 to his 1941 races, more than any three-year-old in turf history. If all of the fans who turned out just to watch him in workouts were included in that figure, the total would probably have exceeded one million.

The Narragansett race would not be an easy one for Whirlaway, even under the best of conditions. First of all, he would be running against War Relic, the horse he narrowly beat in the Saranac Special at Saratoga. Sam Riddle had withdrawn War Relic from further competition in that meet and had brought him to Pawtuckett, where the colt had been in training since the middle of August. While Sam's horse was resting up and becoming thoroughly acclimated to the Narragansett track, Whirlaway had been keeping the rails hot between Chicago and New York. Then there was the added weight disadvantage; Whirlaway would be carrying 11 pounds more luggage in the race than that saddled to War Relic.

As the race began, War Relic got away to an early lead with Whirlaway behind the field as usual. Whirlaway finally passed the two four-year-olds in the race and was only two lengths behind War Relic at the quarter pole. Everything seemed about normal at that point, but instead of catching War Relic, Whirlaway seemed to grow weary and began falling behind, losing by some four lengths at the finish. After the race, jockey Robertson said the champion just didn't have his usual speed in the stretch this time. Whirlaway's load of 11 extra pounds over the mile-and-three-sixteenths route also worked to War Relic's advantage, especially in the last furlong.

Ben Jones seemed unperturbed about Whirlaway losing the race. Afterward, the trainer simply announced that Whirlaway would be shipped back to New York for participation in the Lawrence Realization Stakes on September 20.

The Lawrence Realization Stakes had originated in 1889 as the American counterpart of the world's oldest stakes race, the English St. Leger, which started in 1776, the year American independence was declared. The Lawrence Realization has been considered the autumn distance classic for three-year-olds, much as the Belmont Stakes serves as their first distance race earlier in the year. In 1941, the Realization was for a mile and five-eighths but was shortened in 1969 to the same distance as the Belmont, a mile and a half. In the years prior to 1941, the race had attracted such notables as Sysonby, Man O' War, Gallant Fox, and Twenty Grand.

Whirlaway was once again the favorite in the race, as he had been for 15 consecutive times since leaving Florida back in March. In this race, Whirlaway was required to give up 14 pounds to each of the other three starters, 126 to 112. A large crowd, as usual, of 27,305 was on hand to witness the fall turf classic, and weather conditions were excellent.

The race started in the usual manner for Whirlaway, but to the astonishment of the fans present, Robertson took him out in front at the half-mile marker. That same astonishment turned into disbelief as Whirly kept widening his lead for over a mile of the long race until he hit the finish line ten lengths (30 yards) in front of the other horses. This was Whirlaway's 19th race of 1941, and he had won it by the widest margin of his career.

The Triple Crown champion reflected the ease with which he had won the race as he was paraded to the winner's circle for the 13th time in 1941. Owner Wright took the bridle himself as a long roll of applause went through the stands. For the long route to the unsaddling area, Whirly appeared to be a docile and dignified champion. To say the least, it was a bit incredible that this little horse with the long tail appeared unruffled after traveling 7,000 miles in a railway car and winning the longest race of his career thus far by such a wide margin. But Warren Wright and Ben Jones interpreted Whirly's serene composure to mean the small chestnut was ready for an even longer race one week later.

R. H. Smythe, in his book *The Mind of the Horse*, makes a perceptive statement concerning equine behavior:

> The mental equipment of the horse is, of course, quite incapable of imagining anything at all resembling the muddled emotional upheavals which beset the human mind, but what is particularly extraordinary . . . is . . . that it should be so adaptable, so capable of suiting his moods to those of its master. . . .

Of course, what masters Wright and Jones had in mind was to enter Whirlaway in still another race with the hope of coming ever closer to the world's money-winning title. Victory in the Realization had brought

Whirly's total earnings to $347,661, a fabulous amount for those days, and less than $100,000 away from the existing record.

A victory in the two-mile Jockey Club Gold Cup race would bring Whirlaway nearer to Seabiscuit's money-winning record. The Gold Cup contest was open to three-year-olds and up and was scheduled for the following Saturday at Belmont. In 1941, the Gold Cup was for a distance of a half mile longer than it is today, not a race frequented by many three-year-olds. Whirlaway's chief opponent in this race was Market Wise, a horse he had beaten earlier in the Kentucky Derby and Dwyer Stakes. But as in the case of War Relic before the Narragansett race, Market Wise had been well rested and practicing at Belmont for the Gold Cup contest.

Fenelon, a leading four-year-old, made the first important move in the long race, taking the lead at the mile marker and setting a torrid pace for half a mile. But this did him in. Market Wise and Whirlaway caught up at that point and fought it out in one of the most thrilling stretch runs in turf history. Whirlaway was even ahead for a time, but Market Wise just managed to poke the tip of his nose out in front at the wire. In winning by a razor-thin margin, a well-rested and vastly improved Market Wise had set a new mark for two miles, clipping a full second off the record set by Exterminator 21 years earlier. And it could actually be stated that Whirlaway had also broken the old mark by finishing only a whisker behind the winner.

The renowned equine journalist Salvador, describing the race in *American Race Horses*, wrote:

> Whirlaway went down heroically and, if a champion must be beaten, this was the way it should be done.

After the Jockey Club Gold Cup race, Warren Wright at last decided to close the books on Whirlaway's long and grueling 1941 racing campaign, an unbroken string of 20 races starting in February and ending in late September. A few days later, the Triple Crown champion was shipped home to Calumet Farm in Lexington. Future plans at that time called for the dauntless campaigner to be shipped to California later in the fall to start training for the Santa Anita Handicap, which had been set for March 7, 1942.

Mrs. Warren Wright, giving Whirlaway sugar at Calumet Farm.

Chapter 8

The Blue Grass of Home

WHIRLAWAY'S return to Calumet Farm, after eight months on the racing circuit, was an occasion for spontaneous rejoicing. During Whirly's prolonged absence, life at Calumet Farm had changed drastically. Until 1941, Warren Wright's thoroughbred racing establishment had struggled to stay afloat amid a steadily rising tide of red ink. Whirlaway's winnings in 1940 as leader of the two-year-old juvenile division had started paying

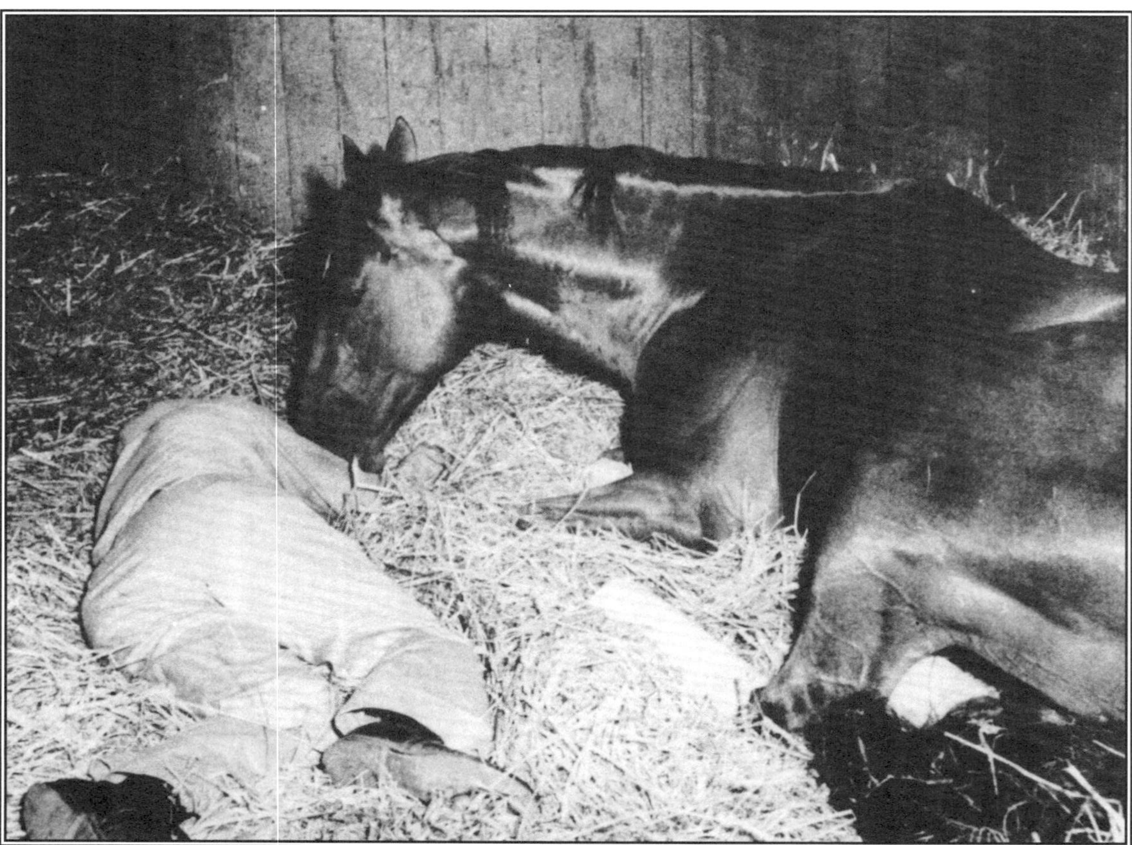

Whirlaway with his groom, Dan Barnett, taking a well-deserved nap.

some of the Farm's major expenses, but his earnings did little to pay expenses for his 156 stablemates. The financial losses for the period 1939 through the first three months of 1941 alone had reached $245,976, a staggering total for that day.

Then on May 3, 1941, a new era in the history of Calumet Farm began. Margaret Glass, long-time secretary at Calumet, announced that the Farm had received its first visitor the day after Whirlaway won the Kentucky Derby. She quipped, "Whirlaway put us on the map." From that polestar of reference, Calumet Farm became the top name in thoroughbred racing with world-record winnings in 1941 of $725,091, due largely to the rich purses won by Whirlaway. On the "flying tail" of Whirly, Warren Wright's lingering deficits were quickly brought under control, and new money could be plowed back into improving his racing stock.

Today, the meteoric rise of Calumet Farm in 1941 is considered a legend in turf history; but for Whirlaway, the road to the top was not built by magic or good fortune. Rather, it was put in place by his strenuous work schedule, coupled with a railway car streaking between the East Coast and Chicago, racing against the clock and the best horses in the land, defying the imposition of heavy weight and clinging mud. Lest we forget.

It is easy to perceive the great human affection expressed by the Calumet Farm family for Whirlaway on his return to Lexington in early October 1941, but wouldn't it be fascinating to know the reaction of Whirly's mother, Dustwhirl, to her son's return after months of absence?

No doubt Whirlaway was glad at last to escape the rapidly shifting sights and sounds of the racing circuit and return to the rolling bluegrass hills of Calumet Farm, the scene of his happy childhood. Life had changed dramatically for Dustwhirl's son during the past eight months. On days between races, the routine for the 1941 turf champion was not too different from that of his stablemates. After the daily workout, he was cooled down by Pinkie Browne, his exercise boy, and then cleaned meticulously by his groom, Dan Barnett, who sponged him down, packed his feet with mud to withdraw any fever from those stout legs, and then combed his mane and long tail.

In 1941 it cost 66 cents per day to feed the sleek, graceful Whirlaway — 21 cents for nine quarts of oats and 45 cents for a measure of hay. On days when Whirly worked particularly well, he received 25 cents worth of carrots as a bonus, carrots being to a racehorse what candy bars are to a child. In all, Calumet Farm spent $4.40 on an average day to maintain the nation's 1941 turf idol. In comparing the minimal cost for Whirlaway's upkeep with his earnings for his first two years of racing, $349,661, it came as no surprise that Calumet Farm was finally operating within its budget.

During the days and months of 1941, when Whirlaway was winning fame and fortune for Calumet Farm, events of profound and lasting impact were transpiring elsewhere in the world, events that would in time greatly alter the future racing career of Warren Wright's first Triple Crown champion.

As if the weather were signaling an omen of things to come, winter made an early call on Colorado the last week of August with a hailstorm of such intensity that a snow plow was called into service to open the highway through Denver. Hailstones piled up eight to ten inches on a nine-mile stretch of the road, and a few flakes of snow fell along with the hail.

This wintry weather out west, however, did not dampen the spirits of the city fathers in Atlantic City, New Jersey. Plans were being made in that East Coast resort for the greatest crowd in history on Labor Day weekend. Attractions would include music by Glenn Miller and his orchestra on Saturday and Sunday, and by Jimmy Dorsey and his band on Labor Day. The 48 contestants for Miss America would be there for Pageant Week, the singing Andrews Sisters were scheduled to head the stage show, and military bands and marching units would be performing all around town.

In early October, Warren Wright made a firm decision to enter Whirlaway in the $100,000 Santa Anita Handicap set for March 7, 1942, billed as the "richest horse race in the world." Owner Wright's decision was obviously influenced by the apparent fact that by winning the lucrative California race, Whirly could take over Seabiscuit's money-winning title.

As a result of the Santa Anita Handicap commitment, Whirlaway's abbreviated visit at home came to an end on October 24. On that day, he was once again loaded on a railway car, his adopted home on wheels, this time attached to the Santa Fe Chief passenger train, on his way to

California to begin training for the winter racing meet at Santa Anita.

It was announced in the October 28 edition of the *Los Angeles Times* that

> Whirlaway, the long-tailed Calumet Cannonball whose magnetic appeal in his parade to the 3-year-old championship has gripped a thoroughbred-loving nation, will arrive this afternoon after a 4-day trip from Lexington, Kentucky.

A royal welcome had been arranged for the "King of American Thoroughbreds" by General Manager Charles H. Strub of the Los Angeles Turf Club, who realized that hundreds of racing fans would jump at the chance to get a close-up view of Warren Wright's great three-year-old. The estimate of the crowd on hand was modest, to say the least: It was said that some 3,500 cheering fans were on hand when Whirlaway arrived at Santa Anita that afternoon. Ben Jones led Whirly off the ramp of his Santa Fe Chief railway car and announced: "Here he is, and no horse ever shipped better."

Paul Lowry, sportswriter for the *Los Angeles Times*, described the cheering spectators as the largest crowd to ever see a horse unloaded from a train in California, perhaps the country. He doubted that those in attendance would ever forget the sight:

> With his head held high, his rich coat gleaming in the afternoon sun, his long bushy tail swinging so low it almost touched the ground. . . .
>
> Newsreels headed the parade, grinding away from atop automobiles as Whirlaway was led to his stable, but the ceremonies didn't stop at the barn. . . .

The royal welcome accorded Whirlaway at Santa Anita made complete the Triple Crown champion's conquest of turfdom from coast to coast. Steady streams of people came to visit him at Santa Anita, and many movie starlets sought to have their pictures taken with Whirly. He proved to be a gracious host, and allowed photographers to shoot pictures at will.

Al Santorro, sports editor for the Los Angeles *Examiner*, in an exclusive visit to Whirlaway's stable, got this description of the champion's serene composure from proud trainer Ben Jones:

> Whirly no longer needs blinkers in a race. He's now as well-behaved as an old plough [*sic*] horse and he's unconcerned no matter how many people come to see him at his barn. Even noisy cement mixers fail to excite him in the least bit.

As Whirlaway began training for the 1942 racing season, the curtain was slowly descending on the 1941 sports year. In baseball, two major league batting records were set that have endured to this day, 53 years later — Joe DiMaggio's mark of hitting safely in 56 consecutive games, and Ted Williams's .406 batting average. Joe Louis was still heavyweight boxing champion, and Craig Wood led the field in golf. It was a vintage year in athletic competition, but from that harvest of stars, none projected a greater light than did Whirlaway and his stellar achievements on the racetrack.

Never before had a racehorse captured the hearts of sports fans and writers on such a broad scale. Thousands of die-hard supporters from sports other than thoroughbred racing had made a rare exception in 1941 by avidly following Whirlaway's races. John Kieran, eminent sports columnist for *The New York Times*, was noted for his perceptive and cool treatment in reporting athletic competitions. His personal interests usually lay in baseball and football. Then Whirlaway came dashing out of Kentucky, and Kieran wrote in one of his columns:

> Ordinarily this innocent bystander plays no favorites at the track, but has to admit a slight weakness for Whirlaway. Not through snobbishness because Whirlaway is an important turf star and up in the money now. No, sir! Rich horse or poor horse, it's all one to this casual racegoer.

He went on to explain Whirlaway's "other attractive qualities," the first of which was his distinctive long tail, which enabled him to be recognized even without jockey colors. Another was the drama that was packed into the stretch, which he described thusly:

> . . . the fourth act . . . with its denouement right under the eyes of the playgoers. Whirlaway is the hero coming to save the girl and tear up the mortgage. He's the United States Cavalry (tantara, tantara) galloping down to . . . capture the already rejoicing enemy, . . . the rightful king, triumphing over rebels and usurpers.

Kieran concluded by saying,

> That stretch run . . . is what makes Whirlaway the star of the thoroughbred circle.

Whirlaway's drawing power in 1941 had caused racetrack turnstiles to click as never before. During his three-year-old campaign, Mr. Longtail had set attendance records for both regular races and workout sessions. Whirly's magic at the gate had established new attendance marks for the Kentucky Derby, Preakness, Henry of Navarre Purse, Arlington Classic, Travers Stakes, and Narragansett Special.

In his book on Triple Crown winners, *The Most Glorious Crown*, Marvin Drager wrote this of Whirlaway:

> He generates more charisma than is likely to be found in a whole herd of thundering thoroughbreds.

For certain, people really knew when this horse came to town, but Whirlaway's wide public acclaim was built on a more solid base than the usual fleeting image of sports celebrities created by the fragile building blocks of charisma, glamour, and excitement. A review of his 1941 racing record will indicate that he participated in and won the most important three-year-old races offered that year. In addition to winning the Triple Crown contests, Whirlaway is the only thoroughbred in turf history to win the fourth most prestigious race for three-year-olds — the Travers Stakes; he set a record for the Kentucky Derby that lasted 21 years, a mark that has lasted 50 years, and his finishing time of 11 seconds for the last furlong of that mile-and-a-quarter race has never yet been equaled.

As a three-year-old, Whirlaway gave new meaning to the racing qualities of courage and durability. He traveled over 10,000 miles in 1941, participated in 20 races at 11 different tracks, was top-weighted in all of them, giving up as much as 18 pounds to opponents, carried 130 pounds in two races, was never scratched from a race in which he had been entered, and ran on tracks ranging from fast to heavy with mud.

No sports star of 1941, and there were many, more fully met the criteria required of a true champion than did Whirlaway. And it must be noted that Whirly's compatriots were not called upon to carry extra weight or participate on endangering surfaces while in competition.

Robert F. Kelley, a leading sportswriter of that day, provided a succinct summary of Whirlaway's 1941 racing campaign in the Jockey Club publication *Racing in America*. He said that Whirlaway's record-breaking Kentucky Derby established Ben Jones as one of the greatest trainers of all time, and that it started Mr. and Mrs. Warren Wright's Calumet Farm on the road to the forefront of racing and breeding.

For his 1941 turf achievements, Whirlaway became the first thoroughbred in turf history to be recognized as a national champion and was rewarded by receiving racing's most prestigious annual award — "Horse of the Year."

Chapter
9

To Race or Not to Race in 1942

BY November 1941, Ben Jones had started training Whirlaway in preparation for the upcoming Santa Anita meet. Little did Ben realize that at an appointed place in the Pacific, Japanese warlords were beginning the countdown to the launching of an aerial attack that would suddenly plunge the United States into global conflict. This unprovoked attack on innocent victims, a cowardly tactic of warfare for which the Axis powers had become infamous, would radically change the "busi-

ness as usual" attitude prevalent at that time throughout most of the nation. And in the long run, it would have a profound impact on Whirlaway's future as a thoroughbred racehorse.

The unexpected disaster occurred on Sunday, December 7, 1941, an unusually warm day on the nation's mainland. Millions were listening to the Columbia Broadcasting System that afternoon when, just as the New York Philharmonic Orchestra was tuning up for Shostakovich's Symphony No. 1, John Daly's familiar voice broke in a few minutes after 3:00 p.m.:

> We interrupt this program to bring you a special news bulletin. The Japanese have attacked Pearl Harbor.

The listeners did not yet know the full, tragic dimensions of that startling announcement, but there were 120 million Americans old enough to understand the significance. The nation was full of outrage and disbelief. Of all the momentous events that would affect American lives over the next four years, this would be the most vividly remembered. It was as if a camera had clicked in their minds and frozen their thoughts in place.

As a direct consequence of these sudden developments, Whirlaway's racing career was placed in serious jeopardy. The bad news came on December 15, when the U.S. Army gave orders to cancel California's Santa Anita Handicap scheduled for March 7, 1942.

Santa Anita track officials had arranged for the richest meet in its history with purses and stakes totaling $1,160,000. The added $100,000 Santa Anita Handicap had drawn the largest number of nominations since the track had begun operating in 1935. More than 1,400 horses had been quartered for the meet. Then to cap the festivities, Colonel Matt Winn, head man at Churchill Downs, had been scheduled to present the winner's trophy after race. Charles Strub, track manager, announced at the time of the cancellation that all seats for the Santa Anita Handicap had been sold out, which would have assured a record crowd. Whirlaway had been established as the early favorite and was, as usual, the prime reason for the anticipated record figures — but this time for a race that was never run.

Grantland Rice, renowned sportswriter, happened to be in California visiting with his friend Ben Jones just before the Santa Anita meet's closing. At that time, Jones told Rice he saw at least $600,000 ahead for Whirlaway in 1942, starting with the $50,000 Santa Anita Derby. By winning the Santa Anita Handicap alone, the long-tailed charger would become the world's leading money-winner. Then Santa Anita was closed.

After the closing, many stables shipped their horses back home; some went to Florida for what remained of the racing season there. Warren Wright and Ben Jones announced that Whirlaway would not leave, but would continue training at Santa Anita. Hope still lingered that California racing might be continued on some basis, perhaps by moving the meet to some track farther inland.

But the national feeling of insecurity continued and was heightened considerably on February 23, 1942, when the war's first direct enemy attack on the continental United States occurred. It happened while President Roosevelt was delivering one of his periodic fireside chats by radio on the war's progress. While he was speaking, a lone Japanese submarine surfaced approximately one mile offshore north of Santa Barbara, California, and fired at an oil refinery.

The submarine attack proved insignificant, but nevertheless it served to intensify invasion jitters and widen hatred of "enemy aliens." After the Pearl Harbor attack, this angry sentiment was directed primarily against the 127,000 Japanese-Americans living in California, Oregon, and Washington where fear of invasion was particularly acute. Finally, in response to public uneasiness and protest, President Roosevelt signed Executive Order 9066 on February 19, 1942, authorizing the Secretary of War to prescribe certain "military areas" and to exile "any or all" persons from those locations.

As a result of this decision, 112,000 Japanese-Americans were designated for removal to temporary camps and then further inland to permanent facilities. Late in March 1942, the Army began rounding them up and transporting them to assembly centers. When General John DeWitt, in charge of West Coast defense, announced that Santa Anita Race Track had been selected as a relocation center for this purpose, Ben Jones knew his hopes for racing Whirlaway in California were doomed. After five months of training at Santa Anita, Whirlaway still had not been entered in a race, and his chances of becoming the world's leading money-winner were dwindling.

It was too late for racing in Florida; the season was over. The only option left was a painful five-day trip by rail back to Kentucky for Ben Jones and the Calumet string of 47 horses. This downcast caravan arrived in Lexington, Kentucky, on March 23. Fortunately, Whirlaway proved once again to be a good traveler. Despite risks involved under such adverse conditions, Whirly arrived in Lexington without injury. After the thousands of miles logged via railway car in 1941, he had become accustomed to the lifestyle. However, some of the other Calumet horses did not fare so well. While at Santa Anita, Ben Jones had eight three-year-olds ready for the Kentucky Derby; but after returning to Kentucky, not one of the eight could be entered in the Derby because of leg injuries suffered on the trip, the long distance traveled, and the sudden change of climate.

Jones obviously was anything but happy. He commented that the less said about Whirlaway breaking Seabiscuit's record, the better. Grantland Rice aptly described his friend's mood:

> Down in Kentucky, Ben was the only thing I saw bluer than Kentucky skies and Kentucky bluegrass.

As April 1942 began, an unanswered question remained for Whirlaway and thoroughbred racing in the U.S. Because of serious wartime conditions, would the sport of kings be shut down?

As a result of the imminent threat, the United States found itself on a collision course in its frantic effort to build up the woefully unprepared Armed Forces. With the rush to train millions of men for combat, civilian life was thoroughly disrupted. Initially, there was widespread belief that most professional sports, including thoroughbred racing, would cease for the duration of the war. When the Army closed Santa Anita Race Track in March 1942, most major tracks had expected to meet the same fate soon thereafter. Ironically, it was this urgency to gear up for all-out war that caused military leaders in Washington eventually to make some unusual exceptions for the civilian sector.

Social life in America was disrupted nationwide in those early months of 1942. Volunteers and draftees from all walks of life were joining up for military service as some seven million troops were rapidly processed for active duty. The list included farm kids and movie stars, professors and students, centerfielders and congressmen. Train stations and bus terminals were bustling with servicemen going in all directions. Girls flocked to soldiers, sailors, and Marines in the training camps. For wives whose husbands were in the service, life was even more disquieting. Many attempted to keep up with their husbands. They would set up housekeeping near the camps as best they could, often paying outrageous rent for that time — $50 a month to live in sheds, chicken coops, or ramshackle barns.

For servicemen who had nowhere else to go for entertainment, there was usually a nearby honky-tonk district. These sections of towns and cities located near training camps featured clusters of bars, dance halls, hotels, and brothels. One of the most notorious such attractions was Phoenix City, Alabama, across the river from Fort Benning, Georgia, which soon became known as Sin City.

However, these seamy conditions on the home front brought quick public outcry. Clergymen and other community service leaders waged an unfaltering war against the fleshpots. As a result, Congress passed the May Act, enabling local communities to shut down houses of prostitution near military installations. As a further means of tackling this widespread social problem, the United Service Organization (USO) announced on March 25, 1942, a drive seeking to raise $32 million to provide hospitality for off-duty soldiers and sailors. John D. Rockefeller, Jr., was chosen to serve as honorary chairman for the drive, and this effort was given official sanction by Paul V. McNutt, director of Defense, Health, and Welfare Services, and by the President's Committee on War Relief Services headed by Joseph E. Davies. Spokesmen for the federal agencies stated that the Army and Navy were depending heavily on all segments of the private sector, including professional sports, to provide vitally needed services. They further emphasized the urgency of the USO drive by stating that nearly all monetary appropriations by Congress, at that time, were earmarked for training and equipping troops for combat duty.

The $32 million called for in the USO drive would be used to meet troop morale needs off-duty and for recreation in the following ways:

1. Half of the total amount raised would be used to build 450

service clubs and 250 smaller units near leading Army and Navy posts and defense plants.

2. Four million dollars would be used to sponsor camp shows within and outside the United States.
3. The remaining funds would be spent to establish emergency USO clubs for women and girls working in defense industries.

Meeting the urgent needs outlined, more than any single factor, prevented the complete shutdown of thoroughbred racing and other professional sports in 1942. Serious consideration had already been given to the closure of horse racing following the closing of the Santa Anita Race Track on January 5. An even stronger case could have been made for closing tracks on the East Coast, where German submarines were creating havoc for our ships, even within sight of curious observers along the shoreline.

Racetrack officials, fearing the imminent shutdown of scheduled races, called together representatives of the country's 22 tracks on March 19, 1942, in Chicago to find a way to keep the racing season open. The crisis brought about the formation of a national association of racetrack operators, something which had met with total rejection in previous attempts. The participants were charged with making recommendations on how the sport could best operate in wartime and make a justifiable contribution to the "nation's war effort." The official name for the group was "Thoroughbred Racing Associations of the United States." Herbert Swope, of the New York Racing Commission, was chosen chairman of the executive committee.

Swope's committee was given the responsibility for setting a monetary goal and establishing methods to be used by the tracks in reaching it. The committee, through Chairman Swope, made its report on April 16. Two million dollars was hoped to be raised for war relief. The report cautioned, however, that wartime restrictions did not favor the attainment of that lofty goal, citing the shutdown of racing in California and the dismal showing of winter racing in Florida and New Orleans, and that starting the drive as late as April 16 did not enhance thoroughbred racing's chances of raising the amount by the end of the 1942 racing season.

Chapter 10

Whirlaway Joins in the Fight for Freedom

WHEN Calumet stable returned from California to Kentucky in late March 1942, Whirlaway had not been entered in a race for six months, and the future of thoroughbred racing was unclear. Nevertheless, Ben Jones started training the Calumet horses with the faint hope that the sport might survive in spite of increasing wartime restrictions.

Fortunately, the spring meet at nearby Keeneland Park

had been allowed to proceed on schedule. This afforded Jones an opportunity to test Whirlaway in a couple of short sprint races, just in case other racetracks would also be allowed to continue with their 1942 meets. The Calumet champion had not been entered in a race of less than a mile since before the Kentucky Derby of 1941. But after the long mandatory vacation from racing, the trainer was elated to find any race still scheduled on April 9, 1942.

Despite the long layoff, Whirlaway showed no signs of deterioration in the Keeneland races, finishing a close second in both three-quarter-mile sprints. Mr. Longtail carried 14 pounds more than the winner in the first race and 17 more in the second; but even with the extra baggage, most track observers agreed he would have won both races had the distance been longer.

Good news for thoroughbred racing was received when, on April 16, the Turf Committee of America issued a press release announcing that racing would be allowed to continue during 1942, primarily for the purpose of raising the $2 million for the War Emergency Relief Fund. The announcement further stated that participating tracks could set their own quotas and choose certain races from their scheduled meets from which proceeds would go to war relief.

An amazing thing happened immediately following the Turf Committee's announcement. Every major track in the country with upcoming meets, including those in New York, Chicago, Maryland, Massachusetts, and Rhode Island, designated special races for war relief and forthwith started negotiations with Warren Wright and Ben Jones to secure Whirlaway as the featured attraction.

This was probably the greatest vote of confidence ever accorded a racehorse. But there were good reasons for Whirlaway to have merited this recognition. In becoming "Horse of the Year" in 1941, he was the obvious favorite for making 1942 the greatest yet in the annals of thoroughbred racing. He had drawn record crowds and purses almost everywhere he had raced, and in those record gatherings were found people of every stripe, people who before had shown only a passive interest in horse racing. And because of his thrilling races and stunning victories, sportswriters from coast to coast called him the national champion, the first time a racehorse had been recognized as such.

All of Whirlaway's accomplishments of 1941 would now pale in significance when compared to the tremendous responsibilities this would-be patriot was to begin carrying. Whirlaway had enlisted in the fight for freedom; he would be racing in a different lane and on a much higher plane.

After the Keeneland Park races, the Calumet stable moved on to Churchill Downs in Louisville, where Whirlaway was entered in the Clark Handicap on April 25. This race served as a springboard for launching Whirly's 1942 campaign in behalf of the War Emergency Relief Fund. The Calumet champion started last in the race, trailed by as much as 15 lengths in the early going, but came on fast in the stretch and won by a head over Aonbarr. In the mile-and-one-sixteenth run, Whirly carried 127 pounds to Aonbarr's 115.

Following the same route as the previous year, Ben Jones wasted no time in moving Whirlaway on to Pimlico in Baltimore to prepare for the Dixie Handicap on May 6. Upon entering Whirly in this feature handicap race, Jones did not realize how much significance would be given to the contest by post time.

When the Calumet team arrived in Baltimore, the sportswriters had already started building up the race as even more attractive than Pimlico's Preakness Stakes, which would follow the Dixie Handicap by only three days. Don Reed's column in the May issue of *The Baltimore Sun* carried this pre-race assessment:

> Any race which can shove Pimlico's Preakness into the background this week must be a fair sort of contest and today's Dixie Handicap has done just that.
>
> Class with a capital C . . . oozes from the lineup of 11 performers scheduled to compete . . . for a prize that will run around $20,000. . . .

Besides Whirlaway, there were three other entries in the race with outstanding records. Challedon had been "Horse of the Year" twice, in 1939 and 1940, with 18 stakes wins including the Preakness in 1939; Mioland was leader of the handicap division in 1940 with impressive victories in California; and Attention had been one of Whirlaway's strongest foes in the past, snapping Whirly's string of victories at six during the previous summer by capturing the Arlington Classic in

Chicago. Never before had that many leading horses of different seasons come together in the same race. The match race between War Admiral and Seabiscuit in 1938 was of that category, but only two horses had competed in that contest.

Usually a lineup of such star attractions in any encounter would generate abundant interest for the occasion, but a Whirlaway race, almost without exception, offered the fans an extra element of surprise or suspense. The Dixie Handicap merely added to the tradition. In the May 6 morning edition of *The Baltimore Sun*, the entry list for the Dixie, scheduled to start in the afternoon about 5:00 p.m., conspicuously showed Whirlaway without a jockey. Imagine the race favorite without a rider only a few hours before post time! That was the ultimate in raw suspense.

In 39 consecutive races, since the start of his career in 1940 as a two-year-old, Whirlaway had never been withdrawn from a race in which he was officially entered. But the business of having a designated rider had been a problem throughout his brilliant three-year-old campaign. Sometimes this had meant latching on to some jockey relaxing in the track's clubhouse after a hard ride or contracting a rider as he dismounted from a horse in the previous race on the day's program.

For the Dixie Handicap, the rider became available from the same race in which Whirly was entered. One of the entries, Century Note, was scratched on the day of the race, thereby freeing the jockey to ride another horse. But there's more to this continuing drama. The liberated jockey turned out to be Eddie Arcaro, the same daring young man who had arrived at Churchill Downs one day before the 1941 Kentucky Derby and jumped astride Whirlaway for the first time.

Actually, a year had passed since Arcaro and Whirlaway, the Triple Crown combination, had last worked together. Eddie was back on the circuit doing most of his riding for Greentree Stable, with whom he was still under contract. By coincidence, the horse scratched from the Dixie Handicap was a Greentree entry, thereby allowing Eddie to be back in Whirly's saddle again.

Without further surprise or suspense, the 39th running of the mile-and-three-sixteenths Dixie Handicap got under way before a crowd of 20,000. When the horses went by the stands for the first time, the lead was contested tightly by Air Master, Best Seller, and Sir Alfred, with

Attention and Impound close up. Mioland was in the middle of the pack, while Challedon and Whirlaway brought up the rear.

The pace battle was a hot one for the first three-quarters but then began to take its toll as the early leaders dropped back and Attention loomed as a strong threat. But from the rear, Mioland, Challedon, and last of all, Whirlaway were beginning to close the gap.

Arcaro moved up to fifth entering the home stretch and waited for an opening. When none developed inside, he swung slightly out and Whirlaway began his charge. Don Reed, *The Baltimore Sun* sportswriter, described the final stages of the race from that point:

> . . . there was no withstanding that chestnut colt making his bid. . . .
>
> A sixteenth of a mile from the line it was apparent Whirlaway was going to win and the roar that went up from the thousands in the stands was testimony enough that a real champion was being greeted.

The Dixie was typical of Whirlaway's great races as a three-year-old in that he came from 20 lengths back of the leaders with a terrific rush in the final half-mile to win. In so doing, Whirly carried top weight of 128 pounds and was timed at the distance in 1:57, just a fifth of a second slower than the track record. It appeared the Triple Crown bearer was in good form for the long campaign ahead.

There were the usual accolades for Whirlaway after the race, reminiscent of those he had received a year before when he had won the Preakness in similar fashion.

Jesse Linthicum, *The Baltimore Sun* sports editor, gave this outpouring of praise:

> Thrills have been provided by . . . other great stakes races, but none . . . overshadowed the finish yesterday . . . of the Dixie.
>
> Whirlaway, the horse with the beautiful flowing tail, came from out of the clouds to beat the greatest collection of handicap stars assembled in years for a race.

He added,

> . . . when he stepped on the gas he found he had airplane fuel. He was simply flying down the stretch. Whirlaway, the express train, passed his rivals as if they were slow freights.
>
> . . . The horde of fans . . . were limp in their seats. . . . They rent the air with cheers. . . .

The Associated Press column in *The New York Times* carried this description of Whirlaway's Dixie Handicap:

> They threw a million-dollar field of handicap horses at Whirlaway today and "little long tail" made his rivals look like [they were standing still] selling platers as he boomed along the road toward Seabiscuit's all-time money winning record.
>
> Hooked up with the best collection of handicap horses since Seabiscuit and War Admiral were stepping along, Whirly turned on the same crushing kick that had made him the head man a year ago, went right around the entire field and galloped home by three-quarters of a length in the thirty-ninth running of the $25,275 Dixie Handicap.
>
> He passed them all — Challedon, Mioland and Attention — so easily he made it look more like fun than work.

Bert Clark Thayer, noted horse photographer and author of that day, gave this account of the race:

> In the stretch Whirlaway picked off horse after horse as each tried desperately, tired, and fell back. Then in one of his spectacular dashes he passed Challedon and Mioland, overtook Attention and won.
>
> Even old-timers, who delight in living over past glories, admitted they could recall no race equal to this one; four handicap stars so evenly matched that there were only four pounds difference at the finish between the first and fourth horse.

Dave Woods, public relations director for Pimlico, offered a tinge of sarcasm for those fans who had passed up the opportunity to attend the Dixie with this remark: "A racing fan who missed this one is a sap."

The Dixie Handicap marked the fifth consecutive time Whirlaway and Eddie Arcaro had teamed up to score an impressive victory in a feature stakes race. Once again Whirlaway found himself the undisputed leader of the handicap division, the same position he had held during his previous two years of racing.

Today, thoroughbred owners are squeamish about their horses becoming leader of the handicap division. They are well aware that once a horse achieves that status, the thoroughbred is required to carry considerably more weight than opposing horses in most stakes races, thus becoming susceptible to injury and more likely to be defeated by a competitor possessing less natural speed. This rationale also explains why most leading three-year-olds are not permitted to show up at the track as four-year-olds.

Whirlaway carried top weight of 128 pounds in the Dixie Handicap, and if he continued his winning ways, the handicappers would be waiting for the division leader after each victory, eager to assign him even more weight for his next race.

After the Dixie Handicap in Baltimore on May 6, Whirlaway and his entourage entrained for Belmont Park in New York. There he would be entered in the Suburban Handicap on May 30. Memorial Day fell on a Saturday in 1942, and a crowd of 51,903 was on hand to see Whirlaway race, the largest crowd ever to see a horse race in New York state. Whirly, as usual, was the favorite and carried a weight of 129 pounds, five more than his formidable opponents, Market Wise and Attention. It was a mile-and-a-quarter race, and Eddie Arcaro was aboard. A field of 11 horses was entered in the Suburban, including Whirlaway's leading foe as a two-year-old, Our Boots.

The race got off to a clean start, but Arcaro allowed Whirly to leave the gate leisurely. Our Boots and Can't Wait set the early pace until reaching the far turn. After a half mile, Whirlaway was dead last, some 20 lengths off the lead. Attention came up on the outside to challenge the leader. At almost the same time, Market Wise came up along the rail. Our Boots dropped back from the double challenge. Whirlaway was underway, but it was only three furlongs to the finish.

Bryan Field of *The New York Times* describes the race as Whirlaway came around the outside:

> Into the stretch Market Wise dashed. . . . Whirlaway was . . . going full blast and passed horse after horse. There was little chance for him to get to Market Wise . . . but his final rush was electrifying and Whirlaway's name was on many a lip as thousands rose to their feet.

Whirlaway was coming on in one of those "awful drives," as Clem McCarthy would say, but missed by a couple of lengths catching Market Wise at the finish. It must have appeared to the fans that Arcaro had started his horse's powerful drive too late to catch the leader; otherwise, it is difficult to explain why those in attendance gave Whirly such a resounding ovation for finishing second in the race. Sid Feder, Associated Press staff writer, wrote later in his column that Arcaro had given Whirlaway "anything but a brilliant ride in the Suburban." Feder further explained that it was expecting too much for Whirlaway to make up as much as 20 lengths in a mile-and-a-quarter race.

The major problem for any jockey riding Whirlaway was to decide at what point in a given race to turn this phenomenal stretch-runner loose. To Arcaro's credit, it must be stated that he had guided Whirly almost perfectly in the five previous races in which he had ridden, four in 1941 and one in 1942, before losing the Suburban. There is little doubt that Warren Wright and Ben Jones would have been elated to have had Eddie as Whirly's rider in all of the colt's races. But the luxury of having a regular mount was something this horse never experienced. Whirlaway rarely knew who his jockey would be until the day of a particular race.

After the Suburban Handicap at Belmont, Whirlaway's next stop would be the Aqueduct Race Track, home of the prestigious Brooklyn Handicap scheduled for June 27. Ben Jones had decided Whirly still needed more fine tuning for this upcoming feature, and thus the trainer entered Mr. Longtail in two races that were scheduled in the weeks preceding the main event at Aqueduct. The first was a seven-furlong sprint, the Carter Handicap set for June 13. Track observers were surprised when they found out Whirly would be running in the short race, knowing that the horse had been carefully trained for distances beyond a mile. Under similar circumstances, most trainers of champion racehorses would not permit their racers to enter such a contest for fear they might sustain defeat or injury in the race. Ben Jones gave little thought to such concerns. By following this format, Ben had successfully prepared Whirly for most of his greatest races, classics like the Kentucky Derby, Belmont, Travers, and Dixie.

With the announcement of Whirlaway's entry in the Carter Handicap, suddenly a relatively minor race became a major attraction. A crowd of 25,298 showed up to see Whirlaway run in a race some thought he had little chance of winning. In this race, he would be facing two of the leading short sprinters of the day, Doublrab and Swing and Sway; he would be carrying 130 pounds, 10 to 18 more than the other 8 opponents; and the *coup de grace* would be furnished by a lesser-known jockey of the day named Leon Haas, who had gained the distinction of becoming Whirly's twelfth racing-career rider.

The fact that Whirlaway was the favorite in the race against such odds illustrates the high esteem accorded this true champion of the turf by his host of loyal fans. He was risking injury and almost certain defeat in a relatively minor race when compared to the important traditional ones coming later. But the fans knew that every race in which Whirlaway was entered during that crucial summer of 1942 meant more money for the War Emergency Relief Fund. Money for the war chest would come from the record crowd attracted by this exciting competitor and apportioned from the track gate receipts, betting totals, and tax collections. In addition, Whirlaway would make an individual contribution — ten percent of the earnings from each of his races went for the purchase of War Bonds. To the racing fans of the day, Whirlaway, through his owner and trainer, embodied more than the means to raise large sums of money for the war effort. At that time of great national crisis, Whirlaway, by his gallant efforts on the track, represented the qualities of character marked "Top Priority": self-sacrifice and courage.

As post time approached, spectators were eager to see how Whirly would fare in a meet designated primarily for sprinters. As the horses broke from the post, a horse named Sheriff Culkin led the way, but Doublrab was not far behind. Whirlaway was last in the early going, at one time as far back as 30 lengths from the leader. This was certainly no way to run a seven-furlong race, but Whirly had been specifically trained to save his explosive speed until the rider gave him the signal to "turn it on." Finally at the far turn, his latest rider did just that. Whirlaway was still last but began gaining ground fast.

As the horses came into the stretch, Doublrab was in the lead with Swing and Sway coming closer and closer. After reaching the stretch, Whirlaway seemed to fly by other horses and took after the leaders. The official chart, which of necessity must be impartial, described Whirlaway's finish with these words: "Whirlaway closed with a brilliant burst of speed and was fairly running over his field at the end." Doublrab managed to cross the line a head in front of Swing and Sway, but once past the finish line, here came Whirlaway sweeping by both sprinters with his incredible but belated burst of speed.

Bert Clark Thayer commented about Whirlaway's run in the Carter Handicap:

> His dashing effort sent the customers in such gales of applause that you would have thought he had won the race by a city block.

Doublrab won the race as expected by the professionals, but he had to equal the track record in doing so. Considering the conditions of a short race, extra weight, and an untried rider, Whirlaway seemed to be more glorious in defeat than if he had somehow managed to win the race. Sid Feder concluded in his column that ". . . in many ways, this was the most remarkable race Whirly ever ran."

Ben Jones still wanted Whirlaway entered in another race before the Brooklyn Handicap. That opportunity presented itself with the announcement of the Celt Purse for June 22, five days before the main event at Aqueduct. The Celt Purse would be a mile-and-one-eighth race, a distance more suited to Whirlaway's racing plan. This race would furnish the crowd of 14,924 with a preview of the Brooklyn Handicap, in which Whirlaway and Attention, two old rivals, were scheduled to meet again.

Whirlaway had another change of riders for the Celt. This time his mount was a veteran jockey named George Woolf who had ridden Whirlaway once before when he brought the long-tailed star home first in the Walden Stakes at Pimlico in 1940. At the start of the race, Swing and Sway was away fast with Attention close by. In the field of five, Whirlaway started last, but this time he was only some five lengths off the pace. Down the backstretch, Woolf moved Whirlaway up to third place, and he was only a length or two back of the leaders. Then in the stretch run, Whirly passed Swing and Sway and nosed out Attention at the wire in a thrilling finish.

A great howl of tribute went up from the crowd as Whirlaway was declared the winner, and in the process he had set a new track record of 1:49 2/5, clipping 3/5 of a second off of the old mark. In riding Whirlaway to victory, George Woolf demonstrated that it was not necessary to keep the horse back in the next county before making the finishing drive to the wire, as in the Celt Purse. Whirlaway was never farther than five lengths off the pace. As usual, Whirly was top-weighted in the race, giving up five pounds to Attention and nine to Swing and Sway.

Aqueduct's summer racing meet would be coming to a close on June 27 with the 54th running of the Brooklyn Handicap. This historic race, dating back to 1887, still is considered to be one of the most important tests for horses in the handicap division. In 1942, the race took on the added dimension of being the special race of the Aqueduct meet from which all proceeds over and above the purse outlay would go to Army-Navy Relief and USO funds. With Whirlaway as the featured attraction, the track had set a lofty goal of $100,000 (at least $600,000 in 1994 dollars) to be raised for the war charities.

The good news for Whirlaway was the presence of George Woolf as his jockey. Imagine Mr. Longtail having the same rider for two consecutive races! As favorite, Whirly carried 128 pounds, spotting the other 7 entries from 6 to 17. Woolf did another superb job of handling Whirlaway; he kept his charger no farther away from the lead than seven lengths in the early going. Bryan Field of *The New York Times* describes the stretch run as Swing and Sway continued to lead:

> . . . Woolf had Whirlaway straightened away and turned him loose. On he came! Attention attempted to run with him, but couldn't. Whirlaway picked up the ones ahead. . . . He was in front inside the eighth pole . . . and he was going easily at the end.

Sid Feder of Associated Press gave a colorful account of the stretch run:

> Turning loose his famous kick down Aqueduct's "killer" straightaway in tune with the "Here Comes Whirlaway" cry from the stands, Little Mr. Big Tail galloped home by nearly two lengths.

In winning, Whirlaway set a new track record of 2:02 2/5 seconds, lopping 3/5 of a second off of the mile-and-a-quarter time. By smashing two records in races only five days apart, Whirly had given the fans at Aqueduct a bountiful supply of thrills. But Bryan Field noted in his column that Whirlaway had given more than just thrills to those attending the 1942 Brooklyn Handicap:

> The soldiers and sailors of our country benefited to the extent of at least $100,000 yesterday at Aqueduct when the long-tailed chestnut smothered his opposition to take the historic Brooklyn Handicap big feature on the Queens County Jockey Club's Army-Navy Day.
>
> Many service men of all ranks were in the crowd of 22,054 who wagered $1,546,194 on the final day of Aqueduct's most successful race meeting.

In addition to his considerable contribution to the war effort, Mr. Longtail had brought joy to his owner and trainer by picking up the winner's paycheck of $23,650 and becoming the second horse in racing history to go over the $400,000 mark in earnings. Many who saw the race expressed the opinion that Whirlaway would soon gain the top place in the equine world.

But there was no time to bask in reflected glory for this soldier of the track. He was reminded that there was a war on and that thoroughbred racing was counting heavily on him to raise its share toward construction of some 700 USO service clubs urgently needed to provide wholesome off-duty recreation, a home away from home, for millions of our soldiers and sailors in training camps throughout the country.

The next race on Whirlaway's heavy schedule was the Butler Memorial Handicap at another New York City track, Empire City. This mile-and-three-sixteenths race had been held on Independence Day for over 25 years. It was most appropriate in 1942 that the Fourth of July race was billed in behalf of Army-Navy Relief. Another $100,000 goal was set for war charities by track officials, despite the fact that Aqueduct had staged its $100,000 attraction for the war chest only seven days earlier, and in spite of the elimination of free bus rides to the track, a factor that might have cut down on attendance for the special race. But once again the decision for the $100,000 target was based on the knowledge that Whirlaway would be entered in the race.

As always, this champion kept his appointments. Some cause for alarm was created for the Calumet camp when prior to the start of the race it was announced that Whirlaway would be required to carry an extra-heavy load of 132 pounds over the mile-and-three-sixteenths course. Whirly was a small horse, and the risk of injury to him under such a burden was indeed great. Unfortunately, horse racing is the only professional sport in which superior performance is penalized with a weight handicap. But no complaint was lodged with the judges. To be sure, it was no longer uncommon for this little competitor to carry top weight in a race. He had taken on extra baggage throughout his racing career. It is true that Whirlaway was smaller in size than most racehorses, but few could match his strength of heart and legs.

So, on the Fourth of July 1942, Whirlaway showed up for the 45th consecutive race of his career. Whirly's drawing power at the gate was never more in evidence. Not in all the years since James Butler first began staging races at Empire City a generation before had there been such a turnout for the Butler Handicap. A packed crowd of 34,728 was on hand in spite of "no free bus rides" to the track. It was by far the largest gathering to witness a race at Empire City in the track's long history. The significance of the Empire City crowd is put in better perspective when compared to Belmont Park's special race for Army-Navy Relief. That more renowned racetrack had chosen the Belmont Stakes for its war-charity race, featuring a duel between the two leading three-year-olds of 1942, Alsab and Shut Out; this was a showdown encounter since Shut Out had won the Kentucky Derby and Alsab the Preakness. But attendance for the Triple Crown race at Belmont was only 27,812, nearly 7,000 less than that for the Empire City feature. Whirlaway's entry in the Butler Handicap at Empire City was a major factor in accounting for that difference.

In spite of the weight handicap, Whirlaway was made the favorite in what would be his third race in the past ten days and his second $100,000 war-relief effort in only one week's time. George Woolf was on hand to ride Whirly in the field of seven, and in the race's early stages things proceeded mostly according to plan. It was when the horses reached the stretch that Whirlaway's heavy load took its toll. As Bryan Field wrote for *The New York Times*: "A tired Whirlaway pounded his dogged way through the Empire City stretch." Due largely to his weight handicap and loaded racing schedule of the past ten days, he couldn't muster the needed speed for the final drive. He made a gallant bid in the stretch, but couldn't catch Tola Rose at the wire. Even at that, the front runner had to break the track record to win.

Again, under conditions similar to those in the Carter Handicap at Aqueduct, Whirlaway transformed a lackluster race into a thriller. Whirly had given up an unbelievable 29 pounds to the winner. According to the Handicappers' Weight Formulas, in a mile-and-one-sixteenth race, one pound of extra weight in the saddle slows a horse one-fifth of a second or one full length (nine feet). As determined by the formula, if Whirlaway had run the distance with weight equal to that of Tola Rose, he might have won the race by a margin of ten lengths or more.

Regardless, the real winners in the Independence Day race were the soldiers and sailors of the Armed Forces. For the second successive week, it was Whirlaway's entry in a race that helped make possible another $100,000 contribution to their relief fund. Also, it should be noted that while no one has mentioned it during the past 50 years, it was Whirly's tremendous drawing power at those early summer races in 1942 that gave thoroughbred racing a decided edge over other professional sports in raising money for war charities. Baseball was definitely recognized in those days as the national pastime, but teams from both the American and National leagues were counting heavily on raising their money for war relief from games scheduled later in the season when the pennant races would start heating up. By then, horse racing had raised hundreds of thousands of dollars.

After the Butler Handicap, Warren Wright and Ben Jones decided to enter Whirlaway in races outside New York in order to give other tracks a boost in raising money for the war-relief fund. By the summer of 1942, wartime restrictions on travel and gasoline and rubber shortages prevented many of the racetracks, especially the smaller ones, from attracting much of a crowd for a war charity race unless Mr. Longtail was there at post time. By generously offering the services of Whirlaway in support of the war effort, Warren Wright and Ben Jones reflected a profound sense of national commitment. Grantland Rice, commenting on that point, referred to Wright, Jones, and Whirlaway as a "triple combination of class."

Chapter 11

Life in the Handicap Division

THE Butler Handicap had marked the ninth race for Whirlaway since the beginning of his 1942 campaign in support of the War Emergency Relief Fund — a continuous string of races that had started on April 9 at the Keeneland track in Lexington, Kentucky, and extended through Independence Day at Empire City, in New York. He had been the feature attraction at each stop, being largely responsible for raising large sums of money for war charity.

By midyear, the interval between Whirlaway's races had been narrowed to less than a week. Starting with the Carter Handicap and extending through the Butler Handicap on July 4, Mr. Longtail had run in four races within a period of 21 days, an average of one race every five days. Not only were the races occurring more often, but with every turn around the track, Whirly's burden was heavier. He was being saddled with as much as 29 pounds more than the weight carried by opposing horses, when covering distances of over a mile. So far, the indomitable campaigner had shown remarkable courage and durability in meeting all obstacles thrown at him in the fast lane, but how much longer could the handicap division leader be expected to continue at such a torrid pace, carrying unusually high weight loads imposed on him by the merciless track handicappers?

As summer settled in on that fateful year of World War II, Whirlaway must have thought he was doing a rerun of his extended 1941 racing campaign. While the dust was still settling on the Empire City track after the running of the Butler Handicap, Calumet stable and Whirlaway were on their way up the coast to Boston, the next port of call on the "extra load" circuit and the site of the Suffolk Downs feature race, the Massachusetts Handicap.

Through the years, most racetracks have followed the custom of annually promoting one race that has traditionally become affiliated with the track of its origin. Just as Churchill Downs is readily identified with the Kentucky Derby, Pimlico the Preakness, and Belmont Park the Belmont Stakes, so Suffolk Downs is best known for its showcase race, the Massachusetts Handicap. Since its inaugural running in 1935, the Masscap had already attracted several outstanding thoroughbreds by 1942, including Seabiscuit, War Admiral, Discovery, Challedon, and War Relic, holder of the track record set in 1941.

The Massachusetts Handicap was scheduled for a weekday in 1942, but with Whirlaway as the attraction, Suffolk Downs officials were confident that the day of the week would have little effect on track attendance. Mr. Longtail had already set new attendance marks at most of the country's major tracks, whatever day of the week he happened to race. During that time, he had also established other viewing records, such as the number watching a racehorse in a workout, attending some other public appearance on or off the track, and witnessing a thoroughbred being loaded onto or unloaded from a railway car at various locations throughout the country, day or night.

Still another factor served to heighten fan interest in the 1942 Masscap. Whirlaway had come to Suffolk Downs with total career earnings of $410,406, which he had accumulated in a little over two years of competition; and by winning the Boston Classic, he would surpass Seabiscuit's world-record total earnings of $437,730, attained over six years of racing. Modern horsemen give little credence to what a thoroughbred might earn by competing in major stakes races. Today, racehorses are rated on their potential value for breeding purposes. Devil's Bag was syndicated as a sire in 1984 for a record $36 million without having to run in a single Triple Crown race. When Seabiscuit and Whirlaway raced, however, the money-winning title was recognized as thoroughbred racing's greatest achievement. But for a horse to gain that distinction, he had to win many handicap races over an extended period of time. In those days, a racehorse made money the old-fashioned way — he really earned it! The possibility of seeing Whirlaway capture the earnings title did much to fill the stands to capacity at Suffolk Downs that July weekday in 1942.

The publicity given the 1942 Masscap was comparable to that afforded the World Series in baseball, the Rose Bowl in football, and the Kentucky Derby in horse racing. But the main theme in most columns that year focused on the viable possibility of the money-record title changing horses as a result of this race.

Several days before the race, Grantland Rice used his column to compare the racing styles of Whirlaway and Seabiscuit, whom he thought had in common the fact that they were both tough and could run. He wrote:

> . . . Seabiscuit liked a fast track. Whirlaway can run over broken bottles, dust or mud, rain or shine; he doesn't care.
>
> Whirlaway apparently has only one set ambition, that is to spot the field from 100 to 200 yards, and then wait for the stretch.

Eddie Welch, sportswriter for *The Boston Globe*, gave this tribute to

Whirlaway in his column one day before the Masscap:

> There's a horse running for $50,000 at Suffolk Downs this week who may surpass Seabiscuit's all-time record. I refer . . . to Whirlaway. And Whirlaway is a case where a great money record represents a great horse. He always races good horses, the best to be found and he works fast.

In the days preceding the highly publicized race, sports columns of newspapers in the area were filled with human interest stories on Whirlaway and his past performances on the track. One such narrative must have particularly interested those who happened to read it. The column appeared in the morning edition of *The Boston Globe*, just hours before the race, and was written by Herbert Ralby. It carried this eye-catching headline: "WHIRLAWAY INTERVIEWED IN STALL, PRAISES TRAINER."

Ralby did not reveal what language, if any, was used as a means of communication in the interview, and nobody bothered to ask. Since no third party witnessed the "closed-stall" conversation, Ralby's purported interview was immediately deemed suspect by traditionalists. Whirlaway loyalists, on the other hand, probably believed every word their hero was quoted as saying in the exchange.

When placed in the context of Whirlaway's past record, the responses attributed to him in the offbeat interview were at least plausible and somewhat worthy of belief. For instance, when Ralby asked Whirly to comment on his chances of winning the Masscap and becoming the world's leading money-winner, he is quoted as saying:

> I am ready and will have no excuses if I lose. I want very much to win the Massachusetts Handicap, not so much for myself but to justify the faith my trainer, Ben Jones, has had in me.

When he was asked if he had a preference for a particular jockey of the many who had ridden him, the colt replied:

> Not at all. I have had twelve different jockeys and have

> done pretty well for all of them. My present rider, George Woolf, has ridden me four times and we have won three races. I won the Derby, Preakness, and Belmont with Eddie Arcaro and for my two-year-old stakes I was ridden by different riders.

Finally, Ralby asked the articulate horse how much, if any, the heavy weight load assigned to him in the next day's race might slow him down over the mile-and-an-eighth distance. To that loaded question, Mr. Longtail gave this confident response:

> I am not one to give tips but here is something to remember. Despite my 130 pounds impost, I am going to do a lot of running tomorrow.

There was consensus that Whirlaway would have "to do a lot of running" to finish ahead of the strong field pitted against him. Ben Jones said he would probably have to run the best race of his career to win. The competition was one of the toughest Whirly had faced thus far that year. Apache, a late bloomer among three-year-olds, would be one of the stronger ones. This newcomer on the circuit had recently broken the mile-and-three-sixteenths track record at Empire City in New York. Others in the field of seven expected to give Whirlaway trouble were his old foe, Attention, a promising colt named Rounders, and Swing and Sway, whose chances were vastly improved with the assignment of Eddie Arcaro as his rider.

By 1942, Suffolk Downs had gained the reputation of being the "graveyard of champions," with such outstanding horses as Discovery, Challedon, and Triple Crown winner War Admiral failing to make it to the winner's circle in earlier runnings of the Massachusetts Handicap. The inability to negotiate successfully the difficult turn of the track in the past had prevented several favorites from winning the race. So Whirlaway would be facing the track jinx in addition to carrying top weight of 130 pounds over the mile-and-an-eighth run.

The handicappers did not relent one bit in assigning Whirly 130 pounds, 22 to 26 pounds more than some of his rivals. By now, though, carrying excess pounds had become old hat to this competitor and did not dissuade fans from installing him as race favorite. Thus the stage was set once again for a landmark race. By winning against formidable odds and strong rivals, Whirlaway could become the world's leading money-winner and add still more prestige and fame to Calumet Farm and his trainer.

Even though it was a weekday, some 33,000 fans solidly packed Suffolk Downs, located within the sight of Boston Harbor and the scene of the famous "tea party" back in 1773. Among the notables attending this richest of New England races were the chief executive of the Bay State, Governor Leverett Saltonstall; former ambassador to Great Britain, Joseph P. Kennedy; and thoroughbred racehorse owners William Woodward and Colonel Edward R. Bradley.

The fans eagerly awaited the start of the feature race, and when it got under way, Whirlaway made his customary leisurely exit from the starting gate. Two of the speedsters, Rounders and Apache, hooked up in a duel out in front for the first three-quarters of a mile. In the early going, Whirly was at one time 20 lengths (60 yards) behind the leaders, so far back that spectators in the stands started asking one another, "Where is Whirlaway?"

Whirlaway answered that question by suddenly showing up in the last three furlongs. Jockey George Woolf had given him the word to go at the far turn of the backstretch. And go he did. The crowd roared as he caught the field and swept by three horses in rapid succession. Halfway around the turn into the stretch, Whirly straightened his six-foot tail like a banner as he swept around the bend of the track. Attention made his move there, but the champion roared right by him, then by Rounders and Apache as they straightened out for home.

Whirlaway's flight down the stretch of Suffolk Downs was reminiscent of his great finishes in the Derby and the Preakness. Down a straight line toward the wire he came as cheers from the crowd became louder and continued long after he crossed the finish line in front of Rounders. Apache faded to fourth in the stretch drive, and Attention finished third.

Some had said before the race that Whirlaway might have to break the existing track record to win. He did! The time posted on the finish board was 1:48 1/5 for the mile-and-an-eighth, lopping 2/5 of a second off the track record set by War Relic the year before in the same race.

Most of the accounts of the race focused on the other record

Whirlaway broke, the surpassing of Seabiscuit's mark by $16,606. The winner's share of $43,850 sent his total in 46 starts to $454,336. Sportswriters found plenty to write about from this race. Sid Feder's column in the Chicago *Daily News* announced:

> WHIRLY DOES IT; NOW LEADING MONEY-WINNER
>
> Whirlaway buried Seabiscuit's all-time money-winning record deep in Suffolk Downs "graveyard of champions" today with a streak of lightning speed that all but set fire to the track.
>
> . . . [He] turned loose his "crusher" kick in one burst of running power to come from almost out of sight and win. . . .

Feder goes on to speculate that Whirlaway might likely become the turf's first half-million dollar racehorse in history. He wrote,

> For, make no mistake about this one — Warren Wright's whizzer had the deck stacked against him.

He went on to explain that in spite of the 130 extra pounds, and the fact that he was spotting the front-runners up to 26 pounds apiece and had never raced at Suffolk's "graveyard" before, Whirly came from 11 lengths back to break the track record.

The stream of metaphors describing Whirlaway's stunning victory continued in Robert F. Kelley's *New York Times* column:

> The flaring long tail of Whirlaway flashed burnished gold in the sun at Suffolk Downs today . . . and thus gained [him] his rightful place among the immortals of the American turf as the greatest money winner of all time.

According to Kelley, Ben Jones said it was the best race of his career and that jockeys aboard the other horses agreed. Reportedly, racegoers came yelling out of their seats, including John (Red) Pollard, seated in the press stand, who had ridden Seabiscuit throughout most of his career. Kelley continued,

> . . . When Whirlaway started he yelled, "Here he comes. He's in," and from that point there was only the thrill of watching the devil's red of the Calumet Farm silks move through straining horses like a flaming bullet.

The Boston Globe carried a sequence of pictures showing Whirlaway winning the Massachusetts Handicap with this caption:

> Whirlaway wins in Whirlaway's own copyrighted fashion — starts last, makes bid on final turn, wins in record time and for record earnings.

Eddie Welch, sportswriter for *The Globe*, added another tribute to Whirlaway in his column:

> The winner and new champion, Whirlaway, the mightiest thoroughbred to dazzle racegoers since the days of Man O' War, established himself as the leading money-winner of all time, when he drove home to a smashing 2-length victory in a new track record for the Massachusetts Handicap at Suffolk Downs.

In his *New York Times* column, Robert Kelley quoted Ben Jones as saying, "This was Whirlaway's greatest race." The trainer did not discuss in detail the reasons for rating Whirly's victory in the Masscap ahead of the champion's other, more publicized, spectacular races such as the Derby, Preakness, Travers, and more recently the Dixie and Brooklyn Handicaps of 1942. Plain Ben was never known for giving lengthy press releases, but neither was he ever guilty of making rash public statements. The passage of time has a way of placing in proper perspective emotionally laden statements made in the wake of some astonishing triumph or rare accomplishment.

Even after running in the Masscap, Whirlaway still had several important racing engagements left on his 1942 schedule. Years and then decades have drifted by since that memorable race of over 50 years ago. A check with the Public Relations Office at Suffolk Downs during the summer of 1985 led to the discovery of some surprising information about that track's centerpiece of thoroughbred racing.

The Suffolk Downs Yearbook reveals that Whirlaway's record of 1:48 1/5 for the mile-and-an-eighth Massachusetts Handicap set in 1942 remained unbroken for 43 years. After 31 years, Riva Ridge, winner of the Kentucky Derby and Belmont Stakes in 1972, equaled Whirlaway's time in the 1973 Masscap. At last, on June 22, 1985, a horse named Bounding Basque shaved 3/5 of a second off of Whirly's mark by posting a new record time for the race of 1:47 3/5. During the 43 years that Mr. Longtail held the record, no other horse ever carried as much as 130 pounds in the race and emerged a winner. In tying the mark, Riva Ridge carried five fewer pounds, and when Bounding Basque broke the record, he was weighted with only 110 pounds.

When the excess weight load carried by Whirlaway in the Masscap is duly considered, his long-standing record at once takes on added significance that goes far beyond the enclosure of Suffolk Downs. A careful examination of track records set by these horses will show Whirlaway to be the only racehorse in turf history to hold the time mark of a major stakes race in this country for anywhere near as long as 43 years. If and when another horse does match or surpass that incredible feat, it is highly improbable and most unlikely that the new champion will be carrying 130 pounds when he crosses the finish line.

Numbers alone do not tell the full story of Whirlaway's Masscap. The horse made liberal use of a broad brush to spread his glory in the rush to victory at Suffolk Downs. In addition to establishing new time and money records, he also gave those witnessing the race enough thrills to last a lifetime, bestowed generous measures of fame on his trainer, owner, rider, Calumet Farm, Suffolk Downs, and thoroughbred racing in general, provided extra funds urgently needed to construct USO and service clubs for Armed Forces personnel — and did it all in less than two minutes. Not bad for a small horse carrying 130 pounds on his back.

After conducting his Massachusetts "clinic," Whirlaway had reached the pinnacle of his racing career, having arrived at that lofty position in just slightly over two years of track competition. During that brief period, he had set new records in almost every category of racing — time, attendance, gate receipts, and finally, top individual earnings. After the Boston race, the 1942 racing season was only at the halfway point. Yet this inveterate campaigner had already run in ten races at seven different tracks.

What motivation and source of renewed power made it possible for a racehorse of his shortened body dimensions — except for the tail — to run week after week, always showing up at the starting gate fit and ready for his next encounter? It is unlikely that he was aware of breaking all those track records and continually winning large purses for his persistent effort. Perhaps the presence of large numbers of soldiers and sailors in the stands had something to do with the fresh supply of strength and courage he brought to each succeeding race. Perhaps Whirly sensed the grave crisis faced by his native land during that fateful summer of World War II. This gallant little champion of the turf acted much like a soldier armed and eager to do battle against the foe every time he lined up at the onset of another run around the racing oval.

Ben Jones, the person who had prepared Whirly for all of his turf engagements, took a few moments from his busy schedule that summer to give a more plausible explanation for the colt's seemingly inexhaustible source of power and speed. The trainer's statement on the subject, the lengthiest press release ever given by this unusually modest and gentle human being, was the focus segment of Grantland Rice's syndicated column of June 27, 1942:

> He's tough. You know how brittle thoroughbreds are. You breathe on most of them and they fold up. Something is always happening to them, including housemaid's knee and the pip.

Ben explained what he looked for in a horse:

> When you're after a real horse, you want three things — speed, stamina and toughness. And I don't have to add heart.
>
> Maybe the finest trait is toughness or durability. . . .
>
> I'm crazy about Whirlaway because Whirlaway likes to run as often as I'll let him. And even oftener.

Ben pointed out that a thoroughbred's main job is running, that "great horses" that keep breaking down are not great horses. No sports figure is any good in the hands of a doctor or veterinarian, on the bench, or in a hospital. He added that Whirlaway didn't know

> . . . what a bench or a hospital looks like. All he knows is that track where he is usually 15 to 20 lengths behind. I've seen him make up a sixteenth of a mile twice this summer, when . . . I didn't believe a guy on a motorcycle could ever catch up.

Few could disagree with Ben Jones's words of high praise in behalf of Whirlaway. Plain Ben had told it like it was, no extras and no frills. Speed, stamina, toughness, and heart — Whirly had shown them all many times. How else could he race week after week, never losing his bearing nor failing to answer the bugler's call for the next race?

But after running in four races in 23 days, breaking track records in three of the four, and lugging 130 pounds or more in the last two, would it be asking too much to grant this frontline soldier a few days leave from active duty? Probably not, but it didn't happen. It was back to the railway car and off to Chicago for the Arlington Handicap.

Why Chicago? There were other races scheduled at Eastern tracks later in the season. No problem, Whirly would be back in time for them, too. Actually it was a matter of commitment, the unique part of Whirlaway's 1942 racing campaign that has no parallel in the total sweep of thoroughbred racing. At the start of the racing season that year, all participating tracks had sought the 1941 Triple Crown champion as feature attraction for their war-charity races. Warren Wright and Ben Jones at that time had agreed to enter Whirly in as many of those races as possible. So far Mr. Longtail hadn't missed a one. The Arlington Handicap in Chicago was next in line. He would be there. It should come as no surprise that Grantland Rice had called them a triple combination of class.

As Whirlaway and supporting cast journeyed westward to Chicago for the third time in the past 12 months, the war was at a low ebb on all major fronts for the United States and her fighting Allies. Japan had overrun and occupied most of Southeast Asia, and Rommel and his desert panzer army had routed the British at Tobruk in North Africa, while in Russia, the German Wehrmacht had finally broken through the stubborn Red Army defenses around Sevastopol and occupied that key

Black Sea port. Even as Whirlaway went to the post to run in the Chicago race, the mightiest military force ever assembled by Nazi Germany was speeding toward Stalingrad and what Hitler was heralding as the end of the war in Russia.

The Arlington Handicap was set for August 1 and would be the feature race, ending the track's 34-day summer meet. In the days preceding the race, heavy rains had turned that track into a soggy mess, increasing the danger of injury to both horses and riders. Turf conditions were so foreboding that four of the owners promptly withdrew their horses from the original field of nine. The entry of Whirlaway in the race probably saved Arlington Park from what would otherwise have been a financial disaster at the gate. But after running in 46 consecutive races without being scratched, this horse's credibility was no longer a matter of conjecture. In the past, he had bailed out other tracks at the ticket window on days when the race was run on terrain where sudden downpours of rain had left the racing oval looking like a newly formed river basin. As a two-year-old, Whirlaway had run through the rain at Pimlico in the Walden Stakes; and the following year he plowed through heavy mud at Saratoga before a record attendance in the Travers Stakes.

The treacherous condition of the track wasn't the only obstacle confronting Whirlaway in the race. His record-breaking performance in the Massachusetts Handicap of two weeks before had cast serious doubts on the validity of formulas used by handicappers in assigning weights to leading horses of that day. Nowhere in the handicappers' handbook did it state that small racehorses like Whirlaway were supposed to break track records while carrying 130 pounds on their backs. Those charged with doling out weights for horses running in the Arlington Handicap were determined that "Little Mr. Bigtail" was not about to break the speed limit on their track. This time they would make Whirly lug his top load of 130 pounds over the distance of one mile and a quarter and lessen the burden over the same route for opposing horses by as much as 27 pounds.

Rounders was considered to be Mr. Longtail's chief opposition in the race, so based on impost differences, he would be allowed to start the race 81 yards in front of Whirlaway, or would be given 5 2/5 seconds more time to reach the finish line.

Despite Chicago's inclement weather, the soggy track, and several withdrawals from the race, a crowd of 30,000 showed up for what appeared to be the Arlington Park "water carnival." And even though Whirly would be saddled with all those extra pounds, his loyal fans still installed him as an absolute favorite at 1-3 odds. Then, as if to give the event a crowning touch of surprise, the old change-of-riders routine was added to the Whirlaway scenario. Word had come to Calumet stable that George Woolf, Whirlaway's rider in his last four races, would not be available for riding duty in the Arlington Handicap. But a rather surprising coincidence would occur.

This was the same track where Eddie Arcaro was to have ridden Whirly in the 1941 Arlington Classic for three-year-olds, but he was under suspension at the time and could not honor his commitment. A substitute jockey had taken his place as the Triple Crown champion's rider for that race.

A year later, when Ben Jones went in search of Whirlaway's replacement rider for the Arlington Handicap, the chosen one turned out to be Eddie Arcaro, Whirly's racing partner in the great Triple Crown victories of 1941.

All other considerations aside, the feature race began at last. As often happened, Whirlaway was last out of the starting gate and last in the field of five going into the first turn. Arcaro, impatient with the slow pace, took Whirly up faster than usual, and midway along the backstretch Arcaro passed everyone except Rounders. As the Associated Press reported it,

> . . . Both went wide on the curve into the stretch and once straightened out, Rounders began to draw away to the surprise of the open-mouthed spectators. . . . Arcaro, anxious now, used his whip. Both horses straightened out and Whirlaway was left behind as Rounders came sailing home. . . .

The sloppy condition of the track and the 27-pound impost advantage given Rounders were undoubtedly contributing factors to Whirlaway's defeat, but there was something else, not reported at the time, that might have really sounded the death knell to the colt's chances of winning the race. At some stage of the race, once again Whirlaway was struck in his right eye by a small stone or some other solid object, probably launched

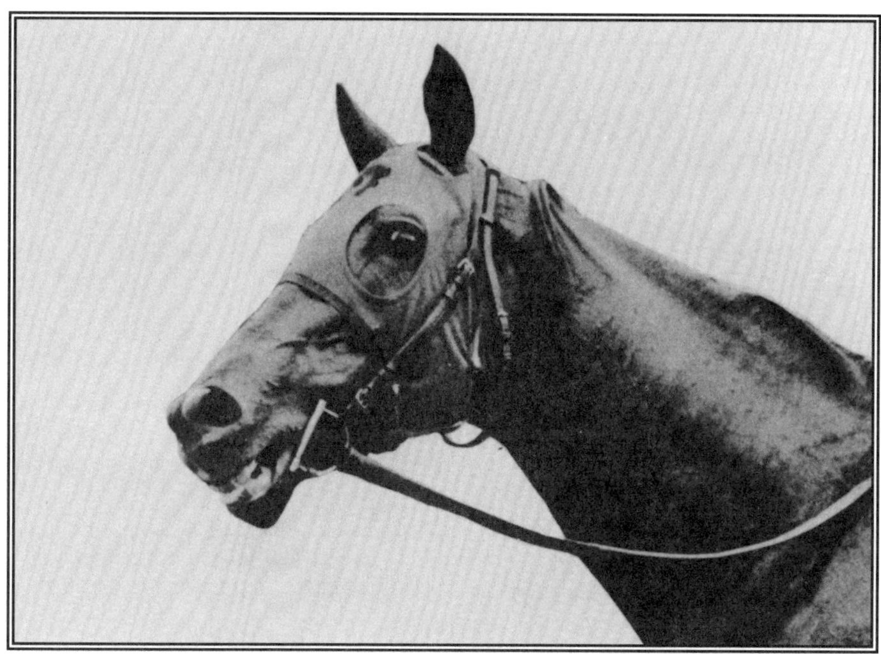

Whirlaway giving what appears to be "the old horse-laugh."

from the soggy track by the flying heels of the front-running Rounders. The hit could have occurred as the two horses began their stretch run, for it was at that point that Whirly began to falter and fall behind. The incident was never mentioned in subsequent news releases on the race, nor did Calumet stable offer it as an excuse for Whirlaway's defeat. Nevertheless, the projectile that had caromed off the colt's right eye was made of stronger stuff than a soft piece of mud or a crumbling dirt clod. In several of his races following the Arlington Handicap, Whirlaway was still wearing an isinglass blinker over his right eye to protect it from further infection.

Despite Whirlaway's defeat, his entry in the Chicago race had saved Arlington Park from certain financial disaster on that final day of its summer meet and thus had enabled the track to finish its richest racing season in history with a total pari-mutuel handle of $20,740,000 and a contribution of $126,695 to the War Emergency Relief Fund. The Arlington Handicap also marked another milestone in Whirlaway's racing career, for as time would tell, this race turned out to be Eddie Arcaro's last ride on his first Triple Crown winner. Because of his full schedule of riding duties for Greentree Stable, Arcaro had only been able to ride Whirlaway in three of the champion's 1942 races. Throughout his racing career, Whirlaway had never enjoyed the luxury of a regular rider, but from the first time Eddie and Whirly met, they seemed ideally suited for one another. In the Triple Crown races of 1941 and the Dixie Handicap of 1942, they had teamed up to produce thrills and excitement seldom seen on a racing oval. A few weeks following the Arlington Handicap, Eddie received a one-year suspension from racing given to him by the Jockey Club stewards for his use of rough riding tactics in a race at the Aqueduct track in New York.

The Arlington Handicap would serve to be the midpoint of Whirlaway's campaign on behalf of thoroughbred racing's effort to raise money for the War Emergency Relief Fund. Already this soldier of the track had participated in 11 races at 8 different tracks, nearly every week competing against top horses of the day, having precious little time to rest and prepare for his next start, and always carrying heavy freight over turf that was at times life-threatening to both horse and rider. But battle fatigue had finally caught up with this courageous campaigner as he struggled his way to the finish line in the Chicago race.

A prolonged vacation from track activities seemed almost mandatory for Whirlaway, but procedures zealously demanded by other owners and trainers for their prize racehorses were never accorded this equine champion. There remained other tracks, some not as large and well known as the Arlington Park enclosure, that counted heavily on Whirly's strong hoofs to assist them in raising their quota for the war fund by running in at least one of their feature races.

So as if to heed the poetic injunction of Robert Frost, "But I have promises to keep, And miles to go before I sleep," Whirlaway was not long in making his way to the starting gate for his next race. Soon after the running of the Arlington Handicap in Chicago, Whirly was loaded into his familiar railway car and shipped to the Saratoga track in upstate New York.

His arrival there signaled to most turf observers that the Calumet champion would be running in the Saratoga Cup race on the last day of the spa's meet, August 29. But after a few days of rest and recuperation at Saratoga, Ben Jones suddenly announced a change of venue for Whirlaway's next start. Instead of running in the Cup race at Saratoga, the champion would be a starter in the Trenton Handicap at Garden State Park, a new outdoor enclosure in New Jersey that had opened its gates for the first time to thoroughbred racing only weeks before on July 18.

Why would Calumet Farm want to enter Whirlaway in a race at a track that could add little traditional and monetary worth to the colt's record at that stage of the racing season? This last-minute decision could only make life more hectic for the weary champion. It was back to the railway car and a 300-mile safari to another location with little time left to prepare for the upcoming race. Add to this list of negatives the strong possibility of losing a relatively unimportant race, and Whirly was immediately cast into a no-win situation.

Ben Jones's rationale for choosing the Trenton Handicap over the Saratoga Cup race was that he was bringing the champion to Garden State out of friendship for Jimmy Loftus, the track's press agent, and more specifically for the purpose of lending the fledgling track a helping hoof in their frustrating effort to raise money for the War Emergency Relief Fund.

Garden State was certainly in dire need of all the support it could muster. The track had been in the news almost since ground had been broken for the $2 million facility in November 1941. Initial work on the structure was restricted to materials on hand before the declaration of war and the June 6 deadline for new construction. Finishing touches were still in progress on opening day.

Problems continued to pile up at the site. War rationing of gasoline hit the park with the elimination of the special trains, buses, and cars that were to carry fans to and from the races. Restrictions even hit newspaper reporters on hand to cover the opening, since no wire communications were allowed from the track. Messengers and carrier pigeons had to be used to deliver accounts of the races to Philadelphia and wire offices in Camden.

But when Jimmy Loftus dispatched the Garden State pigeons to spread the word that Whirlaway would be running in the park's feature race, the wartime problems of travel, rationing, and communications that had plagued the new track from the day of its opening seemed to vanish. Suddenly Garden State's Trenton Handicap was receiving equal space on the sports pages with the Cup race at Saratoga; and for one day at least, the newest racetrack on the circuit could successfully compete with the oldest.

Garden State officials were all smiles on August 29, as they watched 18,492 fans file through the park's turnstiles, occupy all 10,500 grandstand seats, and overflow on to the track's graded lawn area. It was a classic Whirlaway crowd representing all strata of home-front USA society of that war year, including such prominent persons as Senators Hayden Proctor and Grant Scott, Mayor Frank Hague, and the comedy team of Bud Abbott and Lou Costello.

Whirlaway was heavily favored by the Garden State partisans at 3-10 odds to win the mile-and-an-eighth feature, marking the 38th time, the last 28 in succession, that the chestnut colt would be so honored. But the burdens and requirements of being number one in the handicap division at this juncture of Mr. Longtail's racing career were unparalleled, and still are, in the history of thoroughbred racing. He had been top-weighted in most of his two-year-old races, in all but one of his three-year-old races, and thus far in all 12 of his entries at age four. Prior to his appearance at Garden State, Whirly had carried from 22 to 29 pounds more than that required of his opponents in his last three efforts. By post time for the Trenton Handicap, no race could be considered a cakewalk for this relentless campaigner.

The upcoming meet was not without its special problems for the champion, as well. In addition to his usual impost of 130 pounds, Whirlaway would be without the guiding hands of George Woolf, his most recent regular rider, or Eddie Arcaro, sidelined by suspension. Wendell Eads, the Calumet apprentice jockey of 1941, was called upon to serve as Whirly's racing partner. Another complication was the unusually short homestretch of the Garden State track that figured to bother the notorious stretch-runner. Nevertheless, on August 29, Whirlaway was at the starting gate, ready to make the 48th consecutive run of his racing career.

As the race got under way, Whirlaway trailed the field, which was his usual custom. But at the first furlong, he startled his fans and the opposition by making his move toward the front-runners. The crowd roared as he made up more than three lengths and quickly changed his position from last to first at the quarter. Louis Effrat, reporter for *The New York*

Times, gave this account:

> . . . Eads did not have to punish the long-tailed hero and proceeded to win rather easily.
>
> The fans had been treated to a different Whirlaway in the Trenton Handicap. Not different because he won, but different because he ran out in front of the other horses throughout most of the race.

After the race, Eads was asked why he took Whirlaway to the front so early. The jockey replied,

> Whirly got excited and was full of running. I couldn't hold him anyway, so I just set back and let him go. He ran a great race.

A great race it was. Whirlaway had given the Garden State fans a special treat by extending his famed stretch drive for a full mile of the mile-and-an-eighth run. The victory only netted Mr. Longtail $8,500 and a blanket of violet asters, but what this racehorse did for Garden State and thoroughbred racing on August 29, 1942, far transcended his personal achievements. Whirly's appearance at the New Jersey track had set a new meet record of $883,962 for the mutuel handle, assuring the park of a successful opening and making possible a sizable donation of $57,457 to the War Emergency Relief Fund.

As September arrived, Whirlaway had already been entered in a total of 12 races at 9 tracks, almost singlehandedly leading the charge for thoroughbred racing in raising money for the war-chest fund. Beyond helping many tracks raise their quotas, Mr. Longtail was also making a considerable individual contribution to the cause by virtue of his charter membership in the Ten Percent Club, which required its members to pledge that amount of their earnings for the purchase of War Bonds.

But even at this late stage of the racing season, there were still other tracks seeking Whirlaway's tremendous gate appeal in meeting their desired goals for the war fund. The decision-making process that determined Whirly's entry in his races of 1942 was again operational. Trainer Jones consulted owner Wright, and, taking for granted the approval of their star performer, agreed on the choice of Narragansett Park in Pawtuckett, Rhode Island, as the site for Whirlaway's next race.

Mr. Longtail's presence at Narragansett Park in September of the 1942 racing season is a classic example of the Calumet colt's tremendous contribution on behalf of the War Emergency Relief Fund during that first year of U.S. participation in World War II. When confirmation was made for Whirly's entry in the Narragansett Special on September 12, the track asked for and received permission to move its Army-Navy Relief Fund benefit up a week to the 12th, in order to take full advantage of professional sports' number one box-office attraction of the day. All gate receipts accruing from an expected crowd of 45,000, the track's share of the mutuel handle, and all other revenues were to be turned over to the service funds. Beyond that total would be added a cash donation from everyone employed or quartered at the track — quite a magnificent expression of faith in the small racehorse with the long tail and an equally unique commitment by a racetrack to a nation and world in crisis.

According to some turf observers, Whirlaway would be hardpressed at every stage of the mile-and-three-sixteenths race. He would be carrying his usual top weight of 130 pounds and competing against such strong contenders as Valdina Farms's speedy double entry of Valdina Orphan and Rounders. On Friday, the day before the race, the track also announced that Alsab, considered by many to be the turf's three-year-old star, had been added to the list of starters in the Special. Late Friday afternoon, it appeared that the Pawtuckett track had put together the most attractive racing card of the season.

But just minutes before the eight o'clock deadline the next morning, Sarge Swenke, Alsab's trainer, declared he was scratching the three-year-old colt on orders from owner Albert Sabath. Swenke's last-minute action came as a shock to track officials, especially since the trainer had stated the day before that Alsab was in the "best condition of his career." This left a bad taste with many fans looking forward to seeing the long-awaited Alsab and Whirlaway match-up, but the unexpected move did little to dampen the enthusiasm and size of the crowd at Narragansett Park that day. Most of the assembled throng were there to see Whirlaway run, and they knew they wouldn't be disappointed because Whirlaway had established an impeccable reputation for keeping track appointments.

In the early furlongs of the race, Whirlaway trailed the field by some 60 yards, and even some of Whirly's most feverish backers were beginning to doubt their hero's ability to make up so much ground. But at the half-mile pole, George Woolf brought Whirly forward and closed the dozen lengths that separated him from the last horse. At this point, Woolf made his move, and the Calumet charger picked up his field one by one and came flying down the stretch to finish two lengths ahead of Boysy with Valdina Orphan third. Spiral Pass faded in the last sixteenth to fourth, and Rounders finished a distant last.

The Boston Globe headline read:

$101,804 WAR AID AS "WHIRLY" WINS
Longtail Comes From Behind;
Boosts Earnings to $491,136

And in the column, sportswriter Eddie Welch heaped tribute upon the winner:

> King of the American turf and the greatest horse . . . on the American track since the days of Man O' War, . . . Whirlaway rose to supreme heights in the eighth renewal of the Narragansett Special . . . coming from last place to first in a mighty surge that the field . . . could not match.

The $24,300 victory increased his all-time money-winning record to $491,136. Welch credited Whirlaway with the $101,804.10 added to the Army-Navy Relief Fund, saying it was his presence that attracted the 30,000 racing fans to the track. He went on to point out that added to the $42,000 Spring contribution to the Fund, the Narragansett had contributed a total of $143,804.10, topping all other racetracks in America.

The New York Times sports column, calling it "just a romp," described the race in different terms:

> The year's "dream race" failed to develop today, when Alsab refused to tangle with Whirlaway in the $25,000 added Narragansett Special — he's lucky he didn't.
>
> For little Mr. Longtail ran one of his greatest races to come

from a couple of city blocks back and win going away.

Whirlaway's great victory in the Narragansett Special painted with bright colors his true character and quality as a racehorse. Before coming to Rhode Island, Whirly had run in four successive races at tracks in four different states (New York, Massachusetts, Illinois, New Jersey), served as a catalyst at each location for raising large sums of money for war relief, then brought his class act to Pawtuckett on September 12, where he was loaded again with 130 pounds, from 16 to 27 pounds more than that required of the opposing horses. Still wearing a protective cover on his injured eye, he proceeded to run what was adjudged to be one of his greatest races.

As the leaves of autumn began to fall in 1942, Whirlaway's copyrighted weekend special, "the Great Race," had already been seen at most racetracks on the circuit.

Chapter 12

The Match Race

THE withdrawal of Alsab on the day of the race had disappointed Narragansett Park officials and many fans who had hoped to see Alsab and Whirlaway run in the same race. As a result, Track President James E. Dooley that day announced that Narragansett Park would put up a $25,000 purse for a match race between Alsab and Whirlaway the following Saturday, the 19th. It is interesting to note that Al Sabath, Alsab's owner, immediate-

ly agreed to the proposal when just hours before he had withdrawn his horse from the highly publicized Narragansett Special.

One can only speculate about the reasons for Sabath's reversal. The rise of Alsab was one of those rare rags-to-riches stories with a special appeal to many who lived through the Great Depression of the early 1930s. The horse had been bought as a yearling at the 1940 Saratoga Sales for only $700 by Al Sabath of Chicago, after whom the colt was named. That purchase would be recorded as one of the greatest bargains in the annals of thoroughbred racing.

Owner Sabath and trainer Sarge Swenke soon learned that they possessed the goose that laid the golden egg. Alsab was entered in 22 races at the tender age of two in 1941, winning 15 times, including the last 10 straight stakes races. He was named colt of the year for two-year-olds with a winnings total of $110,600.

At the close of Alsab's sensational two-year-old campaign, he was being hailed as a certain Triple Crown winner in 1942. With full confidence in their Cinderella horse, Sabath and Swenke started racing Alsab in early February 1942. But things did not go well for the wonder horse in those early months. He lost seven straight races leading up to the Kentucky Derby in May. His fans remained loyal, but he lost to Shut Out in the Derby. Racing fans began to fear that something had gone wrong with Alsab's three-year-old campaign.

Some observers said the horse was not handled properly. It had been common talk during the winter season that owner Sabath had interfered with Swenke's training of Alsab, and his poor showing during the winter months was blamed on this interference. Following the loss to Shut Out in the Kentucky Derby, Alsab seemed to regain his earlier form. He won the Preakness in record time and followed that with another victory in the Withers Mile at Belmont. But Alsab's comeback was interrupted when he went to the post as favorite in the Belmont Stakes and lost to Shut Out for the second time in the Triple Crown races. Worse yet, Alsab was sidelined after the Belmont due to popping a splint (a foreleg injury). Sabath said the injury was slight and that Alsab would return to racing soon. But the colt's absence lasted two months and kept him from running in some of the more important summer races for three-year-olds.

Alsab finally returned to the track on August 9 at Washington Park in

Chicago. He participated in three preparatory races, losing the first and winning the next two. Sabath believed his horse was back in top form. The colt was then entered in the American Derby on August 29 where he won by three and a half lengths.

But then came a slight setback when Alsab lost to a horse named Marriage on September 8 in the Washington Handicap. Owner Sabath must have been concerned about Alsab's loss in this race. He probably realized that Alsab needed a big victory soon or the chances of his colt winning the leading three-year-old title would be gone forever. Thus, on September 8 Sabath had made a quick decision to enter his horse in the Narragansett Special on September 12, setting the stage for the long-awaited match-up of Whirlaway and Alsab.

This decision by Sabath was even more surprising because back in May, before Alsab's injury, the owner was not interested in racing his horse against Whirlaway. But in the four months since then, Whirlaway had been through the most intensive schedule of races any thoroughbred had ever endured. Sabath must have thought the time had arrived to take him on. Alsab had been resting up for two months, and even Swenke, his trainer, had stated the day before the Narragansett race that Alsab was in the best condition of his life. But perhaps in his pre-race workouts, Whirly looked better to Alsab's team than they had anticipated, for Alsab was suddenly withdrawn.

Most turf writers on the scene sided with Sabath for withdrawing Alsab abruptly from the 'Gansett, giving lack of time for race preparation as the excuse. From a detached viewpoint, however, it would seem rather obvious that Whirlaway had achieved a status in his career where his readiness was literally taken for granted. Normal considerations zealously demanded and received by owners and trainers of other prize thoroughbreds were never accorded Whirly. Rest between races and carrying reasonable weight loads were foreign to his lifestyle. Mr. Longtail was indeed treated like "a breed apart" — but therein lies the true quality of his character.

When the offer for the match race with Whirlaway to be held a week later came, Sabath jumped at it, perhaps thinking he would surely have the advantage. But the most surprising element of the drama came with the announcement that Warren Wright and Ben Jones would indeed allow Whirlaway to run in the proposed match race.

As usual, Whirlaway was not given any consideration in scheduling the proposed race. No owner or trainer in the history of racing had ever allowed a horse of Whirly's caliber to run a match race on such short notice. Why should an owner like Sabath be rewarded for withdrawing his horse from a featured race just hours before post time? Alsab certainly had been more rested for the Narrangansett Special than was Whirlaway.

By running in a match race on September 19th, Whirlaway would have only a few days to prepare for the September 26th Manhattan Handicap at Belmont Park in New York. This race on the first Saturday of the fall meeting would be another effort to raise money for the War Emergency Relief Fund. The race would be over a mile and a half, with the leader of the handicap division scheduled to carry 132 pounds.

A good case could have been made for not entering Whirlaway in the proposed match race, but that didn't happen. After Sabath agreed to the match race, Ben Jones secured Wright's consent in a telephone conversation with the owner, who was at home in Lexington. The trainer announced that he would stay at the park all week with Whirly, adding, "We will run even if it snows." A statement like that made in summertime could easily be classified as *firm*.

One important requirement for the match race, the primary reason for Whirly's appearance in the contests just concluded, was the stipulation that a percentage of the gate receipts should be contributed to Uncle Sam's soldiers and sailors. Track President Dooley agreed that the track's 6 1/2 percent cut of the betting handled in the race would be donated to the cause.

The week went by quickly, and on September 19, 35,000 fans showed up at Narragansett Park to see the delayed match-up. For the 50th consecutive time, Whirlaway had kept a racing appointment. He was still wearing the isinglass protective cover for his right eye and was the favorite, as usual, at 3-10 odds. George Woolf was whirly's rider, and Carroll Bierman was aboard Alsab.

At the start of the race, Alsab went to the front, as expected. Whirly was going along easily in Alsab's wake only a length and a half away until shortly after the three-eighths marker. At that point, Bierman jumped the margin to three lengths over Whirly; then, on entering the stretch, that lead was reduced to two lengths.

As both horses straightened into the stretch and headed for the wire, Eddie Welch, *The Boston Globe* sportswriter, described what he called "the most sensational turf battle in history":

> Three-sixteenths of a mile away the finish line was in sight and down the brown ribbon the pair tore. At the 18th pole Whirly was only a head away and the crowd, accustomed to his patented finishes, were sure he had his adversary and they roared "here he comes."

But this time, it was not to be as Alsab only allowed an inch a stride. Whirly cut the margin to a foot, then half, but at the wire Alsab was in front by what Welch termed an "infinitesimal margin." In the next stride, Whirly was in front, but it was too late.

The finish of the race was so close that the naked eye could not discern which horse was ahead. Many observers thought Whirlaway had won because he was in front just after the two horses passed the finish line. Others thought it was even, but the photo showed that Alsab had won by only the tip of his nose at the wire.

The Associated Press column in *The New York Times* caught the excitement and drama of the finish as Alsab beat Whirlaway

> . . . by the width of a whisker today in a . . . thriller that you had to see to believe.
>
> Not even a movie script . . . could have done justice to the way the . . . colt from Chicago and the Kentucky cannonball fought it out in one of the most smashing drives ever seen. . . .

Both horses were clocked at the same time for the mile and three-sixteenths, 1:56 2/5. The final three-sixteenths was covered in 18 seconds with Whirly's time at least 2/5 of a second faster since he was still behind at that marker. *The New York Times* added: "That's just about as fast as any horse can go."

George Woolf, Whirly's rider, was near tears after the race and admitted that something that had never happened to him before in all his years of booting home winners had just cost him his greatest race. He was quoted as saying:

> For the first time in 12 years I had a horse in the air instead of on the ground at the finish. If Whirly had been at the end of his stride, instead of in the middle of it with all four feet off the ground, we'd have won.

He said he was fooled by the length of Whirly's stride. Mentally he was picking off those strides to make sure he'd be on the ground at the finish. But he said Whirly's stride gets longer as it picks up speed, and that's what made him miss this time.

Ben Jones congratulated Al Sabath and Sarge Swenke on Alsab's victory. The trainer said he believed Whirly would have won in another sixteenth of a mile. Ben told his son later why he thought the race was lost. Jimmy recalls,

> That was a farce. . . . In a match race you ride differently than in other races. You run from the start because you have only one horse to beat. But George Woolf just . . . kept laying back. . . . Alsab just dropped back and stole another 1 1/2 lengths before George realized what was happening.

There have been four so-called match races in turf history in which Triple Crown winners have been pitted against another leading horse of their day. In all four two-horse races, the Triple Crown champions have lost. This result seems surprising, but in reality, the facts show vividly that in each match race the winner had a distinct advantage from the outset.

The first match race was between Sir Barton, first Triple Crown winner, and Man O' War, great three-year-old colt of 1920, but not a Triple Crown winner. The mile-and-a-quarter race was held on October 12, 1920, at the Kenilworth Track in Windsor, Ontario. Man O' War was finishing his brilliant three-year-old campaign, while Sir Barton as a four-year-old had experienced a miserable campaign, winning only five and losing eight. As a three-year-old, Sir Barton had become the first Triple Crown winner in history, winning eight times with three seconds and two thirds. In winning the Belmont Stakes, Sir Barton had set a new

American record of 2:17 2/5 for the mile and three-eighths. John McClelland, owner of Eternal, the horse finishing second to Sir Barton in the Kentucky Derby of 1919, later paid this tribute to Sir Barton: "That's the best 3-year-old I've seen in my thirty years on the turf, and I've seen some great horses."

Commander Ross, Sir Barton's owner, had thought of retiring his colt at the end of 1919 because of the horse's sore feet, which required carefully handmade shoes with piano felt pads inserted between his shoes and soles. Ross, a Canadian, knew Sir Barton didn't have much of a chance against Man O' War in October 1920, but was willing to gamble on the slim chance of winning the race and the purse of $75,000, which would enhance his country's position as a leader in thoroughbred racing.

Sam Riddle, Man O' War's owner, had carefully orchestrated his colt's racing schedule in 1920, avoiding races in which his star performer would be pitted against strong opponents. Riddle had even refused to enter Man O' War in the 1920 Kentucky Derby because he felt long races like the Preakness and Derby were scheduled too close together, and he wasn't going to send his horse "way out west" to run in the Derby.

Man O' War had breezed through his 1920 season with ten consecutive victories against mediocre opposition. That particular year, there was only one horse that had much of a chance at beating him, and that was Exterminator. Although a five-year-old, Exterminator was having his greatest season, including victories in two straight handicap contests at Aqueduct. In the Saratoga Cup, the gelding had set a new American record time for two miles, which lasted for 21 years. Needless to say, Sam Riddle would not consider racing Man O' War against Exterminator.

When Sir Barton arrived at Windsor five days before the race, he became the target of several adverse newspaper stories. It was reported that trainer Guy Bedwell had been handling the horse poorly and that the Kenilworth track was too hard for his sore feet. To add to the complicated state of affairs, owner Ross announced one hour before post time the replacement of Sir Barton's regular rider, Earl Sande, with jockey Frank Keogh.

These pre-race speculations and activities resulted in Man O' War being made an overwhelming favorite at 5-100. The predictions were true.

Man O' War was never fully extended and still won by a margin of seven lengths. It was a ridiculously easy victory, labeled by some as a "farce." One press report called it a "great spectacle, hardly a great race."

The second match race between a Triple Crown winner and another leading horse was held on November 1, 1938, at Pimlico in Baltimore. This time the contenders were War Admiral, 1937 Triple Crown winner, and Seabiscuit, a horse similar to Exterminator in that he had hit his stride as a five-year-old. War Admiral, a son of Man O' War, had won all eight of his races including the Triple Crown races. Seabiscuit did not become "big time" until his four-year-old campaign. The first opportunity for the two leading horses to meet came in October 1937. They were named for the Washington Handicap at Laurel Park, a weight-for-age event. But Charles Howard, Seabiscuit's owner, withdrew his horse because rain during the week of the race had interfered with Seabiscuit's workouts. War Admiral, on the other hand, stayed in the race with the remaining contenders and won handily.

Racing fans were keenly disappointed, and clamor for the match race continued into 1938. Several offers were made from leading racetracks around the country, and finally in April 1938, an offer of a $100,000 purse for a match race at Belmont Park on May 30 was agreed to by both Riddle and Howard. In approving the race, C. V. Whitney of the Westchester Racing Association stated:

> We are offering this race because public interest is high and the two horses are sound and at the top of their form. Why wait for one of them to break down?

Immediately the press started building up the race between War Admiral and Seabiscuit as a real championship match. But a bomb was dropped on May 24, when Charles Howard again called the race off because Seabiscuit's legs were bothering him. Experienced turfmen said the excuse was valid because Seabiscuit had shown a lack of speed in his workouts. Remembering the farcical conditions of the match race between Man O' War and Sir Barton, all parties got together and decided that if it couldn't be a really good race, there would be no race at all.

In order to ease the disappointment caused by the race's cancellation, Sam Riddle came up with another sporting gesture. He announced that

War Admiral would start in the Suburban Handicap on May 28 against his old rival Pompoon. The second bomb in this saga fell on the day of the race when War Admiral was scratched at the last moment. The reason given was the condition of the track, but sportswriters disputed this, saying the real reason was that War Admiral would be required to carry four more pounds at 132 than Pompoon's 128.

Riddle's announcement really upset turf fans and writers. Murray Tynan, of the *New York Herald Tribune*, wrote this accusation about Riddle's decision:

> The turf believes there was only one reason War Admiral was scratched. It feels certain that the Riddle stables feared a defeat and simply couldn't take it.

It was assumed that a defeat might lessen War Admiral's importance as a sire. *Newsweek* magazine added another strong criticism on the development of events surrounding the proposed match race:

> Turf fans soured on their sport last week. What promised to be one of the most glorious events in horse racing history faded into mediocrity, then to washout.

The saga faded but remained alive. There was another glimmer of hope for the match-up in July. Both War Admiral and Seabiscuit were entered in the Massachusetts Handicap at Suffolk Downs, but again Seabiscuit was withdrawn by Charles Howard, this time a half hour before post time, because of a "fever-wracked tendon" in his leg. Someone suggested it might have been because the track was muddy. War Admiral did run in the race but finished fourth, having cut his right forefoot with the sharp edge of his rear hoof plate. After this unfortunate series of events, it appeared likely the two horses would never meet.

Back in 1938, most people still demanded a happy ending to a story, and behold a match race was finally arranged between the two horses that had been badly maligned for decisions in which they had taken no part. The long-awaited race between Seabiscuit and War Admiral was set for November 1 at Pimlico Race Track in Baltimore. This time there were no withdrawals.

After two false starts, the race was under way. For over half of the mile-and-three-sixteenths distance, it was close. But as they rounded the turn, Kurtsinger, on War Admiral, brought his whip down sharply. The Triple Crown winner could not respond, and George Woolf, on Seabiscuit, began opening up the lead. Seabiscuit charged down the stretch to an easy victory by four lengths. But it must be added that Seabiscuit beat a different War Admiral in November than he would have faced back in the early months of 1938 or any time in the Admiral's great year of 1937. Howard had out-maneuvered Riddle this time. Seabiscuit was definitely in top form, and it had been all downhill for War Admiral since he had finished fourth in the Massachusetts Handicap at Suffolk Downs in July. Largely on the strength of his victory over War Admiral, Seabiscuit became "Horse of the Year" in 1938 — quite an accomplishment for a five-year-old. But it did little to prove Seabiscuit's superiority over War Admiral.

After the match race between Whirlaway and Alsab in 1942 came the fourth and last such encounter between a Triple Crown winner and another leading horse of the day. This one was between Assault, Triple Crown winner in 1946, and Armed, a leading horse in the handicap division that year.

Assault had become the first Texas-bred horse to win the Triple Crown. He had won the races in good style, then faded, but won his last two races as a three-year-old, including a victory over Stymie in the Westchester Handicap. Assault closed out the year with 8 firsts out of 15 starts. The pride of Texas had ended the year by being voted by writers as the "Horse of the Year," having amassed total winnings of $424,195 from inflated purses, which had doubled after the end of World War II.

As the 1947 turf campaign began, highly inflated handicap purses would be the dominant factor in determining year-end honors for competing horses. The contest for leader of the handicap division was waged by three horses — Robert Kleberg's four-year-old Assault, Warren Wright's five-year-old gelding Armed, and Hirsch Jacob's six-year-old Stymie. In races between Assault and Stymie, Kleberg's horse had seemed to have the advantage. But by June of 1947, Armed had entered the money-winning derby by amassing total winnings of $487,755.

Armed's stunning success started talk about a match race between Assault and Armed. Warren Wright and Robert Kleberg agreed on one to be held August 30 in Chicago at Washington Park for a purse of $100,000. It was assumed that the winner would more than likely end up as the year's top money-winner. But, the contest was postponed when Assault injured his foreleg; the race was rescheduled for September 27 at Belmont Park in New York.

On September 22, after a workout, Assault suddenly came up lame. Because of the race's uncertain status, the owners were unhappy about continuing with it. However, Kleberg finally issued a candid statement:

> Because of the great public interest and long preparation for the race, we have decided to run Assault and hope he will be at his best. In an ordinary stakes or other race, I doubt that I should start him.

The owners made other stipulations concerning the race. Neither would hold the purse if his horse won. Rather, the money would be split between the Red Cross and the Damon Runyon Cancer Fund. Finally, no betting would be allowed on the race. Instead, it would only be an exhibition. Things became so confusing and unusual that the ASPCA showed up at the track on the morning of the race to demand proof that Assault was in condition to run.

The race went off on schedule, but it should never have been held. Armed won by eight lengths — a hollow victory at best. Assault's rider, Eddie Arcaro, eased up on him when he found out his horse could not keep up. Ironically, the race proved to be a sad ending to an otherwise glorious year for Assault. He did not race again in 1947 and lost out to Armed for "Horse of the Year" honors.

In all four so-called match races, victories over the Triple Crown champions gave the winners unjustified benefits. Man O' War ended his great career with a victory over a disabled Sir Barton. Seabiscuit's victory over a fading War Admiral garnered him "Horse of the Year" honors in a fashion similar to Armed's shallow win over Assault. Alsab's "whisker victory" over Whirlaway rescued the Sabath colt's three-year-old campaign from oblivion.

These races were not in any sense valid match races. To be so, both horses should be the same age. The Triple Crown races alone meet the requirements of a match race for thoroughbreds. In those races, the horses must be the same age, carry the same weight, have the same amount of previous training, and are usually in the best condition of their careers. And rarely do horses like Affirmed and Alydar come along at the same time, as was the case in 1978 when that duo ran the three closest Triple Crown races in history, Affirmed winning over Alydar by one and a half lengths in the Kentucky Derby, by a neck in the Preakness, and by only a head in the Belmont Stakes.

The sad exhibition between Assault and Armed in 1947 was the last special match race held between a Triple Crown winner and another leading horse. Most likely no owner of a Triple Crown horse will ever again risk the animal's reputation in that kind of encounter, because a loss or injury could lessen the thoroughbred's value as a sire. Only promoters like this sort of fight-to-the-finish between champions. Commander Ross, owner of Sir Barton, made this statement about such races:

> Match races are wonderful in prospect — that's why they are run — but, as good racing goes, they are often terrible duds.

Most assuredly, one thing can be said about the match race between Whirlaway and Alsab: It was not a dud. Whirly was at a distinct disadvantage by facing a well-rested Alsab with only a few days rest himself and giving his opponent a seven-pound weight advantage, but those observing the race would never have guessed it by the way Mr. Longtail ran. Eddie Welch's comment in *The Boston Globe* after the race still holds true today:

> The race between Whirlaway and Alsab was the greatest match race in the history of the turf, one that will live forever in the memories of those who were fortunate enough to witness the event.

Chapter
13

Where Have the Other Horses Gone?

IT requires a good measure of diligence to keep an accurate account of significant contributions made by Whirlaway to the sport of kings in 1942. To be sure, there were no kings around to see him race; but as a substitute for royalty, there were thousands of commoners who crowded racetracks during that war year to see Little Mr. Bigtail in action. They were a garden-variety crowd composed mostly of soldiers, sailors, and shift workers in defense plants, just ordinary people upon whom the future of freedom in the world depended heavily at the time. This new breed of racing fan came not necessarily to bet on Whirly, but just to see him race. After all, to watch Mr. Longtail in one of his stretch drives was the best remedy available to counteract the grim war news of the day. Also, these special fans were much more aware than the general public that Whirly was out there running to help raise money for their benefit. They knew he was working fast and often, helping thoroughbred racing raise vitally needed money for War Emergency Relief. He could bring in more than the total amount raised from a strong baseball rivalry like the Dodgers and Giants.

To update the tally sheet, by participating in the special match race at Narragansett Park on September 19, Whirlaway made significant contributions to racing:

— he had prevented the sport and Narragansett Park from receiving further negative publicity generated by match races of another time;
— he had allowed owner Al Sabath a second chance;
— he had made possible an additional contribution to the War Emergency Relief Fund;
— he had run the race in spite of the disadvantage of carrying seven extra pounds with only a few days' rest;
— and he had provided Alsab the opportunity he needed to regain his former prestige on the track.

It is difficult to identify a loser in a race of such high caliber. To this day, no horse has ever done that much for racing in one afternoon.

The match race had been the last thing Whirlaway had needed tacked on to his weighty racing schedule in late September 1942, with his next meet scheduled for September 26 at Belmont Park in New York. He would again have only a few days for preparation. The best way to explain the circumstances is to say that times were not normal and that the usual criteria hadn't applied to Whirlaway throughout his racing career. Whirly was entered in the September 26th Manhattan Handicap and would show up at post time as he had in every race he had been entered in.

The featured race of a mile and a half was scheduled to initiate the fall meeting at Belmont Park. As usual, it was arranged with the hope of having Whirlaway on the card. When the weights were assigned to the eight entries, many suspected Whirly might be withdrawn, because Whirly would be carrying 132 pounds, giving up from 17 to as much as 37 pounds to the other horses. At such a frightening prospect, most owners and trainers would have scratched their horses immediately. But Ben Jones, already spoiled to the core by his pride and joy, stated that he was not afraid in the least for his horse to carry this top weight and that, after all, Whirly was a "natural stayer" who had always done well over a long distance.

The heavy weight handicap, the race's long route, and the short interval of rest between races should have been obstacles enough to throw at this little competitor. Then, on the day before the race, the rider for Whirlaway was once again in doubt. Eddie Arcaro was still under suspension, and George Woolf was not available. But no need to fret, this had happened before. Finally, a jockey named Jack Westrope was contracted to ride Whirly, the 13th different rider for Mr. Longtail in his three-year career.

In what had to be a personal tribute to Whirlaway, the fans again installed him as favorite in spite of the excess weight he was required to carry, the guiding hands of a new rider, and the fact that he would be facing strong opposition, which included Bolingbroke, The Rhymer, and Staretor with Johnny Longden aboard.

The race turned out to be a duel between Bolingbroke and Whirlaway. As Bryan Field wrote in *The New York Times* column:

> The chief difference was that Bolingbroke carried 115 pounds and Whirlaway 132. . . . Even so it was a battle . . . but after doing his gallant best, Whirlaway could not reach Bolingbroke at the wire.

But Jockey Herb Lindberg had to drive Bolingbroke for all he was worth to reach the wire ahead of Whirly, to the extent that Bolingbroke had to break the existing American record for one mile and a half. By running the distance in 2:25 3/5, Townsend Martin's horse set a new Belmont Park track record that lasted for 15 years.

By late September 1942, it should have been clear to most turf observers that carrying heavy loads of excess weight was about the only reason Whirlaway lost a race. Different riders, racing long distances, lack of rest between starts, long-distance travel between engagements, competing on dangerous turf, and being hit in the eye by flying missiles didn't seem to perturb this dauntless competitor of the racing oval. According to widely used Handicappers's Formulas, in the Manhattan Handicap Mr. Longtail might have won the race by 15 lengths and set a record that would still be intact had he not been saddled with the extra weight.

The next race on Whirly's "weekly" schedule was the prestigious Jockey Club Gold Cup race set for October 3. At least it would be run at the same track so travel wasn't necessary, but this time the distance would be two miles. It had been the year before in this same race that Whirlaway had lost by a nose to Market Wise at the end of his grueling three-year-old campaign. Then a well-rested horse had run the race of his life and had to break the existing American record for two miles to beat Mr. Longtail.

As had been the case in practically every important race in which Whirlaway had participated, there would be something of a dramatic flare added to the upcoming Gold Cup race. Whirly approached the race needing only about $6,000 to become the first half-million dollar race-horse in history. He could easily reach that goal by winning the contest; and in so doing, he would make Warren Wright and Ben Jones, owner and trainer, the two happiest people in the world of thoroughbred racing.

But there was more. Alsab was also entered in the race. Naturally, interest would be high for this encounter after their previously thrilling race at Narragansett. Alsab's comeback seemed secure at this point. He had won the Lawrence Realization a few days before and appeared to be in top form. However, the scale of weights used for the Jockey Club Gold Cup race would not put Whirlaway at such a disadvantage this time. It would put 124 pounds on Whirlaway and 117 on Alsab. Whirly would still carry seven extra pounds, but that's certainly a vast improvement over having to tote 130 or 132 pounds for a distance of two miles. Most observers believed this two-mile test would do more than their match race had to put to rest existing doubt as to which was the better colt. To increase the interest level, two other strong horses would be in the race, Bolingbroke and The Rhymer.

A crowd of 30,805 was on hand to see the return meeting of Whirly and Alsab. The same riders that had been aboard in the match race were to ride — George Woolf on Whirlaway and Carroll Bierman atop Alsab. For the 16th consecutive time in 1942, Whirlaway was the favorite.

At the start of the race, The Rhymer went to the front and set the pace for the first mile and a quarter. Alsab stayed close up to The Rhymer most of that distance while Whirly stayed nearer the front than usual, trailing by about three lengths for the first mile and a quarter. It was not until the field was a half mile from the finish line that the real battle began. At that point, Woolf attempted to send Whirly up to Alsab, but he couldn't. Biding his time for an eighth of mile, he tried again and this time got alongside, but Alsab drew off.

Bryan Field of *The New York Times* described the stretch run:

> . . . it was Alsab by more than a length. Whirlaway came on once more. . . . They battled for fifty yards . . . but Alsab couldn't hold on. . . .
>
> They were inside the eighth pole now. Suddenly Whirlaway went a neck to the front and as they pounded over the line, Whirlaway was slowly drawing away.

When Whirlaway flashed across the finish line as winner of the Jockey Club Gold Cup race, he became the turf's first half-million dollar baby. By picking up the purse of $18,350, he had earned a total of $511,486. That seems paltry compared to the highly inflated purses won on the racetrack today. On the modern scene, a half-million dollar purse is rather common for one stakes race; but when the inflation rate is applied to Whirlaway's total, it increases sixfold or more to over $3 million, and Whirly had to race three years to reach his mark. Arthur Daley, sportswriter for *The New York Times* in the 1940s and 1950s, discussed, in one of his columns, inflation's ballooning effect on purses of stakes races after World War II. He ventured the belief that Whirlaway would have been the first thoroughbred to reach the goal of $1 million, had he enjoyed the luxury of winning $100,000 purses instead of half that amount offered in his races.

Warren Wright had run out of goals for his "little horse with the big bankroll." In less than three years of racing, Whirly had achieved for Calumet Farm the loftiest goals offered to a stable by thoroughbred racing — first Kentucky Derby winner, first Triple Crown winner, world's leading money-winner, and on October 3, 1942, the half-million dollar pinnacle. But there was still unfinished business for Whirly and his barnstorming act. Other racetracks besides Belmont Park were still desperately hoping Mr. Longtail might find time to help them raise their quotas for the War Emergency Relief Fund.

Whirly's racing program into October 1942 had not slowed one bit. Instead, the weary champion was averaging one race per week. The grind continued with the October 10 race becoming Whirly's fourth start at Belmont during 1942, giving that track a decided boost in meeting its war-relief quota. The first Belmont race had been the Suburban Handicap back on May 30, which drew a record crowd of 51,903, the largest to that date to see a horse race in New York state.

The October 10 feature at Belmont was to be the New York Handicap over an unbelievable distance of two miles and a quarter. At that stage of the racing season, handicappers were having great difficulty finding a race long enough in distance and weight heavy enough for Whirlaway to make betting attractive. In spite of long distance and excess poundage, Whirly had already won five of the most prestigious races open to four-year-olds in 1942 — the Brooklyn, Massachusetts, and Dixie Handicaps, the Narragansett Special, and, most recently, the Jockey Club Gold Cup race. Those who set the requirements for the upcoming New York Handicap must have been confident they had found the correct formula — saddle Whirlaway with 130 pounds and race him for two miles and a quarter, a distance that has long since become extinct at the racetrack.

There is no known record of an owner or trainer risking a thoroughbred of Whirlaway's caliber in a race under these conditions. Mr. Longtail had nothing to prove. But Whirly's owner and trainer knew how dependent the racing establishments had become on Whirlaway's presence at the track in order to raise money for the War Emergency Relief Fund and thus consent was given for Whirly to continue racing.

On October 10, a crowd of 26,456 turned out for the New York Handicap to see Whirlaway. There was a strong field opposing him, including Alsab, Bolingbroke, Lochinvar, and Obash. George Woolf was not available to ride Whirlaway, so Jack Westrope, who had guided him in the Manhattan Handicap two weeks before, was called upon. But Westrope's lack of experience on Whirlaway showed up quickly as he took the little competitor to the front at the start of this very long race.

Whirly led for a mile and a half with Lochinvar close by. At that point Lochinvar faded, and on came Alsab and Bolingbroke; but Whirly continued in front until the stretch. It was then that Whirlaway faltered under the stress of the heavy weight and long distance. Alsab faltered, too, but did manage to nose out Obash, who was coming in a rush at the finish carrying only 106 pounds. At that, Whirly was only a length behind the front two at the wire.

Whirlaway had carried 130 pounds, giving up 9 to Alsab and 24 to Obash. He had been ridden very differently from the way he had been trained to run. By setting a fast pace for a mile and three-quarters, Westrope had used up Whirly's reserve speed and had allowed the other contenders to wait until the stretch before going to a drive. Mr. Longtail had been beaten by the same technique he had executed flawlessly in his great races. Jack Westrope, Whirly's rider, said after the race that the weight alone beat Whirlaway over the long distance. When a racehorse is speeding around a track, all the weight of a horse lands on one foot at a time. The thoroughbred weighs about a thousand pounds. On top of that half ton, Whirlaway carried 130 extra pounds. It is difficult to imagine how much agonizing punishment Whirly's legs absorbed, pounding for two and a quarter miles, and carrying 130 extra pounds. It is safe to assume that many horses would have dropped out of contention or broken down under the same circumstances before reaching the finish line.

The persistent task in recounting Whirlaway's story lies in the importance of keeping his racing career feats and concurrent historical events in proper perspective. Mr. Longtail's racing agenda and the early years of World War II formed a remarkable parallel, one that is unique for a racehorse and one that most assuredly will never occur again.

Whirlaway and the war were still going strong in October 1942. Whirly had reached his earnings milestone just as the battle for Stalingrad was entering its most crucial stage. It would seem the proper time for Whirlaway to bring his 1942 racing season to a close. He had already achieved the highest honors racing could offer; he had raced without interruption in 16 consecutive contests, bearing unconscionable weights in almost every race. But there still remained unfinished business on Whirly's loaded racing card.

Because other tracks besides Belmont Park had feature races scheduled to raise money for the War Emergency Relief Fund, owner Wright and trainer Jones decided that the race at Belmont on October 10 was Whirlaway's last appearance at a New York track in 1942, thus making it possible for Whirly to give an assist to smaller tracks in their war-relief efforts. The next stop for Whirlaway would be the Laurel track just outside Baltimore on October 24; then four days later at Pimlico, Mr. Longtail was scheduled to run in the Special, a race that appeared to be shaping up as one of the year's major turf attractions. Earlier in the year, Pimlico had sent out invitations to all the leading thoroughbreds to run in the Special, with proceeds going for war charity.

Whirly's next race was at a much smaller track in Laurel, Maryland, located about halfway between Baltimore and Washington, D.C. The occasion was the 29th running of the mile-and-a-quarter Washington Handicap, and, as might be expected, this race was billed as Laurel's special race for the War Emergency Relief Fund. With Whirlaway as the feature attraction, some 20,000 fans attended on October 24, despite the obstacle of wartime travel restrictions, showing their appreciation for Whirly joining them in their war-relief effort.

Don Reed, sportswriter for *The Baltimore Sun*, described the running of the Washington Handicap with Whirlaway in a strong field of nine as "just the kind of race that a big crowd likes to see."

Whirly continued to retain his title as race favorite, but would be facing strong opposition from Tola Rose, Riverland, Thumbs Up, and Vagrancy.

George Woolf returned to ride Whirlaway, and Warren Wright's champion made his customary casual exit from the starting gate. As the horses headed through the backstretch, the battle began to shape up with Whirlaway, Riverland, and Thumbs Up making their moves for the lead at about the same time. Woolf made his bid for victory on Whirly at the far turn of the track, and from there the Calumet Comet thundered down the stretch, passing Riverland and Thumbs Up on his way to the finish line where he led by half a length.

Whirlaway carried his accustomed 130 pounds in the race, giving up 20 pounds to second-place winner Thumbs Up and 12 pounds to third-place Riverland. Don Reed, in his *Sun* column, gave this assessment of the thrilling race:

> Whirlaway proved not only his speed and stamina but that he has a heart as big as his body by the way he stood off his two chief challengers through the last three-sixteenths of the race from the head of the stretch to the wire.

The soldiers of our rapidly growing Army in 1942 were once again winners as Whirly's appearance at Laurel helped raise $30,000 for war relief. Beyond the champion's many personal achievements on the track, he had already added significantly to thoroughbred racing's total contribution to the War Emergency Relief Fund — and there was more to come.

Whirlaway's next appearance was scheduled for October 28 at Pimlico in Baltimore. The attraction was the Pimlico Special, which had come to be known as the "Rose Bowl" of horse racing. It was always held near the end of the season, and the nation's leading horses were customarily invited to enter.

Since 1942 was a banner year for outstanding horses, nine with the best records, including Whirlaway and Alsab, were invited to participate in the running of the Special. Pimlico had weeks before designated the race as the one from which the net proceeds would be donated to the War Emergency Relief Fund. But a discouraging thing happened by the eve of the contest. All of the invited horses except Whirlaway had been withdrawn from this highly publicized race. Pimlico officials had counted on having at least Whirlaway and Alsab to draw a large crowd for the benefit event. But Al Sabath belatedly withdrew Alsab, saying he was keeping his horse in New York for a race the following Saturday.

This was the second time in recent weeks that Al Sabath had withdrawn Alsab from a featured war-relief race. At the Narragansett Special there had been other topnotch horses in the race, so it proceeded on schedule. Then, for the sake of war relief, owner Wright had allowed Whirlaway to remain at Narragansett Park a week longer for the match race with Alsab. But Sabath's withdrawal of Alsab from the Pimlico Special forced track officials to make other arrangements for their War Relief Day.

C. M. Gibbs's column in *The Baltimore Sun*, titled "Gibberish," contained some speculation as to what should happen if Whirlaway, running alone, would be unable to finish. What would become of the $10,000 purse? He offered these biting words on Sabath's action and the Pimlico Special:

> While no one knows just what would be done in such a case, they all seem to agree that the track would make a mistake in donating it to Al Sabath . . . who withdrew his horse and ruined today's War Relief Day for Pimlico, because he wants to win . . . on Saturday.

The Special could have developed into the super race of that year, if some of the invited horses had joined Whirlaway at post time. Warren Wright could have entered Whirly in some of the more lucrative races in New York, but owner and trainer alike had decided from the start of the 1942 racing season that the War Emergency Relief Fund would have priority in determining Whirlaway's schedule. Apparently, other owners did not share that commitment or sense of national urgency.

Pimlico officials were naturally disappointed over the Special failing to attract two or more horses. A great crowd had been anticipated, and a duel between Whirlaway and Alsab was to have been the magnet. After the other entries were released, War Relief Day was switched to the following Saturday. The decision was then made to go ahead with Whirlaway's walkover, since the majority in attendance were there to see him run, whatever the circumstances.

For the 19th time, without exception in 1942, Whirlaway was present for a race to which he had been committed. In paying honor and appreciation to Whirly's class act, the Maryland Jockey Club named two of the secondary races for his sire and dam, Blenheim II and Dustwhirl. Pearl Kroll's article in *Time* magazine, titled "$10,000 Cakewalk," gave this description of Whirlaway's uncontested victory that day:

> Rose Bowl of racing is Pimlico, outside Baltimore, at the end of the racing season. Invited to run this year were nine of the nation's headliners. At post time only one answered the bugle.
>
> In a stake race, the show goes on even if there is only one

> performer. In the stands 10,000 fans watched the track — not so much to see the rarity of a walkover (only 18 in the U.S. since 1910) as to see the popular headliner who had scared away eight rivals: Warren Wright's twinkled-toed Whirlaway. A sort of Veronica Lake of the turf, Whirly can draw a crowd even if he does nothing but swish his long golden tail.
>
> Last week he strutted to the post, cakewalked around the track until he reached the stretch, then with nothing to pass but the grandstand, put on the famed finishing sprint that has made him the turf world's top money-winner. Time: 2:05 2/5 for the mile-and-three-sixteenths.
>
> For his personal appearance, Whirlaway got $10,000 — the biggest purse ever won in a walkover.

Thus, despite the fact that he had no opposition in the Special, Whirlaway put on a good show for the crowd. And the fans responded with gusto to the race, whose outcome had already been determined. The fans cheered him both times he passed the stand. Afterward, Whirly returned to the unsaddling area to receive a blanket of chrysanthemums.

What had to be a touch of irony for Al Sabath and Alsab took place in the Westchester Handicap three days after the Pimlico Special. In that race, which Sabath had thought his horse would win easily, Alsab finished third. By November of the 1942 racing season, Mr. Longtail seemingly had completely worn out the other leading horses competing in the handicap division, which is what had happened to Alsab. Sabath's horse had made a gallant comeback after an injury had sidelined him for two months during the summer. But after three sessions with Whirlaway, it was mostly downhill. After winning the New York Handicap at Belmont on October 10, Alsab lost two straight races, the Gallant Fox Handicap at Jamaica and the Westchester Handicap at Empire City, both in New York. Shortly after those races, Alsab was retired.

A similar fate befell the other leading horses of the year. Market Wise was not entered in a race against Whirlaway after the Suburban Handicap in May. He was out with an injury for most of the season. Attention, one of Whirly's strongest rivals spanning three years of racing, faded from the turf scene after the Massachusetts Handicap in July. Rounders looked strong in July but went downhill in August. Shut Out was thought by many to be the leading three-year-old of 1942, having won the Kentucky Derby, Belmont Stakes, Travers, and Arlington Classic; but then he disappeared from the track until October. After losing in the Gallant Fox Handicap on October 21, Shut Out was retired from racing for the year.

There were other competitors like Swing and Sway, The Rhymer, Tola Rose, and Bolingbroke that tried a few races with Whirlaway, then dropped out of the circuit. It had been a vintage year for outstanding racehorses, including a two-year-old named Count Fleet who had flashed impressive victories in 1942 and who would continue doing the same into the following year until injury forced him to retire after winning the Triple Crown.

By November 1942, Whirlaway's earlier rivals had left the track scene, but Whirlaway, the horse for all seasons, was still out there giving his all for the War Emergency Relief Fund.

After the Pimlico walkover on October 28, Whirlaway remained at the track for two additional races. This gesture was made by Warren Wright and Ben Jones as an act of generosity to help the track make up for the loss sustained by the failure of other leading horses to compete against Whirlaway in the Special. Whirly was entered in the Riggs Handicap on November 3 and finished second, but trailing the winner, Riverland, by only half a length — a remarkable performance that late in the racing season, considering he had carried 130 pounds once again, 14 more than Riverland, over a treacherous, muddy track for a distance of one mile and three-sixteenths.

As the first signs of winter appeared in 1942, 20 races had been completed, and the hoofbeats of Whirlaway could still be heard on the track. The champion made his last appearance in the East at Pimlico on November 11, the same day General George S. Patton and his inexperienced American troops successfully took control of the port city of Casablanca in North Africa from Vichy French forces without firing a shot. In this 30th running of the featured Governor Bowie Handicap, Whirlaway abandoned his usual style and took the lead after less than a mile of the long-distance race of one mile and five-eighths, proceeded to show his heels to three pursuers, and crossed the finish line with speed to spare. Whirlaway won by three lengths over Dark Discovery, who had been a recent victor over Alsab. In this contest, Whirly had carried 23 pounds more than Dark Discovery.

With this race, Whirlaway raised his world-record winnings total to $548,461 and made still another contribution to the war effort on behalf of thoroughbred racing. After the race, Whirlaway was shipped to Florida, indicating to most turf observers that his remarkable, and at times unbelievable, racing campaign of 1942 had finally reached journey's end. But once again established protocol didn't apply to this equine wonder's racing career — and lest we forget, a few days of the year still remained for something to take place.

Naturally, something had to happen. Whirly's 1942 scenario demanded further action. On arrival in Miami, Ben Jones received a plaintive request from Tony Pelleteri, vice president of the Fairgrounds Racing Association in New Orleans. The previous winter racing season at the Fairgrounds had been a colossal failure, and thus far 1942 had offered little hope for improvement. The Fairgrounds management at that late date was still trying to attract leading horses and racing fans. Officials were offering the added incentive of raising money for the War Emergency Relief Fund. Pelleteri was in desperate straights in his attempt to procure a top drawing card for the Louisiana Handicap set for December 12 at his track. Whirlaway was his first choice by a wide margin, but the track manager had seen little chance of obtaining his help while he was still racing in the East.

Imagine the great joy that swept New Orleans when Tony Pelleteri received the most welcome news from Ben Jones that Warren Wright had given consent for his beloved horse to run in the Louisiana Handicap. William Keefe, sportswriter for the New Orleans *Times-Picayune*, described the public reaction to that announcement in his December 11 column:

> New Orleans, which has always gone all-out for top attractions, will show its appreciation Saturday for the first big racing feature held here in many years. The great Whirlaway, whose name will probably be listed among the immortals of the turf, will meet one of the finest fields of rivals. . . .

He went on to say that it was too bad that the Fairgrounds Track didn't have 10,000 reserve seats to sell, because many could be sold to people who would like to see the "champion of champions" perform.

All of the qualities ever attributed to a true champion of any sport came to the track with Whirlaway on December 12, 1942. Before his appearance in New Orleans, this rare specimen of thoroughbred racing stock had run 21 races at 11 different locations, competed in all the major handicap contests available that year, set three new track records in spite of the extra baggage he was required to carry, attracted record crowds to his races in spite of wartime restrictions on travel, and raised more money on behalf of War Emergency Relief than the combined efforts of all other leading sports figures of the day. The Louisiana Handicap, regardless of the outcome, would be recorded as race number 22 of Whirlaway's 1942 class act. But in the flurry of excitement preceding the race that day, someone must have posed this question — How much longer could Whirlaway's small equine body contain the heart that knew no boundaries?

Entered in the Louisiana Handicap were some of the best horses racing at the time. Most of them, with the notable exception of Whirlaway, had not raced much in the earlier months of the year. Riverland and Marriage had both beaten Alsab in previous races, and Staretor had finished second to Whirlaway in the 1941 Kentucky Derby. All in all, the card of eight starters was considered strong. And no horses were withdrawn after it was announced that Whirlaway was entered in the race.

The *Times-Picayune* carried this prospectus of the race:

> The program looks like the best racing card ever offered in New Orleans. Of course, Whirlaway is the most prominent horse ever to perform here. He probably is the most prominent horse of modern times next to Man O' War, and Man O' War did not race here. . . .

Predictions about the race came true. A record crowd of 20,000 turned out, the largest gathering ever to witness a race at the Fairgrounds. Whirlaway was the favorite, as he had been in all 22 of his races in 1942, and carried top weight of 130 pounds. He was once again ridden by Wendell Eads. William Keefe of the *Times-Picayune* described the race:

> Trailing the field after the start . . . Whirlaway moved up on

> the outside . . . as the leaders swung into the stretch, and a great cry went up from the crowd of 20,000. . . .
>
> Then, when Whirlaway . . . started mowing down the leaders, it became apparent no horse . . . could stand in the way. . . .

Whirlaway had run his usual race, almost a carbon copy of many previous races. He came from far behind, turned on the power with another of his famous stretch drives, and won going away at the finish. He beat Heartman by a length and a half in the mile-and-an-eighth race.

Following the race, Whirlaway was given a great ovation when he came back to the stand for the Louisiana Handicap trophy presentation. Keefe wrote this closing remark about the exciting race:

> The immense crowd, able to spread out because of the perfect weather, was for the most part out to see the great Whirlaway perform. A made-to-order day, a brilliant crowd, a grand horse race, and a real champion thoroughbred! That was Saturday's offering at the Fairgrounds — and more.

Of all the people who were happy with Whirlaway's appearance in New Orleans, probably the happiest was Tony Pelleteri. He lost no time in contacting Warren Wright by phone. He told the happy owner, who was in Chicago:

> It was magnificent. And we owe it to you. I can't tell you how much we appreciate your kindness. . . .

Owner Wright asked if they liked Whirly. Pelleteri almost yelled,

> Did they? They acclaimed him like a king.

He went on to say that he'd never be able to thank Mr. Wright enough, but that he knew the trophy Whirly won meant more than the purse. He added that by sending Whirlaway there he had done more for racing fans in New Orleans than anybody had done in a long time.

Later, Pelleteri's official press release reflected the same feeling of appreciation for Whirlaway's appearance at the Fairgrounds. It said that Warren Wright and trainer Ben Jones had gone

> . . . a long piece out of their way to help Fairgrounds racing. Shipping a million-dollar horse here from Miami for a purse that could not exceed $13,000 was about as friendly and generous a gesture as could be made with a horse whose purse winnings were $545,000 before he came here.

Since leaving California early in the year after the Santa Anita races had been canceled, Whirlaway had journeyed almost 8,000 miles appearing in 22 races at 12 different tracks on behalf of the Army-Navy Emergency Relief Fund. But in none of the other races had the fans shown more genuine gratitude for his gallant effort than those 20,000 spectators who had seen him come streaking down the stretch at the Fairgrounds in New Orleans on that beautiful December afternoon.

Chapter
14

1942 — A Year of Crucibles

PARTICIPATION in the Louisiana Handicap at the Fairgrounds in New Orleans marked the end of Whirlaway's 1942 racing campaign, a racing schedule that had started on April 9 and had stretched out nonstop through December 12. During that eight-month period — a most crucial time of World War II for the United States and her fighting Allies — decisions, battles, innovations, and movements transpired that would eventual-

ly change the outcome of the war and alter the course of history forever.

With the extensive use of planes, tanks, and long-range automatic weapons in World War II, little notice was given to the wartime contributions made by animals, especially in the early years of the war. During the winter of 1941-1942, Russian cavalrymen had used 200,000 horses effectively in stopping the German advance on Moscow. The Soviet horsemen tore through a breach created by the infantry southwest of Moscow and cut off a key road to Smolensk at the German army rear. From that position, the Russian horsemen harassed the Germans throughout the winter.

After the Japanese invasion of the Philippines, the 26th U.S. Cavalry Regiment of the Philippine Scouts was used to cover the American retreat to Bataan, marking the last time horses were used in battle by U.S. troops. After that heroic action, the regiment withdrew inland, and eventually the men were forced to slaughter their noble steeds for food, a most unbefitting end to a breed of warriors that had served heroically, without complaint, in the defense of the United States since the days of the American Revolution.

During those dark days of 1942, a voluntary organization called Dogs for Defense, Inc., had recruited dogs to aid in the war effort. The organization set a goal of 300,000 canine recruits for use as guards at war plants, storage warehouses, and military camps and for activity at fronts throughout the world. A report by Dogs for Defense issued on December 20, 1942, noted:

> Members of the canine fraternity are represented in every branch of the armed forces and in all departments on the home front. Individual dog owners are numbered by the millions in the United States and their collective efforts cannot be estimated.

Help for America's war mobilization during this time of crisis also came from the bird kingdom. The Army had announced during the summer of 1941 that Thunderbolt, the first fighting falcon, was being trained at the pigeon lofts of Fort Monmouth, New Jersey. Thunderbolt was described as a veritable dive bomber that could spot a mouse a quarter of a mile away. Falcons were trained to blitz enemy carrier pigeons and fight parachute soldiers by tearing into their parachute "umbrellas" with some sort of secret weapon. It was rather fitting that a master of the skyways should be enlisted to thwart the greatest aerial threat ever released against freedom-loving people on the earth below.

The year 1942 was filled with commendable individual home-front efforts on behalf of war mobilization, but none from the animal kingdom made a more significant contribution to the War Emergency Relief Fund than Whirlaway. From the lowest point for the United States in World War II, the surrender of American troops to Japan in the Philippines after the fall of Bataan in early April, Whirlaway led thoroughbred racing through its most glorious year, a year in which racing contributed immensely to the war-relief fund.

As a result of his many accomplishments on the track, Whirlaway received many awards. Four days after winning the Louisiana Handicap in New Orleans, he was selected "Horse of the Year" for the second straight year by 128 sportswriters in the annual poll of *Turf and Sports Digest*. *The New York Times* named Whirlaway's victory in the Massachusetts Handicap, which made him the world's leading money-winner, the sports headline of the year. He was also named Best Four-Year-Old and Best Handicap Horse. But for some unexplained reason, no annual sports review made mention of Whirlaway's noteworthy contribution to the War Emergency Relief Fund during that crucial war year.

The New York Times year-end review did note that thoroughbred racing had led the way in raising money for the Fund. The article mentioned that American racing had contributed $3 million to the beneficiaries of the fund — the Army, Navy, USO, and Red Cross. The amount given more than doubled the $1,314,825 donated by major league baseball, with other professional sports giving lesser amounts. John Drebinger's *New York Times* column of December 20 described thoroughbred racing's most successful year:

> American racing . . . yielded staggering financial figures. Racing in . . . New York alone produced $10 million in taxes, the result of wagering which reached the incredible total of $175 million. All this . . . at a time when transportation grew increasingly difficult — . . . perhaps the most fantastic year the sport of kings has ever had.

The National Turf Committee was quick to take a bow for racing's magnificent contribution to the war effort, but not the slightest mention was made in the committee's report concerning Whirlaway's role in raising that "incredible total."

The lack of recognition for Whirlaway's war-effort role in 1942 can be explained by rationalizing that the racing establishment must have reached the point where Whirly was simply taken for granted. Whirlaway was always at the starting gate, in sun or storm, ready to race in race after race designated for war charity. But the National Turf Committee failed to recognize and acknowledge that therein lay the primary reason $3 million had been raised for the cause.

The amounts Whirlaway helped to raise by facing strong competitors in war-relief races varied from $30,000 to over $100,000. In three of those special races alone, he was largely responsible for raising over $300,000. An aside on Whirlaway's tremendous drawing power at the track was highlighted in *The New York Times* on November 22, 1942. It noted that attendance at Eastern tracks had dropped 50 percent in recent days. In connection with that announcement, it was no ordinary coincidence that Whirlaway had run his last race in the East on November 11.

Whirly's magic at the gate, with the help of strong competition, had helped attract well over 500,000 people to his 1942 races. That half-million attendance figure tells quite a story. Including tax revenues collected, gate receipts, and betting totals accruing from those sources for support of the war effort, it is well within reason to state with confidence that Whirlaway was a major factor, directly and/or indirectly, in raising at least $5 million ($30 million at today's rate) toward meeting the immediate and critical wartime needs of the United States during that crisis-filled year of World War II.

That year had produced heroes of many species, sizes, colors, and nationalities. Countless individual efforts emerged from the heat of battle on land, sea, and air that boldly depicted selfless devotion to the rescue of freedom and human dignity from ruthless and evil forces let loose in the world. But amid the throes of struggle, an equine knight arrayed in his natural armor came forth, armed with weapons of rare speed and indomitable courage, and on 12 different racetracks created a glorious lane of national honor and self-sacrifice unparalleled in the spectrum of thoroughbred racing history.

The deeply disturbing days of 1942, days of uncertainty and anguish that seemed at times to extend into months and years, at last drew to a close. In the United States, the usual joys of Christmas observance yielded to thoughts of men at war. The spirit of that time was reflected in a generous gift of $1 million made by Bernard Baruch, renowned adviser to presidents, to "Fighters for Freedom Throughout the World" — Refugees, Russians, Chinese, British, and Americans.

Chapter
15

The Whirlaway Legacy

ALTHOUGH the Louisiana Handicap turned out to be Whirlaway's last race of 1942, Ben Jones had already made plans for the horse to continue racing that winter. The trainer announced that Whirly would probably race for two more years and might earn a million dollars before being retired. Jones added confidently, "Whirly has never been scratched in three years of hard racing. He is sound, ready for everything." The proud trainer had really convinced himself that Whirlaway was indestructible.

But most impartial observers were well aware that the horse could not continue much longer at his 1942 pace. He was top-weighted in all 22 of his races that year. A further breakdown of that amazing campaign clearly discloses just how much extra weight Whirlaway did carry in those races. In 15 of the 22 races, he carried 10 pounds or more over the amount carried by his nearest competitors; in 10 of those 15 races, he carried 17 pounds or more, and in one race 27 pounds more, and in two races 29 pounds more than his best company. There were times during the year when Whirly was averaging one race per week; during one stretch he participated in three races at two different tracks within a period of only 10 days. In those 22 races he covered distances up to two miles and a quarter. Whirlaway's 1942 racing campaign was undoubtedly, and is to date, the most grueling agenda to which a thoroughbred racehorse of his caliber has ever been subjected. No wonder Ben Jones thought Whirlaway was indestructible.

A careful examination of these statistics would convince most critics that Whirlaway had indeed exhibited a unique, if not rare, brand of durability on the racetrack. But at some point, even the kingdom of fantasyland has an exit gate. While waiting for the next race planned for him by his trainer, the "iron horse" developed a problem in his left foreleg, later diagnosed as a bowed tendon. The injury might have occurred during the running of the Louisiana Handicap in New Orleans. In past races, injuries had never stopped this courageous competitor. Even as a two-year-old, Whirly had continued on to victory in the Hopeful Stakes in spite of being hit in the eye by a stone at some point during the race.

When the tendon injury was finally detected weeks after the Louisiana Handicap, Ben Jones thought Whirly would recover as he always had before. But this was to be different. The redoubtable trainer tried to nurse the horse back to his former fitness, but Whirlaway never fully recovered, no doubt due largely to overwork under heavy loads for three straight years.

Ben Jones had become so accustomed to having Whirlaway fit and ready for the next race that for many months he could not accept the horse's injury as permanent. Finally, Whirlaway was entered in a trial race on June 22, 1943, at Washington Park in Chicago. He finished third, and showed no signs of favoring the injured leg. Jones was elated and expressed confidence that the horse had regained his form. But his next race four days later caused considerable concern. Obviously struggling in the Equipoise Mile at Washington Park, Whirlaway finished fifth in a field of 12. But what was most disturbing was that he had pulled up at the finish with a noticeable limp.

Jones was visibly shaken and worried about Whirly after the race when he didn't respond to treatment. The trainer called Warren Wright in Lexington, and the decision was immediately made to retire Whirlaway. Jones issued a statement to the press, explaining the decision:

> Whirly pulled up noticeably sore. He didn't respond to treatment. I called Mr. Wright . . . and . . . he agreed with me that the only logical course was retirement. After all, it would be little short of inhumane to continue such a great horse and run the chance of permanently maiming him.

Later the same day, Wright made the retirement official, explaining that Whirlaway had not fully recovered from an injury received at New Orleans. He went on to say,

> . . . Rather than punish him in trying to bring him back to racing form, or run the risk of breaking him down, we have decided to retire him and give him his much needed rest. . . . He is entitled to this, and [we] believe he has made a great contribution to racing.

For Ben Jones, it was extremely difficult to put aside personal feelings and recommend retirement for Whirlaway. But not wanting to take further risks, he concluded:

> Whirly has been very good to me, so it is only fair to the horse and Mr. Wright to retire him while he is still sound.

The relationship between Ben Jones and Whirlaway had become very special, even unique, in the annals of thoroughbred racing. Grantland Rice, in one of his 1942 columns, described this "man and horse" saga:

After retirement ceremonies, Ben Jones bids his good friend a fond farewell.

You've likely heard of Damon and Pythias, Amos and Andy, Mike and Ike, Smith and Wesson, Jones and Keeler and other inseparables of history and sport. Now I can give you a man and a horse. They are Ben Jones and Whirlaway.

And he said that while Whirlaway's opinion of the men was not known, Ben's opinion of the horse was:

> . . . It goes back to what George Ade once gave me as nature's greatest romance — a man and his dog. . . . Jones almost got sore last fall when Whirlaway wasn't picked for the All-America backfield. I know he will be squawking if Whirlaway isn't named to one of the [baseball] All-Star teams. . . .

When the news of Whirly's retirement was officially announced, the fans in Chicago clamored for one last look at their idol. In a moving ceremony at Arlington Park on July 5, 1943, Whirlaway was paraded before a cheering crowd, and Mr. Longtail pricked his ears to the applause from the stands as he stood in the winner's circle for the last time.

A few days later, Whirlaway was shipped to Lexington to begin his retirement. He arrived on July 13, and not since Man O' War had a horse received such a triumphant return to Kentucky. An official homecoming day for Whirlaway was set for August 8. The mayor's proclamation read:

> WHEREAS, the citizens of Lexington and Fayette County desire to pay tribute to the achievements of Warren Wright's WHIRLAWAY of Calumet Farm, — one of the greatest of all race horses, and
>
> WHEREAS, all Kentuckians are justly proud of their homeland — the beautiful Blue Grass State of Kentucky — proud of its historical associations, its culture, its gallant men and lovely women — taking special pride in its splendid stock farms, famed throughout the entire world for their beauty and successful breeding of innumerable record-breaking thoroughbreds of all classes, and

WHEREAS, high on the list of favorites of the racing world stands WHIRLAWAY, the greatest money-maker of them all, of whom we are specially proud, and who added inestimable value to the fame of the Blue Grass,

NOW, THEREFORE, I, R. Mack Oldham, Mayor, take pleasure and consider it a privilege to proclaim Sunday, August 8, 1943, as WHIRLAWAY DAY in Lexington, and invite the participation and interest of all horse-lovers in the festivities and ceremonies which will welcome the homecoming and retirement of this great horse to the green pastures and meadowlands of Calumet Farm.

Several thousand people flocked to Calumet Farm that day to welcome Whirlaway home. The occasion attracted horse-loving celebrities and well-wishers from near and far. The roads leading to and from Calumet Farms held hitchhikers and local people walking on their way to see this champion. Undoubtedly, the event would have attracted even more had not gasoline and transportation shortages interfered.

Among those present was Whirly's "assistant trainer," movie actor Don Ameche, who was interviewed on a nationwide radio broadcast immediately preceding the celebration. The program included tributes to Whirlaway by several of the outstanding horsemen of America and civic leaders as well as a "welcome home" address by Kentucky Congressman Virgil Chapman. Before the program ended, Warren Wright expressed his sincere thanks to all who had had anything to do with making "Whirlaway Day" possible. Then, as photographers' bulbs flashed and the crowd strained in anticipation of seeing the champion, Whirly was led, nodding as though he sensed the importance of the event, down the cinder path directly in front of the speaker's platform.

As part of the celebration, Lexington's *Herald-Leader* carried a special section on "Whirlaway Day," featuring tributes by Clem McCarthy, nationally known sports commentator, and Alex Bower, sports columnist for *The Herald-Leader*.

Whirlaway's last public appearance on home-coming day, put on for him by the town.

McCarthy, whose staccato voice had long become legendary calling horse races, wrote an editorial for the event in which he tells what he admired greatly about Whirly:

> . . . his speed, his gameness, his innate consistency, his good manners about the stable, in the paddock, on post parade, at the starting gate, his endurance and his soundness. But the two things I liked best were his grand heart and good sense.

He went on to say that Whirlaway was among the greatest American racehorses of all time:

> . . . He broke records and forced others to break them; he carried weight-a-plenty; he was consistent and raced like a true champion.

Alex Bower's tribute to Whirlaway was a poem he wrote for *The Herald-Leader*, which appeared adjacent to Clem McCarthy's editorial:

WHIRLAWAY

Swift as a tempest he swirled through the stretch
Like a hurricane gust that the wire rushed to meet.
Living his name as he whipped round the bend
Forging his fame in the contest's white heat.
Poise snugged the reins as the field left the gate
Mocking the vanguard that fought for the lead.
Then fury unfettered the lightning that blazed
Down the lane with a searing, unquenchable speed.
Tail flaunting wide in the wake of his course,
Throngs screaming shrill as the pacemakers died,
Matchless in courage, unflagging, alert
He winged past the weary with lengthening stride.
Cast in the mold of a thoroughbred king —
Trained for the battles that search out the heart,
Charged with the sureness that dwells in the strong,
He looked like a titan and lived to the part.

— Alex Bower

It is interesting to note that at the time Warren Wright had made Whirlaway's retirement official, he had only mentioned his horse's "contribution to racing." It would have surprised no one if the master of Calumet had instead used the occasion to highlight Whirly's money-winning record, his great Triple Crown victories, and other significant individual accomplishments. Under similar circumstances, other owners might have seized the opportunity to praise their horse's achievements on the track. When Warren Wright introduced the concept of "contribution to racing" in evaluating Whirlaway's track career, he raised thoroughbred racing to a plane it had never before enjoyed. And that is the level on which Whirlaway must be judged in order to appreciate fully his stature as a thoroughbred racehorse.

After carefully detailing Whirlaway's career through 60 races, it is no small task to summarize his many achievements in a few paragraphs. There are several factors to be considered in evaluating a thoroughbred's record as a racer: speed, durability, courage, consistency in performance, caliber of competition, and ability to carry extra weight in handicap races. Two criteria unique to Whirlaway's accomplishments must be added to this list: the instinct to sense the importance of a given race, and his deeds of valor on behalf of the Armed Forces, USO, and Red Cross during the 1942 racing season.

Speed is the starting point for judging racehorses. The other factors always follow the ability to finish first in the race. Whirly possessed an abundance of speed, but it was his innate ability to accelerate in the late stages of a race that set him apart from other greats of the turf. His explosive speed showed itself in his first race as a two-year-old. He was all over the track during the race, but still won. It took a year to find a jockey who could manage this speed to advantage. When Eddie Arcaro rode Whirlaway to victory with consummate ease in the 1941 Kentucky Derby and set a track record that lasted 21 years, Warren Wright and Ben Jones knew that at last such a rider had been found.

Whirlaway is the only thoroughbred in turf history to establish a consistent pattern of finishing races faster than he started them. A few horses have accomplished this rare feat occasionally during their racing careers, but Whirly made it a habit.

In his book *Ainslie's Complete Guide to Thoroughbred Racing*, Tom Ainslie describes the sight of a thoroughbred coming on strong to pass four or five others in the stretch as

> . . . mostly optical illusion. It obviously is running faster than the others. But it may be actually slowing down. It passes its rivals because they are "backing up" — decelerating more rapidly. . . . The stretch-runner in no circumstances runs as rapidly as it did in the earlier stages of the race.

In most cases, Ainslie's theory about the stretch run is true, but Whirlaway's speed in the stretch was no illusion. Whirly performed this so-called impossible task in three of his greatest races as a three-year-old, the Kentucky Derby, the Preakness, and the Travers Stakes. He repeated the feat often as a four-year-old, including his stunning victories in the Dixie, Brooklyn, and Massachusetts handicaps.

Even as a two-year-old, Whirlaway showed great finishing speed. Ben Jones was quick to take advantage of this talent and trained the colt to save his explosive speed for the stretch, where Mr. Longtail usually bid farewell to the other horses.

After demonstrating Whirly's spectacular and explosive stretch-running ability by riding him to victory in both the Kentucky Derby and the Preakness within a week's time, Eddie Arcaro commented on the colt's talent for increasing his speed in the mad dash for home:

> When you speak to this horse, he gets to the other horses faster than any horse I ever rode.

Whirlaway's racing career is resplendent with displays of instant speed. Even with over 50 years as a backdrop, his electrifying Kentucky Derby finish remains unequaled. In 1942, Whirly set two track records at Aqueduct, the mile-and-an-eighth Celt Purse and the mile-and-a-quarter Brooklyn Handicap, races run only four days apart. Then 17 days later, he set another track record in the mile-and-an-eighth Massachusetts Handicap. In addition, he set a new Dwyer Stakes record in 1941 and later that year tied Cavalcade's 1934 track record for the American Derby, both races run over a distance of a mile and a quarter.

Whirlaway kept sportswriters busy leafing through amplified dictionaries looking for words to coin new expressions that would adequately describe his dazzling speed: Calumet Comet, Kentucky Thunderbolt, the Flying Tail, Monarch of the Stretch, Bronze Bullet, Ghost Horse, Express Train, and Jet Propulsion in Horseflesh.

When Whirlaway's speed records alone are taken into account, it becomes more difficult to understand why modern sports analysts continually neglect to recognize him as one of the truly great thoroughbreds of turf history. This oversight cries out for redress when Whirly's 1942 records are placed in proper perspective. In the three record-breaking races of that year, Whirly carried from 5 to 22 pounds more than his nearest competitor and still won the races and set track records in all three. In the Massachusetts Handicap he carried 130 pounds, 22 more than the second-place finisher, and set a record for the mile-and-an-eighth distance that remained unbroken for 43 years.

Add durability and consistency to the mix, and Whirlaway's track feats take on an even brighter glow. His record of never being withdrawn from any of the 60 career races in which he was entered stands alone in the annals of the turf. He gave new meaning to the title "iron horse." In his three prime years of racing, he is the only thoroughbred of championship quality to win 32 races. Clem McCarthy said, "Whirlaway never turned in a bad race." John Kieran depicted the colt's consistency and durability in these words:

> Here's a horse that gets around, starts regularly, picks up heavy weight and goes to the races where the competition is keenest.

Among his credentials, Whirlaway possessed another rare quality for a racehorse: the ability to sense the importance of a particular race. In 1940, Ben Jones started training Whirlaway as a two-year-old with one main goal in mind, that of eventually entering him in the 1941 Kentucky Derby. This had been the race Warren Wright had wanted a horse of his to win for ten years, without success. Running in the Derby, Whirlaway seemed possessed with winning. As Eddie Arcaro, Whirly's rider in that race, said later, there was no way he could hold the colt back once they had entered the stretch and headed for the finish line.

In much the same manner, Whirlaway won the other Triple Crown races and later that year, the Travers Stakes. Then as a four-year-old he won the Massachusetts Handicap with the same kind of performance, dethroning Seabiscuit as the world's leading money-winner. A few starts later, in the same vein, he became the turf's first half-million dollar thoroughbred by winning the Jockey Club Gold Cup race, carrying top weight over the two-mile distance and beating a strong field, which included the champion three-year-old of 1942, Alsab. Overall, out of his record-breaking total earnings of $561,161, all but $12,825 was won in the most important races of his day.

Courage, constant and renewable, was required for Whirlaway to meet the standards suggested by John Kieran of starting regularly, picking up heavy weight, and going to races where the competition was the keenest. It was Whirlaway's courage and durability that endeared him most to his loyal racing fans.

Whirlaway's fearless action on the track is best illustrated by his ability to carry heavy weight, in race after race, over long distances. He was top-weighted throughout his racing career, in most of his races as a two-year-old and in all of his races at three and four; in his 22 races of 1942, he carried from 10 to 29 pounds more than his best of company, was weighted with 128 pounds or more in 13 of those races and 130 or more pounds in 10 of the last 15. In 19 of the 22 races he ran that year, he covered distances of over a mile; four of them were from a mile and a half up to two miles and a quarter.

Despite the imposition of heavy weight and having to race continually without adequate rest between starts, Whirlaway still won most of the important races of that day open to three- and four-year-olds. It's quite conceivable that he could have won even more of his 1942 races if he had not been required to carry burdensome weight so often over such long distances on tracks that were at times threatening to both horse and rider.

Whirly's performance in the Washington Handicap on October 24, 1942, at the Laurel Race Track in Maryland, was typical of his class act on the turf. After running in 18 consecutive races, including all the big feature races for the War Emergency Relief Fund, Whirlaway came to Laurel late in the racing season for the express purpose of helping the smaller track raise its quota for the war fund.

Another important criterion should be used in evaluating records of champion racehorses; that is the caliber of opponents faced in competition. Some modern turf writers have suggested that Whirlaway's opposition was generally weak, thereby discounting his racing stature. It would be far more accurate to say that overall, Whirly faced stronger competition than that of most thoroughbreds of championship caliber.

Our Boots, Porter's Cap, Dispose, and Market Wise faced Whirly in the Kentucky Derby, all with outstanding records to that date. War Relic had just set a new record for the Massachusetts Handicap two weeks prior to tangling with Whirly in the Saranac Special during the summer of 1941. Attention was a determined rival who ran many strong races against Whirlaway in three years of competition.

In 1942, Whirlaway faced two great handicap horses in the Dixie Handicap, Challedon and Mioland. He opposed Doublrab, a sprinter who set a world record for five-and-three-fourths furlongs on July 18, 1942. Later in the fall of that year, he ran against Alsab and Bolingbroke. Alsab had set records earlier in the Preakness and Withers Mile. Bolingbroke set a new American record for the mile and a half at Belmont in the Manhattan Handicap on September 26, 1942, a record that stood for 15 years until Gallant Man broke it in the 1957 running of the Belmont Stakes.

Whirlaway was never withdrawn from a single race because of having to run against strong opponents or having to carry extra weight, reasons causing some owners and trainers to purposefully orchestrate the schedule of races for their horses in order to avoid the possibility of serious injury and/or defeat. Whirlaway never enjoyed that luxury in 60 consecutive races, and he faced a strong field in most of those contests.

No valid evaluation of Whirlaway's racing career is possible without the inclusion of the unique role he played in the war mobilization effort of the United States during 1942, something no writer or commentator has mentioned since. When that noble effort on behalf of Armed Forces personnel is placed in perspective, Whirlaway automatically enters the winner's circle as the only war hero in the long history of thoroughbred racing.

At the time of Whirly's retirement, Warren Wright had alluded to the horse's part in the war effort and his contribution to racing. But it should not have been left for Warren Wright or Ben Jones to voice this rather obvious fact. Instead, recognition of Whirlaway's contribution should have come from the National Turf Committee.

Whirlaway had participated in 22 races during 1942 at 12 different tracks. He was always the favorite and feature attraction for the war-relief races because of his tremendous drawing power. As Pearl Kroll of *Time* magazine wrote of Whirlaway's walkover race at Pimlico, "Whirly can draw a crowd even if he does nothing but swish his long golden tail." In those 22 races, Whirlaway's participation was a prime factor in attracting over 500,000 people; therein lies the main source of thoroughbred racing's phenomenal success in raising $3 million for the War Emergency Relief Fund. In races at three separate tracks, Whirly was responsible of raising over $300,000: Brooklyn Handicap at Aqueduct — $100,000; Butler Handicap at Empire City — $100,000; Narragansett Special at Narragansett Park — $101,804.

In other war-relief races in which Whirlaway was featured, varying sums of $30,000 or more were collected. In addition to those amounts, ten percent of Whirly's earnings — which was considerable for those days — was given to the war effort through the purchase of War Bonds.

And what did it cost to maintain this superstar of the racetrack during his nonstop racing campaign of 1942? First of all, Whirlaway asked for no salary and employed no agent; he required no expenses for hospital care and incurred no loss of purse winnings because of absenteeism from work; his only request was for some oats, a measure of hay, and a few carrots now and then — a $4.40 per day expense.

During three years of unremitting hoofbeats around the racing oval, Whirlaway compiled records of unquestioned and lasting values — accomplishments and feats of which legends are made. Yet the passage of time has greatly diminished their glow. Today, over half a century later, Whirlaway's name is rarely, if ever, mentioned in media discussions of great racehorses. A few turf writers have included Whirlaway in anthologies dealing largely with Triple Crown winners, but even those narratives are cursory, failing to place his complete record in perspective and downplaying or omitting certain feats that really set him apart from other thoroughbred champions.

During ten years of thorough research, my greatest thrust was directed at finding an answer to the puzzling question: Why is a racehorse in possession of such imposing credentials not ranked among those deemed to be the greatest thoroughbreds of the century?

Leading sports columnists who witnessed and reported on Whirlaway's performances on the track never questioned the colt's greatness as a racehorse. But unfortunately for Whirlaway, those statesmen of the turf scene are no longer available for comment.

Thirty years after Whirlaway began racing, and several years after Warren Wright and Ben Jones had departed from the earthly scene, *The Blood-Horse* published a series on thoroughbred racehorses called *The Great Ones*. Jimmy Jones, who had assisted his father with the training of Calumet Farm horses, and had praised Whirlaway highly at that time, was asked by *The Blood-Horse* to submit an evaluation on Whirlaway's racing career for Number 75 of the anthology, the one on Whirlaway. Surprisingly, Jimmy referred to him as "a nut":

> The colt wouldn't compare in any way with a lot of good horses we had or a lot other people had. . . . Whirlaway had only one style and you had to set it up his way. He was just a hard bird to handle, that's all.

The *Daily Racing Form's* 20th Century Hall of Fame does not include Whirlaway on its distinguished membership roll; yet only 3 of the 14 horses chosen through 1978 were Triple Crown winners; 4 of those chosen, Man O' War, Citation, Count Fleet, and Secretariat, never ran as four-year-olds, and the other 10 didn't compile outstanding records in both their three- and four-year-old campaigns.

Whirlaway is also missing from another list of great racehorses. The *Book of Lists #2*, published in 1980, contains a list of "the ten greatest thoroughbreds of all time," selected by Sam Lewin. On the list, Lewin names Count Fleet as the greatest thoroughbred of all time. He also includes Secretariat on the list but was hesitant in the selection saying he wasn't sure the top ten should include "a horse who never raced beyond a three-year-old." Based on that premise, it is difficult to understand why his number one selection was Count Fleet, a three-year-old who was retired from racing with an injury after winning the Belmont Stakes in 1943. And if the criterion of racing beyond the three-year-old season were really significant in selecting the greatest thoroughbreds, why was Whirlaway not included, a racehorse that probably compiled the greatest four-year-old record in turf history?

In 1968, Florida's Gulfstream Park staged what was called a "Computer Race of the Century," wherein supposedly the complete records of great horses of the century to that time were computerized to determine the winner. However, no set criteria were given in selecting horses for the race. Most experts would agree that all 12 horses chosen were among the greatest of their day, but based on the horses that were selected, it is difficult to understand why Whirlaway was omitted from the entries.

The computer race was evidently patterned after the Kentucky Derby with all horses carrying equal weight of 126 pounds for one mile and a quarter. Of the 12 entries, only three had been Triple Crown winners — War Admiral, Count Fleet, and Citation; five never ran in the Kentucky Derby — Tom Fool, Kelso, Equipoise, Buckpasser, and Man O' War; the other four entries were Exterminator, Swaps, Nashua, and Native Dancer. Exterminator and Swaps won the Kentucky Derby, while Nashua and Native Dancer finished second in that prestigious race.

In the "Computer Race of the Century," Citation electronically defeated Man O' War with a time of two minutes. Notably, not one of the 12 horses entered in the computer race who actually ran in the Derby came close to covering the mile-and-a-quarter distance in two minutes. Citation ran the 1948 Derby in 2:05 2/5. Man O' War was not entered in the 1920 Derby, but in his match race with Sir Barton that year, he won that mile-and-a-quarter race in a time of 2:03 carrying 120 pounds to Sir Barton's 126. Whirlaway, not among the electronic race entries, had won the 1941 Kentucky Derby with a record time of 2:01 2/5, a faster time than any of the horses in the computer race, a record Derby time that lasted 21 years, and faster than the times posted by 13 of the last 14 Derby champions through the running of the 1994 classic.

In a seemingly endless search for some tangible recognition of Whirlaway's unique and remarkable racing career, I journeyed to the National Racing Hall of Fame during the summer of 1981. It is part of the National Museum of Racing located in Saratoga Springs, New York. The Museum was founded in 1950 and contains a truly outstanding collection of paintings, sculpture, and memorabilia of thoroughbred racing from this country and around the world. Over 70 thoroughbreds have thus far been elected to membership in the Hall of Fame. Some member horses started racing in the early years of the 19th century. No attempt is made to rank the thoroughbreds, but the list includes all Triple Crown winners and others considered to have compiled outstanding records in their racing careers.

Since Whirlaway had been elected to membership in the Racing Hall of Fame, I expected to find within the Museum's confines some valuable information pertaining to his racing record. Instead, all I discovered was a single name plate, signifying only that he had been elected to membership. All other member horses had at least a portrait or photograph on display by which a museum visitor might identify a certain horse. Several other thoroughbreds on the Hall's honor roll had numerous trophies and awards on display in their behalf. I asked the museum caretaker why something identifying Whirlaway was not in evidence and was informed that all displays at the Museum were originally donated and that nothing as yet had been given in Whirlaway's behalf, an oversight that also seemed strange to the caretaker.

This experience served to intensify my resolve to gain full recognition for Whirlaway's monumental contributions to racing. To treat Whirlaway's many gallant deeds on the track in such a careless and indifferent manner has denied thoroughbred racing a large portion of its richest heritage and certainly its most glorious moment in history. John Madden, Sir Barton's owner, once answered critics attempting to discredit racing's first Triple Crown winner by saying, "Opinions die, records live." But even significant recorded deeds will soon die away if they are not adequately preserved and nurtured for the enlightenment of future generations. It is just such a fate that has befallen many of Whirlaway's historic accomplishments in racing.

After exhausting all known and visible sources of information pertaining to Whirlaway's racing career, I returned to the fount of credible research: archives, libraries, personal interviews, and copies of old newspapers and other publications, many of which are no longer in circulation.

Whirlaway was widely acclaimed in his day as one of the greatest racehorses of the century. Words of praise for his racing prowess filled the columns of leading contemporary sportswriters, including such legendary scribes as Grantland Rice, John Kieran, Bill Corum, Bob Considine, Clem McCarthy, and Red Smith. Even Jimmy Jones voiced a different opinion of Whirlaway in those days when he praised him in an article in the Louisville *Courier-Journal*, following the 1941 Kentucky Derby.

Most modern turf writers tend to classify Whirlaway as a "one-run horse," usually meaning he relied solely on a final burst of speed to win races, and on that basis alone should not be recognized as one of the century's greatest thoroughbreds. Such thinking suggests that Whirly's usual pattern of running a race revealed a serious weakness in his racing ability. A close examination of the horse's total racing career proves just the opposite.

Actually, Whirlaway's wait-until-the-stretch style of racing was by design and did not result from the horse's inability to change his pattern of running. Ben Jones considered Whirly's stretch-running talent his greatest asset. Jones deliberately trained the colt to run that way, and the strategy worked well. Many times opposing horses would wait up to take Whirly on in the stretch drive, but Mr. Longtail did not return the favor. He successfully employed that style of racing in winning the Kentucky Derby and the Preakness. In 1942, he also won the Massachusetts Handicap that way. *The Boston Globe* headline of July 16, 1942, proclaiming Whirlaway's victory in that race vividly illustrates his phenomenal success as a "one-run" horse:

> Whirlaway wins in Whirlaway's own copyrighted fashion — starts last, makes bid on final turn, wins in record time and for record earnings.

Although Whirlaway won many of his greatest races with a blazing burst of speed in the stretch drive, others were won by using a different racing plan. The Calumet colt won each of the Triple Crown races from a different vantage point — the Kentucky Derby from near last, the Preakness from dead last, and the Belmont Stakes by leading for over a mile in the mile-and-a-half race; and he won all three races with consummate ease. In addition to the Belmont, Whirly won four other races in 1941 by leading most of the way: Dwyer Stakes, Arlington Allowance, American Derby, and Lawrence Realization. Following the same pattern, he won the Trenton, Governor Bowie, and Washington handicaps in 1942. In other 1942 races that year, he was close to the front runners during most of the race.

Eddie Arcaro rode Whirlaway to victory in the Triple Crown races without once using the whip. After the Belmont Stakes race, Eddie said,

> It was easy. I found the early pace too slow to suit us there by the quarterpole. . . . I just leaned over and told Whirly "let's get running." That's what he did. . . . When I wanted him to run, he ran. That's about all you can ask of any horse.

Joe Palmer, esteemed writer for *The Blood-Horse*, made an even stronger statement in support of Whirlaway's unusual racing style:

> Whirlaway carries in his armament the deadliest weapon a thoroughbred can have — an annihilating burst of speed which he can apparently turn on at any stage of the race.

Actually, there is scant evidence to support the opinion that "Whirlaway had only one style and you had to set it up his way." In fact, it would be more accurate to state that Whirlaway could win a race in any acceptable fashion, providing he wasn't shackled with too much weight while running and was ridden by a jockey capable of managing the colt's explosive speed at critical stages of a race.

Those privileged to follow Whirlaway's racing career from start to finish never questioned his greatness as a racer. Starting in the early spring of 1941 and continuing until the end of his career, Whirly was the favorite in 40 consecutive races. He was the most popular sports figure of 1941 and 1942, drawing record crowds to racetracks where he appeared, including Churchill Downs, Pimlico, Belmont Park, and Saratoga. Fans flocked to his races, which attracted people to the track who had never been there before and who were there not just to wager on the race's outcome, but primarily to see him run. If there had been an award for a "people's horse," Whirlaway would have most assuredly been its recipient. In *Great Horses of Our Times*, M. A. Stoneridge makes a valid point that Whirlaway's spectacular races alone might qualify him as a great thoroughbred and states:

> Horse racing is, after all, a spectator sport, and Whirlaway was a splendid star performer who invariably put on a great show.

By virtue of his tremendous gate appeal and record earnings, Whirlaway could easily be adjudged thoroughbred racing's first superstar. His average annual earnings were almost $250,000 for 1941 and 1942. The highest paid baseball pitcher of the day was Bob Feller, with an annual salary of $35,000; and Joe DiMaggio, Hall of Fame outfielder for the New York Yankees, signed with that club in 1942 for $42,500.

The Triple Crown victories of 1941 brought into clear focus Whirly's championship qualities, and he became the first thoroughbred to be hailed from coast to coast as the national champion. This eventually led to the creation of a trophy honoring all horses, past and present, achieving that feat. The presentation is made at the end of each racing season at the Thoroughbred Racing Associations dinner. If no horse achieves Triple Crown stature, then the trophy goes to a previous equine hero that had swept the three races. In *The New York Times* column of February 21, 1955, Arthur Daley described the retroactive presentation of Whirlaway's Triple Crown trophy:

> The last horse to be given the Triple Crown trophy . . . in absentia . . . was Whirlaway. . . . Newsreel shots of Mr. Longtail rocketing to victory in each of the classics . . . left folks gasping.
>
> . . . No one would have been surprised if Whirly had come down the homestretch doing cartwheels. . . .

In Whirlaway's day, newsreel film was in black and white. If the "knowing and track-wise" hardboots of today could view those same film shots of Whirly's Triple Crown races in living color on a wide-screen television, some radical changes in lists of great racehorses would, no doubt, follow.

No clear consensus could ever be reached on how well Whirlaway would fare racing against leading thoroughbreds of the modern era. Conditions under which thoroughbreds race today are far different from those of Whirlaway's time. Racetracks nowadays are carefully manicured and favor speed horses in setting track records. Today's leading thoroughbreds race less frequently, carry less weight in handicap races, are never required to enter races over a mile and a half, and are transported by air to the different tracks throughout the country instead of being shipped by rail car, as was Whirlaway. If a thoroughbred of his caliber raced today, very little imagination is required to believe that many track records would fall by the wayside, including records in attendance not only at the racetracks but in the added millions viewing the Triple Crown races on television.

If Whirlaway raced today, turf fans would probably not see him run following the Triple Crown races. Once his great speed had been established in those races, he would undoubtedly be retired and sold for multimillions as a sire to some syndicate. If this present policy is continued by owners of potential thoroughbred champions, racing fans may no longer be privileged to witness the best thoroughbreds race against strong opposition, and there may be no entries in the four-year-old column for such horses.

The apparent obsession for instant wealth practiced by horse breeders in the past 10 to 20 years reached new heights when Devil's Bag was sold to a breeding syndicate for $36 million long before he had reached maturity. And yet this thoroughbred billed as the next superstar of racing somehow never even made it to the starting gate of the 1984 Kentucky Derby. Devil's Bag was retired from racing, reportedly with a minor leg injury, just days before he was to unleash his vaunted speed in the first major test for three-year-olds.

In his *Los Angeles Times* column of May 8, 1984, Jim Murray pointed out that a thoroughbred racehorse's sole function is to run, that he doesn't earn his keep any other way. He explained that thoroughbred racing is presently losing its true identity and sense of direction because:

> . . . Breeding has now overtaken the real purpose. . . . They now breed for breeding's sake, not for racing's. It's like making soldiers so handsome and gloriously mounted that you're afraid to send them to war. . . . Super horse never gets to prove he's Super Horse. His papers just say so.

Thoroughbreds of Whirlaway's day were rated more for their long-term track records against worthy opponents than for their potential worth as a sire with only a few runs around the track. Warren Wright could easily have been justified in deciding on retirement for Whirlaway long before the end of the 1942 racing season, but fortunately for race fans, he continually gave in to the popular demand for another Whirlaway race. The master of Calumet demonstrated a commitment to horse racing as a spectator sport by allowing Whirlaway to run in 16 races as a two-year-old, 20 as a three-year-old, and 22 back-to-back races at age four. Such dedication to the true spirit of thoroughbred racing is no longer prevalent on the track today. Instead, the sport of kings now operates in a vacuum of changed values.

The handling of Spend A Buck, the 1985 Kentucky Derby winner, presents an interesting comparison to Whirlaway. When owner Dennis Diaz took Spend A Buck to Garden State for entry in the Jersey Derby instead of continuing the quest for Triple Crown honors by running him in the Preakness at Pimlico, the prime goal of horse racing in the 1980s was placed in true perspective. As a part of the promotional management by Robert Brennan, securities investor, who had reopened Garden State Park on April 1, 1985, Dennis Diaz could, and did, as a result of Spend A Buck winning the Jersey Derby on May 27, pick up an all-time record purse of $2.6 million.

Following his Jersey Derby win, Spend A Buck did not run in any of the remaining traditional races for three-year-olds in 1985. He was retired to the breeding farm before the running of the Breeders' Cup Classic at Aqueduct, which by winning, could have added countless millions to his value as a sire — certainly an amount far in excess of the $2.6 million won at Garden State earlier in the year.

Spend A Buck became horse racing's instant leading money-winner in 1985 by narrowly finishing first over a less-than-strong field in Garden State's Jersey Derby.

In contrast, by 1942, Whirlaway had already become top-money horse when he raced at Garden State. And his trip to turfdom's money-winning circle was accomplished through his hard work and championship abilities, though it had taken almost three years of continuous racing to reach that monetary pinnacle. During that time, Whirlaway had to start 46 times and win practically all the big-purse races of his day, including the Triple Crown races, the Travers Stakes, the American Derby, and the Massachusetts Handicap.

This tale of two horses contains other interesting contrasts. The $130 million Garden State track of 1985, with its glassed-in paddock, overhanging balconies, and 17 different levels of restaurants and cafes, from nacho stands to a marble and crystal dining room, is light years away in appearance from the bare-bones structure of 1942. When the New Jersey track, first built at a modest cost of $2 million, held its opening race in that crucial war year, finishing touches on the steel and wood structure were still in progress, and carrier pigeons had to be used to dispatch racing results to the wire offices in Camden and Philadelphia.

With the seemingly unlimited financial backing of Wall Street, securities investor Robert Brennan actually bought success for Garden State's reopening by enticing Dennis Diaz to enter the Kentucky Derby winner Spend A Buck in the Jersey Derby and try for an almost sure chance of winning the $2.6 million prize.

In 1942, Ben Jones, with permission from owner Warren Wright, brought Whirlaway to Garden State's first meet out of friendship for Jimmy Loftus, the track's press agent, but more specifically for the purpose of helping the new racing oval raise its pledged contribution to the War Emergency Relief Fund.

It could be said that the Garden State track paid dearly for Spend A Buck's Jersey Derby victory in 1985; yet just the appearance of Whirlaway at the site in 1942 had rescued the struggling track from serious financial loss at the gate. An overflow crowd had turned out to watch Whirly run in the Trenton Handicap on the last day of the meet, resulting in record receipts of $883,962, thereby enabling Garden State to make a sizable donation of $57,457 to the war fund. And the cost to Garden State Park for Whirlaway's victory there in 1942 was a token sum of $8,500, plus a $200 War Bond awarded to Ben Jones by track president Eugene Mori.

Thoroughbred racing has come a long way since 1942, but the values used to assess a thoroughbred's track record has undergone major revision in the past 50 years.

But in spite of his incredible record, Whirlaway is not a household word among contemporary turf fans. His name will not be found in syndicated columns of sportswriters when comparisons are drawn between leading racehorses of today and those of the past. After being allowed to suffer the erosion and oversight of over 50 years, Whirlaway's legacy has now become only a blur on the pages of thoroughbred racing history.

Clem McCarthy, who probably called more important horse races than any track announcer in turf history, commented on Whirlaway's reputation as a racehorse, and at the same time spoke for bona fide racing fans everywhere when he said he feared American racing would not see his like in many a year. He said,

> I only wish it were given a thoroughbred like Whirlaway to have strong legs and feet that would enable him to campaign until he was eight, nine or ten — I like to have my good horses stay around a long time!

Arthur Daley of *The New York Times* expressed the universal acclaim given Whirlaway by racing fans of that day:

> . . . Whirlaway was one of the great horses of the century. Certainly he was one of the most beloved.

The best appraisal of Whirlaway may have been Ben Jones's:

> . . . There may be better horses, but for me there can be only one Whirlaway.

Whirlaway, 1944.

Epilogue

AFTER his retirement from racing in 1943, Whirlaway spent the next seven years enjoying the peace and quiet of Kentucky's Blue Grass countryside, a striking contrast to his life on the racetrack with its special community of sights and sounds. By 1949, Whirly had made the list of 20 leading sires, having produced 52 winners out of 71 starters, including 7 stakes winners.

During those years immediately following retirement,

Whirlaway remained high in public favor. In a poll taken by the Lexington *Herald-Leader* in 1948, Whirly was voted the "Most Famous Horse in the Blue Grass," succeeding Man O' War, who had died the previous year. He was chosen by a substantial margin over such other famous retirees as War Admiral, Count Fleet, Alsab, and Armed.

One year before Whirlaway received this honor, Marcel Boussac, one of Europe's most celebrated thoroughbred breeders and owners, came to the United States in search of a sire needed to help rebuild the French thoroughbred stock that had been seriously depleted during the German occupation. While in Lexington, Boussac became an immediate captive to Whirlaway's charm and exclaimed in his native language, "*C'est pour moi.*" The French textile magnate began negotiations at once with Warren Wright to lease the Calumet stallion. After three years of turning down offers, Wright finally acceded to Boussac's wishes. The agreement was announced in Louisville's *Courier-Journal* on July 14, 1950:

> Whirlaway, Calumet Farm's great Triple Crown Champion of 1941 and for five years the top horse on the list of the world's leading money-winners, will be sent to France for three seasons at stud. The horse is expected to be returned here on expiration of the lease with Marcel Boussac.

Later that same year, on December 28, 1950, Calumet Farm received the sad news that Warren Wright had died at his Florida home in Miami Beach. He was 75 years old and had been ill for a long time. The master of Calumet had been hospitalized in New York for several months during the fall and winter of 1949, but he had left the hospital on February 11 and later in the spring had returned to Calumet Farm. It was during his last stay at Calumet that Whirlaway's lease was finalized. He had departed for his home in Florida early in December and died several days later.

Whirlaway's first offspring in France showed such good quality and Boussac became enamored with the famous stallion that an offer was made in 1952, a year before the lease would expire to purchase Whirlaway outright. The September 21, 1952, edition of *The Courier-Journal* announced that Whirlaway had been sold to Boussac. The sale of Calumet Farm's first champion and Triple Crown winner was announced by Calumet General Manager Paul Ebelhardt, who had acted for Mrs. Warren Wright in the negotiations. Whirlaway's correspondence folder at Calumet Farm reveals that although Warren Wright would not have approved of the sale, perhaps it was the best decision to make under the circumstances.

Warren Wright's consent to send his beloved horse to France for three years probably had been done in the spirit of America's Lend-Lease program for her allies in World War II. But it would be almost inconceivable for the master of Calumet, under any circumstances, to have sold Whirlaway for any price. Whirlaway had put Calumet Farm on the map as the leading thoroughbred racing farm, and in three years of racing, he had achieved for his owner all the goals that the sport could offer. Naturally, a first champion was always number one, but not for sale.

The irony of Whirlaway's sale was made complete when on April 8, 1953, only months after the deal was finalized, it was announced that Whirlaway had died unexpectedly at Boussac's stud farm in Normandy. The stable manager, F. De Brignac, said death probably came as a result of a ruptured nerve tissue. Whirlaway had just reached 15, and this writer would like to venture the guess that the horse's death resulted more from a broken heart than from anything else.

From the day of his birth until his shipment to France 13 years later, Whirlaway had been the focus of tender love and adulation from members of the Calumet Farm family, whom Whirly had brought to center stage in the brief period of three years. Even after his retirement in 1943, Mr. Longtail was still the star attraction throughout the Blue Grass country. Then in 1950 he had been abruptly sent to France.

This sudden transplant to a faraway land with a different setting may have caused Whirlaway to experience, for the first time in his life, a feeling of rejection. And in the gamut of emotions operative in both humans and animals, rejection often leads to a broken heart.

If it were any other racehorse, it would suffice to simply say that Whirlaway was the only Triple Crown champion to be buried in France. But for Mr. Longtail, every milestone in his life was marked with a touch of destiny. He was the first colt sired by Blenheim II for Calumet Farm; he created instant fame for Warren Wright, Ben Jones, and Eddie Arcaro by sweeping to victory in the Kentucky Derby, Preakness, and Belmont; he is the only Triple Crown winner in racing history to go on and also win the Travers Stakes; his record in the 1941 Kentucky Derby held for 21 years; and his record for the mile-and-an-eighth Massachusetts Handicap of 1942 remained intact for 43 years, the longest span of time a major track record for that distance has endured in the history of the American turf.

Whirlaway was the first Triple Crown champion to be named twice as "Horse of the Year" and the only one ever to win 32 races in a thoroughbred's three prime years — as a two-, three-, and four-year old. In addition to becoming the world's leading money-winner and racing's first demimillionaire, his gallant campaign on behalf of the War Emergency Relief Fund for Armed Services personnel in 1942 represents an admirable act of patriotism.

On June 6, 1944, some 154,000 Allied troops had stormed ashore on the beaches of Normandy to knock down Hitler's Atlantic wall. The American, British, and Canadian troops launched a concerted attack on D-Day that would soon lead to the destruction of the tyranny with which Hitler had battered the peoples of Europe. Some 2,500 Allied troops lost their lives in that operation and were buried in Normandy.

Many of the Americans resting there may have witnessed Whirlaway race for their benefit during that summer of 1942 when plans were first being laid for the invasion of Europe. Others of those fallen heroes might have enjoyed a few pleasant hours in a service club or USO center made possible by Whirly's gallant campaign for soldiers and sailors who were training for D-Day at the time. From the beginning of his life, Whirlaway seemed led by destiny to his final resting place. In the end, he really belonged with his countrymen buried there in Normandy, France.

Though it was fitting for Whirlaway to be buried there, it is, by the same token, inexcusable for custodians of past glories to bury his magnificent legacy to thoroughbred racing and the land of his birth. Perhaps "out of sight, out of mind" best explains why the Whirlaway record and legacy are not mentioned in today's sports columns, commentaries, or discussions engaged in at the racetrack.

When Warren Wright died in 1950, his wife, Lucille, inherited Calumet Farm and the $82 million fortune realized from oil investments. At that point, Lucille allowed the children to run the farm with her backing when needed. Perhaps their decision to sell Whirlaway to Marcel Boussac was based on expediency and the conclusion by Calumet's new management that their first Triple Crown champion was no longer needed to enhance the Farm's thoroughbred racing empire. By 1951, Calumet Farm had actually raced many winners, including Citation, 1948 Triple Crown champion. And in the intervening years of 1946 through 1948, Calumet had experienced million-dollar earnings. But it should be remembered that when Whirlaway began his racing career in 1940, Calumet Farm was operating in the red. In his first year of racing, Whirlaway had helped support his stablemates and had vaulted Calumet's racing colors from eleventh to third on racing stable charts. Then in 1941, Whirly's winnings as the Triple Crown champion put the farm solidly in a number one position and turned red ink to black for the first time in Calumet's history as a thoroughbred racing farm. Robert F. Kelley, a sportswriter of that day, summarized Whirlaway's impact on Calumet Farm:

> The 1941 season of Whirlaway started, more or less, with the record-breaking Kentucky Derby. . . . and by the same token started Mr. and Mrs. Warren Wright's Calumet Farm toward the point where it would dominate racing and breeding more than any other similar organization in racing's history.

Whirlaway kept Calumet on top during three years of sustained racing in which he won for Calumet Farm and the Warren Wrights practically all the honors thoroughbred racing had to offer. With the momentum provided by Whirlaway, Calumet Farm kept its premier status for two decades, through 1961. Those were the glory years for Calumet Farm.

The year 1961 marked a turning point in Calumet Farm's history. By 1962, Calumet had lost its premier position as thoroughbred racing's leading farm by falling to 17th in racing stable winnings and then tumbled to 28th in 1964. Calumet made a comeback in 1978, the year Alydar, the Farm's last star performer, finished a close second to Affirmed in all three of the Triple Crown races and enabled Calumet to enjoy its seventh million-dollar year in earnings. But Calumet's comeback only lasted through 1979, the last million-dollar year. After that,

Calumet Farm began a steady decline.

The downward turn for the Farm actually began in 1978 with the death of Warren Wright, Jr., and continued four years later with the death of his mother, Lucille. At the time of Lucille's death in 1982, the Farm passed to Warren Wright's widow, Bertha, along with her two sons and two daughters. Because Bertha Wright and her children had no interest in the business, responsibility for running the Farm was left to J. T. Lundy, Bertha's son-in-law.

For the next ten years, things got progressively worse for Calumet Farm as prices for horses and real estate in the 1980s rose sharply, then plummeted. Foreign buyers from Japan and the Middle East became less visible. Risky investments were made, unpaid loans accumulated, and family relationships became strained.

The point of no return was reached in 1990 when Calumet Farm took out a loan of $2.6 million from D. Wayne Lukas racing stables. As a part of the transaction, the Lukas stables took over the responsibility of training and racing a Calumet horse named Criminal Type. Ironically, under the Lukas stable colors, Criminal Type turned out to be the 1990 "Horse of the Year." That same year Calumet sold Strike the Gold for $500,000, a colt that went on to win the 1991 Kentucky Derby for his new owner. But the fatal blow to Calumet's crumbling empire came in November 1990 when the great sire Alydar died two days after he had kicked the door in his stall and fractured a leg. Alydar was 15 at the time of his death and at the peak of his career as a stallion. He had become Calumet's "meal ticket" by earning $20 million a year in stud fees. At the time of his death, owner Bertha Wright was quoted as saying:

> It was a big blow, personally and psychologically. His stud fees were being used to keep the farm running. . . . Where do you get the money to keep it up?

From the time of Alydar's death in 1990 to just before the Keeneland thoroughbred sales in July 1991, a response to Bertha Wright's request for financial help was sought. Finally on July 11, legendary Calumet Farm, faced with reported debts of $127 million, filed for bankruptcy under Chapter 11. At the court appearance, Farm president John T. Ward said that bankruptcy was the only thing that would give management time "to search for a new buyer who can come in and protect the greatest single horse farm in the world."

The search proved fruitless, and eight months later on March 26, 1992, the thoroughbred farm that had produced two Triple Crown horses, nine Kentucky Derby champions, and six winners of the "Horse of the Year" award was placed on the auction block.

But the divestiture of the Calumet legend took an unexpected turn when aviation executive Henryk de Kwiatowski, a Polish native, arrived from his home in the Bahamas and rescued Calumet Farm from dismantling at the auction block with the high bid of $17 million and an additional $210,000 for the Calumet name. He stated that he would keep the Farm's staff and operate it as before. Kwiatowski brought tears from some and a standing ovation from 3,000 as he said,

> When I saw this place being dismantled, it was an offense to me. Not a whisker of this farm will be changed.

And thus the drama of Whirlaway and the kingdom of Calumet was brought full circle. Order was finally restored to the Blue Grass of Kentucky. At last Warren Wright, Whirlaway, Citation, and Alydar could rest in peace. The legend would continue as envisioned by the master of Calumet when Whirlaway won for the Farm its first Kentucky Derby and Triple Crown.

* * *

As I think back over the ten years of research devoted to this story of Whirlaway, many images flash across that inward screen of the mind and heart — in endless procession, images of anticipation, excitement, thrills, victory, disappointment, and heroism unparalleled on the racetrack. And one image always appears without prompting, on a wide screen, in full color.

On the trail of seemingly endless research, one of the first places I visited was Churchill Downs in Louisville. I arrived at that historic racecourse early one day, long before time for a scheduled race. I roamed the empty stands and viewed various areas of the track where over a hundred runnings of the Kentucky Derby had been staged. After a while, my gaze became fixed on the final treacherous turn of the oval where on May 3, 1941, Whirlaway had made his bid for fame.

At that moment, I turned my mind loose in the time tunnel of the turf and could hear yet another track announcer describe the final seconds of the 1941 Kentucky Derby:

> Here comes Whirlaway . . . around the final turn of Churchill Downs, exploding from the host of worthy contenders like sunshine from behind a dark cloud, opening a corridor through the wind, challenging the speed of sound to new horizons. . . .

Bibliography

BOOKS

AINSLIE, Tom. ***Ainslie's Complete Guide to Thoroughbred Racing***. *(New York: Simon and Schuster, 1979).*

Alsop, Joseph. ***FDR: A Centenary Remembrance***. *(New York: Viking Press, 1982).*

Bailey, Ronald H., ***et al. The Home Front: U.S.A.*** *(Alexandria, VA: World War II Time-Life Books, 1979).*

The Blood-Horse Anthology: The Great Ones. (Lexington, KY: Thoroughbred Owners and Breeders Association, 1970).

Collier, Richard. *The War in the Desert.* (Alexandria, VA: World War II Time-Life Books, 1980).

Correspondents of Time, Life, Fortune. *December 7: The First Thirty Days.* (New York: Alfred A. Knopf, 1942).

Craig, William A. *Enemy at the Gates: The Battle for Stalingrad.* (New York: EP Dutton and Company, Inc., 1973).

Drager, Marvin. *The Most Glorious Crown.* (New York: Winchester Press, 1975).

Elson, Robert T. *Prelude to War.* (Alexandria, VA: World War II Time-Life Books, 1979).

Glass, Margaret B. *The Calumet Story.* (Lexington, KY: Calumet Farm, 1979).

Hirsch, Joe and Gene Plowden. *In the Winner's Circle — The Jones Boys of Calumet Farm* (New York: Mason and Lipscomb Publishers, 1974).

Hoofprints of the Century. (Lexington, KY: Thoroughbred Record Company, Inc., 1963).

Lingman, Richard R. *Don't You Know There's a War On?* (New York: G.P. Putnam's Sons, 1970).

Menke, Frank G., comp. *Encyclopedia of Sports.* (New York: A. S. Barnes and Company, 1975).

Mosley, Leonard. *The Battle of Britain.* (Alexandria, VA: World War II Time-Life Books, 1979).

Mosley, Leonard. *Marshall: Hero of Our Times.* (New York: Hearst Books, 1982).

Pepe, Phil and Zander Hollander. *The Book of Sports Lists #2.* (Los Angeles: Pinnacle Books, 1980).

Prange, Gordon W. *At Dawn We Slept.* (New York: McGraw-Hill, Inc., 1981).

Smythe, R. H. *The Mind of the Horse.* (New York: Stephen Greene Press, 1965).

Stoneridge, M. A. *Great Horses of Our Times.* (New York: Doubleday and Company, Inc., 1972).

Thayer, Bert Clark. *Whirlaway.* (New York: Duell, Sloan and Pearce, 1946).

Time-Life Books, editors, *Japan at War.* (Alexandria, VA: World War II Time-Life Books, 1980).

Wallechinsky, David, Irving Wallace and Amy Wallace. *The People's Almanac: The Book of Lists #1.* (New York: Bantam Books, Inc., 1977).

Wernick, Robert. *Blitzkrieg.* (Alexandria, VA: World War II Time-Life Books, 1979).

Wilding, Suzanne and Anthony Del Balso. *The Triple Crown Winners.* (New York: Parent's Magazine Press, 1975).

NEWSPAPERS AND PERIODICALS

The Baltimore Sun — 1941, May 4, 10, 11; June 8, 26; August 17
1942, May 6, 7, 30, 31; June 14, 21, 22, 23, 27, 28, 29; July 5, 16; October 28, 29; November 10, 12; December 13
1948, January 4

Belmont Stakes Press Book, New York Racing Association, June 7, 1980.

The Blood-Horse (Lexington, KY) — 1941, May 10, 17

The Boston Globe — 1941, May 1, 5, 6, 9, 11, 25; June 4; August 17
1942, July 2, 6, 15, 16; August 5; September 11, 13, 20

Chicago *Daily News* — 1942, July 16
1943, June 28

Chicago Tribune — 1940, July 3
1941, May 4; July 17, 27; August 21

The Courier-Journal (Louisville, KY) — 1941, May 3, 4, 5; June 8
1950, July 14
1952, September 21
1953, April 8

Daily Racing Form (Hightstown, NJ) — 1941, May 5, 12
1942, June 24
1943, *American Racing Manual*

Daily Racing Form (cont.)
(Hightstown, NJ) — 1953, April 8
The Herald-Leader
(Lexington, KY) — 1940, June 22, 23; July 27; August 31; September 8, 25, 28; October 4, 12, 19, 25; November 2, 5, 10
1941, February 2, 7, 9, 18; March 22, 28; April 6, 13, 20, 24, 29; May 1, 2, 3, 4, 8, 11, 21, 23; June 8, 10, 22; July 6, 26; August 6, 17, 24, 31
1942, September 22
1943, August 8, 9
1948, January 4
1949, January 23
1950, July 13; December 29
1953, April 8
1991, July 12
1992, April 6
Kentucky Derby Yearbook, Churchill Downs, May 1, 1982.
Look magazine, September 9, 1941: Hallett Abend, "Why We Will Fight Japan — Soon."
Los Angeles *Examiner* — 1941, May 8, 11; October 27, 29; November 12, 14
Los Angeles *Herald Examiner* — 1985, May 21
Los Angeles Times — 1941, May 4; October 28, 29; December 8
1942, January 6
1984, May 8
1985, May 8, 12; August 25; November 1
The Louisville Times — 1941, May 9
Newsweek magazine — 1941, May 12, 19; June 16; August 11
New York *Daily Mirror* — 1941, May 8
New York Daily News — 1941, May 1, 2, 4, 11
New York Herald Tribune — 1941, May 4, 11
1953, April 8
New York *Journal American* — 1941, May 1, 4, 11, 13; June 6, 8
New York Racing Association Media Guide, New York Racing Asso-

ciation, 1982.

The New York Times — 1938 through 1942
1943, January through August
1953, April 8
1955, February 21
1985, April 1, May 8
1991, July 15

New York Times magazine, August 10, 1941: Anita Brenner, "Whirlaway: Problem Horse."

Parade magazine, February 6, 1983: Herman Wouk, "Must Wars Occur?"

Preakness at Pimlico Press Book, Maryland Jockey Club, May 15, 1982.

Racing in America, New York Jockey Club, 1941: Robert F. Kelley, "Whirlaway, Ben Jones and Calumet."

Saturday Evening Post, June 28, 1958: Frank Stanley, "A Visit With Eddie Arcaro."

St. Louis Post-Dispatch — 1941, May 4, 9, 12, 13; June 8

Suffolk Downs Yearbook, Suffolk Downs, Inc., Boston, 1982. U.S. Department of Labor, Bureau of Labor Statistics: "Purchasing Power of the Consumer Dollar," January 15, 1983.

The Thoroughbred Record (Lexington, KY) — 1941, May 10, 17; August 23, 30
1943, July 3

Time magazine — 1941, April 28; May 12
1942, November 9
1943, July 12
1992, April 6

Times-Picayune (New Orleans, LA) — 1942, December 11, 12, 13, 14

Washington *Post* — 1941, May 4

OTHER SOURCES

Audio Cassette: "1941 Kentucky Derby," Race called by Clem McCarthy and recorded by WHAS Radio in Louisville, Kentucky.

Film: "Triple Crown Champions," Thoroughbred Racing Associations, Lake Success, New York.

Video Cassette: "Jewels of the Triple Crown," CBS Fox Video Sports,

1211 Avenue of the Americas, New York, New York 10036.

PICTURE AND REPRINT CREDITS

The Baltimore Sun: May 11, 1941, headlines and pictures of Preakness; May 7, 1942, headlines and pictures of Dixie Handicap.

The Boston Globe: headlines and pictures of Whirlaway's races, July 15, 16, 1942; September 13, 1942.

Calumet Farm: color portrait copy of Whirlaway.

Chicago *Daily News*: Massachusetts Handicap headlines, July 16, 1942.

Keeneland-Meadors: picture of Whirlaway and Warren Wright; profile picture of Whirlaway.

Keeneland Morgan: Whirlaway in Preakness Winner's Circle, in Belmont Stakes Winner's Circle, Travers Stakes finish, and Lawrence Realization finish.

Lexington Herald-Leader: reprint of poem "Whirlaway," by Alex Bower, August 8, 1943.

Louisville Courier-Journal: May 4, 5, 1941 — headlines and pictures of Kentucky Derby.

The New York Times: headlines and pictures of Whirlaway's races; May 7, 1942; June 28, 1942; October 25, 29, 1942; December 20, 1942.

Photograph Inc., Louisville: finish of 1941 Kentucky Derby and Whirlaway in Derby Winner's Circle.

Bert Clark Thayer: book containing original photographs of Whirlaway from birth to end of racing career.

Time magazine: reprint of editorial "$10,000 Cakewalk" by Pearl Kroll, November 9, 1942.

The Times-Picayune (New Orleans): headlines of Louisiana Handicap, December 12-14, 1942.

War Relocation Authority, National Archives: Santa Anita Race Track as Relocation Center for Japanese-Americans.

Index

by Lori L. Daniel